.

Compulsory Arbitration

Compulsory Arbitration

THE GRAND EXPERIMENT IN EMPLOYMENT

Richard A. Bales

ILR Press

an imprint of

CORNELL UNIVERSITY PRESS

Ithaca and London

First published 1997 by Cornell University Press.

Printed in the United States of America

Library of Congress Cataloging-in-Publication Data

Bales, Richard A.
  Compulsory arbitration : the grand experiment in employment / Richard A. Bales.
    p. cm.
  Includes bibliographical references and index.
  ISBN 0-8014-3446-7 (cloth : alk. paper)
  1. Arbitration, Industrial—United States. 2. Labor disputes—United States. 3. Dispute resolution (Law)—United States. I. Title.
KF3425.B27 1997
344.7301 89143—dc21   97-25729

Cornell University Press strives to utilize environmentally responsible suppliers and materials to the fullest extent possible in the publishing of its books. Such materials include vegetable-based, low-VOC inks and acid-free papers that are also either recycled, totally chlorine-free, or partly composed of nonwood fibers.

Cloth printing   10 9 8 7 6 5 4 3 2 1

Contents

Acknowledgments

Special thanks to Stewart Schwab, Laura Cooper, Gregory Crespi, Marc Steinberg, Alan Bromberg, Katherine Van Wezel Stone, and Jennifer Bales for their thoughts and insights on the manuscript; and to Marilyn Mounger and Kathleen Vaughan for their invaluable secretarial assistance.

R. B.

Compulsory Arbitration

One

An Introduction to
Employment Arbitration

ARBITRATION OF EMPLOYMENT DISPUTES IN THE
nonunion sector was virtually unheard of as recently as
five years ago. Today, however, commentators in the
popular press[1] and in various trade journals are concluding that employment arbitration is becoming "the cornerstone of national labor policy,"[2]
"an idea whose time has come,"[3] and that compulsory arbitration "is here
to stay" as a method of resolving employment disputes.[4]

The trend was sparked by two events that occurred in 1991. The first
was that Congress, in the Civil Rights Act of 1991 (the Act),[5] amended
the federal antidiscrimination statutes to provide that "the use of alternative means of dispute resolution, including . . . arbitration, is encouraged
to resolve disputes arising under" the federal antidiscrimination laws.[6]
Although the legislative history of the Act indicates that Congress may
not have intended to permit employers to require employees to sign agreements to arbitrate prospective claims,[7] employers and courts nonetheless
have seized upon the language of the Act as a congressional endorsement
of compulsory arbitration.[8]

The second event was the United States Supreme Court's ground
breaking decision in *Gilmer v. Interstate/Johnson Lane Corporation.*[9] In
Gilmer, the Court enforced an employee's agreement to submit all claims
against his employer to arbitration instead of litigating them in court.
When the employee filed suit in federal court with an age discrimination
claim, the Court dismissed the lawsuit and ordered that his claim be
referred to binding arbitration.

According to one commentator, the *Gilmer* decision precipitated a
"stampede" by employers to draft agreements with their employees that
would require them to submit employment disputes to binding arbitration.[10] This somewhat may overstate employer reaction. Although many
employers, particularly in the securities industry, already have adopted

compulsory employment arbitration policies, many more have proceeded cautiously, waiting until the law becomes more established and the enforceability of arbitration agreements becomes more certain.

Recently, however, as courts continue to render decisions enforcing employment arbitration agreements, employers have become increasingly inclined to require employees to sign compulsory arbitration agreements as a condition of employment. A recent study by the United States General Accounting Office found that although only 1.3 percent of companies surveyed currently use arbitration outside the context of a collective bargaining agreement, an estimated 8.4 percent were considering implementing a policy requiring mandatory, binding arbitration.[11] Another survey of ninety-two companies showed that most presently are considering the use of employment arbitration,[12] and a newspaper reporter's informal survey of twelve Silicon Valley companies revealed that over half recently had enacted a compulsory arbitration policy.[13] The companies that have adopted or are considering compulsory arbitration range from large companies employing tens of thousands of employees, to small companies that worry that the cost of a single litigated case might put them out of business.

As the use of compulsory arbitration agreements proliferates, there is increasing concern that some employers are using the agreements to force their employees to relinquish important employment rights. Pony Express Courier Corporation is a particularly striking example of a company that has used arbitration agreements to eliminate substantive employment rights conferred by statute. Pony Express is a nationwide overnight delivery service. A subsidiary of Borg-Warner Security Corporation, it is headquartered in Charlotte, North Carolina, and employs approximately 4,100 people.[14] The company requires its employees, as a condition of employment, to sign an agreement providing that all employment claims will be arbitrated; that the employee's total remedy will be limited to the lesser of actual lost wages, six months' wages, or reinstatement; and that the arbitration will occur with no opportunity for the employee to conduct discovery of her case.[15] The effect of this agreement, if enforced, would be to wipe out an employee's statutory rights to trial by jury, to seek a broad spectrum of remedies including several years' worth of back pay and punitive damages, and to complete discovery of her case.

Concerns about compulsory arbitration assumed new urgency when the National Conference of Commissioners on Uniform State Laws approved the Model Employment Termination Act (META) to serve as a model for state employment legislative efforts.[16] META was created in part to protect employees from arbitrary dismissal by prohibiting discharges without "good cause" for employees with at least one year's tenure.[17] META is also intended to protect employers from excessive jury awards by waiving jury trials and requiring employment disputes to be resolved by arbitration.[18] Supporters of META have argued that it provides a remedy to blue-collar and rank-and-file workers who previously could not bring lawsuits because of high litigation costs—a barrier which can be overcome by arbitration.[19]

The events leading to the emergence of compulsory employment arbitration have sparked an intense debate in both the academic community and the popular press about whether such arbitration should be encouraged, or whether it should be banned as yet another employer encroachment on employees' rights.[20] This book provides a comprehensive analysis of compulsory arbitration and includes an exhaustive review of its legal background, an examination of how it has been (and should be) implemented, and a discussion of the policy implications of substituting compulsory arbitration for litigation as the preeminent method of resolving disputes that arise in our nation's workplaces.

A. Arbitration Defined

Arbitration is a "simple proceeding voluntarily chosen by parties who want a dispute determined by an impartial judge of their own mutual selection, whose decision, based on the merits of the case, they agree in advance to accept as final and binding."[21] A compulsory employment arbitration agreement is an agreement between employer and employee to resolve future employment disputes by arbitration.[22] Compulsory arbitration provisions can be created as stand-alone agreements, or inserted as part of broader written employment agreements. They can be broad enough to encompass virtually every employment dispute imaginable, or drawn narrowly to encompass only a limited range of disputes (such as those involving discharge from employment). They can incorporate original rules to govern arbitral procedure, or adopt the rules promulgated by a neutral agency such as the American Arbitration Association (AAA) or the Center for Public Resources (CPR).

An arbitration agreement, by itself, does not affect the substantive legal rules that govern the employment relationship.[23] If an employee is employed at-will, that is, she can quit or be fired at any time without notice for any reason (other than one proscribed by law, such as her race),[24] an arbitration agreement does not affect her at-will status. Similarly, an employee does not sign away her right to be free from invidious workplace discrimination or to recover certain damages specified by statute to compensate her for discrimination she has suffered, merely by signing an arbitration agreement. An arbitration agreement, by itself, merely changes the forum where the parties' substantive rights are adjudicated from the courthouse to arbitration, and does not affect those underlying rights.[25]

Some employers, however, have added additional provisions to arbitration agreements, provisions that significantly affect the parties' substantive rights. For example, Title VII, the federal statute making it illegal for an employer to discriminate on the basis of race, color, religion, sex, or national origin,[26] gives victims of employment discrimination the right to recover all of the pay they have lost as a result of discrimination, plus up to $300,000 in punitive damages and those for pain and suffering.[27] The agreement that Pony Express requires its employees to sign would permit a victim to recover only six months of back pay and would entirely eliminate her right to recover punitive damages and damages for pain and suffering. Courts should not permit overreaching by companies such as Pony Express, and should refuse to enforce provisions like theirs that affect parties' substantive employment rights.

The primary distinctive feature of a compulsory arbitration agreement is that both parties, the employer and the employee, agree to submit to binding arbitration any employment dispute that arises in the future. Because this is the final adjudication of a dispute, it operates to the exclusion of other forms of adjudication, such as litigation. As such, compulsory arbitration is a mutually exclusive alternative to litigation, because one signatory to such an agreement can compel the other to submit a claim to arbitration in lieu of litigation, and because an arbitration award is as final and binding as a case that has been litigated to final judgment with virtually all appeals exhausted.

This finality distinguishes arbitration from mediation, which is another alternative to litigation. The purpose of mediation is compromise. Instead of rendering a decision, the mediator attempts to persuade the parties, by proposals or arguments, to settle their differences voluntarily.[28] Mediation often is used by the parties trying to reach agreement before resorting to litigation. If the parties are unable to reach an agreement, however, they still must litigate to resolve their dispute. Arbitration ends the dispute, because the parties have previously agreed to accept the arbitrator's decision as binding, and courts will not permit a party to litigate such a dispute.

It is critical, therefore, that the arbitration be conducted fairly by an arbitrator who knows the area of the law at issue in the case. If the rules of mediation unfairly affect the parties, or if a mediator is ignorant about the law, the parties are free to attempt mediation for a second time under different rules or with a different mediator, or to bypass mediation altogether and proceed directly to litigation. However, if the rules of arbitration are unfair or if an arbitrator is ignorant about the law, the arbitrator's decision is, except under very narrow circumstances,[29] nonetheless final and binding.

B. A Brief History of Arbitration—with Emphasis on the American Workplace

1. Early Use of Arbitration

Arbitration is an ancient form of dispute resolution. King Solomon was an arbitrator.[30] Philip II of Macedonia, the father of Alexander the Great, specified the use of arbitration in disputes arising under his peace treaty with the city-states of southern Greece.[31] George Washington provided that any disputes concerning his intentions in his will would be resolved by a panel of three arbitrators, and that the decision of those arbitrations would be "as binding on the Parties as if it had been given in the Supreme Court of the United States."[32]

The United States inherited arbitration from England, where it had been used, though not always enforced,[33] many centuries before the beginning of English common law.[34] Arbitration has been used regularly in commercial settings as a substitute for litigation since the early 1920s.[35] The use of commercial arbitration in the United States and worldwide expanded significantly when, in 1970, the United States ratified the United Nations Convention on the Recognition and Enforcement of Foreign Arbitral Awards, under which the courts of signatory nations are required to enforce arbitration clauses and awards on the same basis as they would domestic arbitration proceedings.[36] More recently, Olympic athletes were required, as a precondition for competing in the 1996 Games, to agree to arbitrate any disputes between them and Olympic officials, including issues related to eligibility and drug testing.[37]

2. Transformations in the Resolution of Workplace Disputes

By far the most significant use of arbitration in the twentieth-century United States has been in the workplace. There have been three major transformations in the way workplace disputes have been resolved. The first was the unionization of the American workforce in the 1940s and 1950s, and the concomitant use of arbitration to settle disputes between employers and unions.[38] The second was congressional passage of individual employment rights statutes, such as those prohibiting discrimination, which shifted the resolution of employment disputes from arbitration by the union and the employer, to resolution by litigation brought by an employee against the employer.[39] The third, which is the subject of this book, is the return to arbitration for resolving disputes concerning these individual rights.

Although labor arbitration began during the latter part of the nineteenth century, its most rapid advance occurred during World War II through the National War Labor Board.[40] The NWLB decided approximately 20,000 labor dispute cases, most of which were disputes over the terms of collective bargaining agreements. As a precondition to issuing a decision in a labor dispute, the NWLB required the parties to insert into their collective bargaining agreement a clause providing for arbitration of all future disputes. This laid the foundation for the current labor practice of terminating the contract grievance procedure with the final step of arbitration.[41]

The preeminent role of arbitration in resolving labor disputes was confirmed by the United States Supreme Court's 1960 *Steelworkers* Trilogy.[42] In these cases, the Court created a virtually irrebuttable presumption that disputes between employers and unions were arbitrable, and sharply restricted the role of courts in resolving such disputes.[43] The Court also articulated its vision of the American workplace as entirely autonomous—a place where unions and employers would collectively bargain and agree to rules governing the workplace, where all workplace disputes would be settled by arbitration, and where there was very little room (or need) for judicial intervention.

Beginning in the early 1950s and continuing to the present, however, union membership has withered.[44] The union density rate—the percentage of nonagricultural workforce participants who are unionized—declined from a high of 35 percent in 1954[45] to 15.5 percent in 1991.[46] When the recent increase in public sector unionization is discounted, the decline of private sector unionization becomes even more vivid. The private sector density rate currently is 10.9 percent, the lowest figure since 1936.[47] The decline shows no sign of reversal. If the rate of union membership decline over the past twelve years continues, the private sector union density rate may fall to 5 percent by the year 2000.[48]

This dramatic decline has resulted in a much smaller percentage of employees who can avail themselves of union-negotiated grievance procedures, and has made it abundantly clear that unions are unable to provide workers with the minimal terms of employment that they have the right to expect.[49] This does not, however, mean that the employment of the vast majority of Americans is entirely subject to their employers' whims. At the same time that American workers began losing their ability to arbitrate grievances through the auspices of a union, the second major transformation in employment dispute resolution occurred: Congress passed legislation, and courts modified long-standing judicial doctrines, to establish threshold terms of employment that protect employees whether or not they belong to a union.

The trend to legislate in the employment sector began in the first decades of this century, when states began passing workers' compensation statutes. These laws supplanted the tort litigation system and established administrative agencies to oversee compensatory payments to injured workers.[50] The federal move toward employment legislation began in 1908 with the passage of the Federal Employers' Liability Act, which provided remedies for employees of common carriers engaged in interstate commerce.[51] In 1938, Congress passed the Fair Labor Standards Act,[52] which set the minimum wage, required premium pay for overtime work, and restricted child labor. The FLSA, however, merely was intended to provide a floor to support collective bargaining.[53] Statutory protection for broad categories of nonunion workers began in earnest in 1963, when Congress enacted the Equal Pay Act prohibiting wage discrimination on the basis of sex.[54] The watershed event occurred a year later when, in Title VII of the Civil Rights Act of 1964 (Title VII), Congress prohibited discrimination in employment on the basis of race, color, religion, sex, or national origin.[55] Other key federal statutes enacted since then include the Age Discrimination in Employment Act of 1967 (ADEA),[56] the Occupational Safety and Health Act of 1970 (OSHA),[57] the Rehabilitation Act of 1973,[58] the Employee Retirement Income Security Act of 1974 (ERISA),[59] the Pregnancy Discrimination Act of 1978 (PDA),[60] the Civil Service Reform Act of 1978 (CSRA),[61] the Employee Polygraph Protection Act of 1988 (EPPA),[62] the Worker Adjustment and Retraining Notification Act of 1988 (WARNA),[63] the Americans with Disabilities Act of 1990 (ADA),[64] the Civil Rights Act of 1991 (CRA),[65] and the Family and Medical Leave Act of 1993 (FMLA).[66]

State legislatures have followed the congressional lead and, in addition to enacting many state statutes that parallel the federal statutes listed above, have passed legislation protecting employees in a wide variety of other circumstances.[67] As of 1991, twenty-two states made retaliatory dismissal for filing a worker's compensation claim unlawful, thirty-four states protected whistle-blowers,[68] and forty-two states regulated the administration of employment-related lie detector tests.[69] In addition, many states restrict the use of drug testing in the workplace,[70] several have enforced workplace safety and health mandates,[71] and some have enacted statutes to protect employees from the adverse effects of corporate takeovers.[72] Montana enacted the first state statute protecting workers from wrongful discharge,[73] and similar statutes have been passed in Puerto Rico[74] and the Virgin Islands.[75]

While federal and state legislatures have been imposing minimum terms on employment relationships, state courts have applied contract and tort principles to open gaping holes in the doctrine of employment at will.[76] For example, courts in at least twenty-nine states have used contract law to bind employers to tenure promises and discharge procedures outlined in employee handbooks.[77] Eleven states have used contract law's covenant of good faith and fair dealing to give employees a cause of action for wrongful termination.[78] Most states use contract law to enforce employers' explicit oral promises concerning job tenure,[79] and at least one state court has implied such a promise from an employee's length of service.[80]

At least thirty-two states have adopted a public policy exception to employment at will.[81] State courts use this exception, which gives employees a cause of action in tort, to protect employees fired for refusing to commit an unlawful act,[82] for exercising a statutory right,[83] or for performing a public duty.[84] Many states also have given employees tort actions for intentional infliction of emotional distress.[85]

These new minimum terms of employment are called "individual rights"[86] because the individual employee, rather than a union, is responsible for their enforcement. Unlike the grievance mechanism of a collective bargaining agreement, in which conflicts are resolved jointly by employer and union, individual rights rely for enforcement on lawsuits brought by employees against employers. The number of such lawsuits has exploded recently,[87] as press coverage of highly publicized cases has made employees aware of their rights and of the possibility of receiving large damage awards.

Not everyone, however, welcomes the prospect of enforcing these new individual employment rights through litigation. Judges see the employment litigation explosion as adding to a backlog that forces litigants to wait for years before getting to trial.[88] One commentator, predicting the expanded use of arbitration to cover a broad range of conflicts in our society, noted aptly: "The courts cannot handle all of the load now, and even if they could handle all of it well, the judicial process is too slow and too costly. Courts are better at setting principles and establishing procedures in test cases. Private mechanisms need to carry the bulk of the caseload if the whole dispute-setting process is not to break down with serious consequences."[89] This may explain, at least in part, the recent judicial embrace of compulsory employment arbitration.[90]

Many employers are equally happy with compulsory arbitration. They dislike the jury system because they believe that juries are unpredictable, that jurors often decide cases on the basis of sympathy rather than legal merit, and that jurors are "the 'peers' of employees, not employers."[91] Moreover, because arbitration is faster and less formal than litigation, it is a substantially less expensive means of resolving employment disputes. As discussed later in this book,[92] one company slashed its annual expenditure on outside legal fees in half by adopting a comprehensive dispute resolution program that included compulsory arbitration.

Employees and their advocates often are less enthusiastic. This hesitation no doubt stems from the (often justified) fear that employers will draft arbitration agreements that deprive employees of their basic employment rights, and then offer these one-sided agreements to current and prospective employees on a sign-it-or-be-fired basis. The agreement Pony Express requires its employees to sign provides a vivid example of how employers can abuse compulsory arbitration. If arbitration is to become an effective and fair method of resolving employment disputes, courts will have to scrutinize arbitration agreements rigorously and refuse to enforce those that are unfair to employees.

A fairly designed compulsory arbitration system has a great deal to offer to employees. Many employees, especially lower-income workers, are shut out of the current litigation process because their low salaries make their receiving large damage awards unlikely, and this in turn makes it difficult to attract attorneys who will handle these cases on a contingency basis.[93] The speed and low cost of an arbitration award may make even a low-damage case attractive to plaintiff attorneys. Moreover, even if the employee still cannot find an attorney, the relative informality of arbitration makes it far easier to arbitrate a claim without the aid of an attorney rather than satisfy the procedural roadblocks imposed by federal antidiscriminatory statutes as a prerequisite to litigation.[94] Further, the adversarial litigation process forces employees to jeopardize or sever current employment relationships; to pay for attorneys' retainers, expert witness

fees, and protracted discoveries; and to put their professional lives on hold
for years. Arbitration offers a way to resolve disputes quickly, often before
the parties are so entrenched that reconciliation becomes impossible. For
these reasons, employers and employees increasingly are entering into,[95]
and courts increasingly are enforcing, compulsory arbitration agreements.

This use of compulsory arbitration to resolve disputes concerning individual employment rights represents the third transformation in the way
employment disputes are resolved. This transformation, however, is far
from complete, and in fact is quite tentative. As discussed at the beginning
of this chapter, the transformation was sparked by the Supreme Court's
Gilmer decision and by congressional passage of the 1991 Civil Rights
Act. *Gilmer,* however, left several issues unresolved. For example, the
Court did not specify whether its decision permitting compulsory arbitration applies to all employees or merely to a small, narrowly defined group;
or whether all employment disputes (such as those arising under Title VII
and other federal legislation) can be resolved by compulsory arbitration.
A future Supreme Court decision ruling hostile to compulsory arbitration
could bring the nascent era of compulsory arbitration to an end quickly
and effectively. Similarly, it is possible to interpret the 1991 Civil Rights
Act in a hostile manner. If courts reverse their current pro-arbitration
course, or if Congress decides to pass a statute hostile to compulsory
arbitration, it will become a thing of the past. That is why this book is
subtitled *The Grand Experiment in Employment.*

C. An Overview of This Book

Chapter 2 provides the legal background to the enforcement of compulsory employment arbitration agreements. At common law, all arbitration agreements were unenforceable, but this changed in 1925 when
Congress enacted the Federal Arbitration Act.[96] The FAA requires federal
courts to enforce arbitration agreements. For years, courts used the FAA
as authority for compelling arbitration of nonstatutory disputes (such as
contractual disputes) and used other sources of law to compel arbitration
of disputes arising between employers and unions. At the same time,
however, courts refused to enforce agreements to arbitrate claims arising
under statutory law, such as employment discrimination claims, because
the courts considered arbitration an inferior way of adjudicating important
public rights. This rigid divide between arbitrable nonstatutory issues and
nonarbitrable statutory issues began to crumble when, in the late 1980s,
the Supreme Court enforced agreements to arbitrate statutory claims aris-

ing under antitrust, securities, and racketeering laws. These nonemployment cases foreshadowed the Supreme Court's 1991 *Gilmer* decision, in which the Court gave its imprimatur to compulsory employment arbitration agreements by dismissing and ordering to arbitration an age discrimination lawsuit brought by an employee who had agreed to arbitrate all his prospective employment disputes.

Although there now is an extensive body of case law upholding the enforceability of compulsory employment arbitration agreements, two issues remain to be finally resolved before employers and employees can absolutely be confident that such agreements will be judicially enforced. These issues are discussed in chapters 3 through 5. The first issue, discussed in chapter 3, concerns the scope of an FAA clause excluding "contracts of employment of seamen, railroad employees, or any other class of workers engaged in foreign or interstate commerce." Although some commentators have argued which this clause should be interpreted broadly to prohibit courts from enforcing *any* arbitration agreement in the employment context, nearly every court that has considered the issue has interpreted the clause narrowly to apply only to employees *such as* seamen and railroad employees. The Supreme Court, however, has never resolved the issue and there is ample authority for reasoning that the clause should be construed broadly. Chapter 3 examines in detail both the legislative history and subsequent judicial interpretation of this "contract of employment" exclusion. It concludes that neither offers a definitive answer as to how the exclusion should be interpreted, allowing the Court either to continue its tentative endorsement of compulsory arbitration or to reverse course and shut down the experiment.

Chapter 4 discusses whether *Gilmer,* in which the Supreme Court ordered a federal age discrimination claim to arbitration, applies equally to other types of federal claims such as race and sex discrimination claims, and to claims arising under state law. Regarding federal claims, the issue is whether *Gilmer* can be applied to Title VII and other federal antidiscrimination statutes. Since *Gilmer,* the lower courts unanimously have answered this question affirmatively, thus broadening the applicability of compulsory arbitration. The Supreme Court, however, has not definitively resolved the issue, and there are indications in the legislative history of the 1991 Civil Rights Act that Congress may have been opposed to compulsory arbitration. Chapter 4 reviews both that history and post-*Gilmer* extensions of the FAA to various federal employment statutes, and, as with the FAA contracts of employment exception, concludes that it is sufficiently ambiguous for the Court either to bless or condemn compulsory arbitration. Similarly, such ambiguity gives Congress the opportunity to "clarify" its intention in the Civil Rights Act based on how compulsory arbitration works in practice.

The chapter next turns to extending the FAA to employment causes of action brought under state legislation and state common law. The FAA's failure to address its impact on state statutory and common law, and to provide a basis for independent federal question jurisdiction, left open issues such as whether, and to what extent, the FAA preempts contrary state law; whether causes of action based on state law are subject to compulsory arbitration under the FAA, and whether the FAA is applicable to state courts applying state substantive law. The latter part of chapter 4 thoroughly reviews the several Supreme Court decisions that have answered all these issues in favor of arbitration.

Chapter 5 considers the effect of the National Labor Relations Act on employment arbitration agreements. The NLRA, which gives employees the right to unionize, to bargain collectively, and to engage in other concerted activity such as strikes and picketing, might affect employment arbitration in two ways. First, requiring employees to waive their right to litigate statutory claims could interfere with their right to act concertedly. Second, an employment arbitration system, depending on its structure, might be an illegal employer-dominated labor organization. Although the dearth of case law on these issues makes it difficult to predict how the NLRA will affect employment arbitration, it appears more likely than not that the NLRA will not significantly inhibit arbitration's growth.

Chapter 6 examines the role of the Equal Employment Opportunity Commission, the federal agency Congress created to oversee enforcement of federal antidiscrimination laws, in the future of compulsory employment arbitration. Ever since the Supreme Court issued *Gilmer*, the EEOC in two ways has stridently opposed the use of compulsory arbitration agreements.

First, the EEOC has asserted that it has the legal right to circumvent the arbitration agreement without directly challenging the agreement itself. The EEOC's argument is that even if an employee contractually waives *her own* right to litigate her statutory employment claims, that waiver has no effect on the *EEOC's* right to sue the employer on behalf of the employee. After reviewing analogous case law related to class certification and employee settlements, I conclude that the EEOC is correct to assert that it retains independent authority to sue in its own name on behalf of employees. However, in cases where the employee on whose behalf the EEOC has sued has signed an arbitration agreement, the EEOC may seek only classwide injunctive relief, and may not seek damages that the employee might have obtained in arbitration. This limitation, together with the paucity of the EEOC's resources, makes it extremely unlikely that the EEOC will litigate claims on behalf of employees who have signed valid (and fair) compulsory arbitration agreements.

Second, the EEOC has opposed compulsory employment arbitration by issuing policy statements condemning it and by directly challenging the legality of such agreements in court. It mounts direct challenges by litigating cases on behalf of employees who want to avoid enforcement of the arbitration agreements they have signed. But while the EEOC has the authority to litigate cases against employers that have adopted compulsory arbitration agreements, the agency's limited resources leave it unable to do so except in the most egregious cases. Moreover, the policy statements which the EEOC has issued condemning compulsory arbitration have no practical effect, because the agency has no legal authority to interpret the FAA. Although the EEOC has some limited authority to interpret federal antidiscrimination statutes, courts have already interpreted those statutes to favor compulsory arbitration, making the EEOC's opposition moot. For these reasons, an employer whose compulsory employment arbitration policy is scrupulously fair to employees has little to fear from the EEOC.

The next two chapters examine the way compulsory arbitration agreements have been implemented in two different industries. Chapter 7 considers the securities industry, which was the first industry to put these procedures into effect on a widespread basis. It did so almost by accident —the compulsory arbitration system that now resolves employment disputes was created to resolve investor-firm disputes. The provision that was drafted to compel arbitration of the latter disputes is broad enough to cover the former as well, and, since *Gilmer,* has been used with increasing frequency to compel the arbitration of employment claims. This discrepancy between the purpose for which the system was designed and the purpose for which it now is often used has created problems that raise serious doubts about the system's fairness to employees. This chapter discusses the securities arbitration system, its current application to employment disputes, and problems that often lead to the evisceration of employees' statutory rights.

The securities industry approaches arbitration essentially by substituting arbitration for litigation. Brown & Root, a large construction, maintenance, and engineering services company, has developed a radically different employment arbitration procedure. It has worked out a comprehensive four-step dispute resolution process, which culminates in arbitration but which is designed to encourage resolution of disputes by agreement reached, for example, through internal conciliation and mediation. This process has been phenomenally successful in the 3 years it has been used. In addition to slashing the company's outside legal fees in half, it has reduced the personnel turnover by resolving disputes before they result in discharges or resignation. This has not been accomplished at employees' expense; to the contrary, Brown & Root encourages employees to air grievances, contractually guarantees that they will not be retaliated against for doing so, and even reimburses them for legal expenses incurred when their grievance involves a legally protected right. Brown & Root's dispute resolution program is discussed in chapter 8.

Chapter 9 takes a "nuts and bolts" look at various aspects of employment arbitration agreements. Although the cases discussed in chapters 2 and 3 establish that virtually every conceivable type of employment claim is arbitrable, courts are unlikely to enforce those agreements perceived to be unfair to employees. This chapter discusses how employment arbitration agreements should be drafted and implemented, various procedures for selecting arbitrators, discovery options, whether arbitrators should be required to issue written opinions, attempts to limit the arbitrator's ability to award relief, and the scope of judicial review of arbitral awards. For each, the chapter first canvasses the existing case law, then makes recommendations both to courts regarding what procedures should be required prior to enforcement, and to employers regarding how their agreement should be drafted to maximize the probability of enforcement.

Finally, chapter 10 examines the policy implications of the current transition from dispute resolution by litigation to dispute resolution by compulsory arbitration. It begins by discussing the procedural rights that parties waive by agreeing to arbitration and the benefits arbitration offers over litigation, and by assessing the relative effect each right or benefit has on employers and employees. Next, the chapter considers several broader concerns commentators have raised about compulsory arbitration, such as the prospect of employers unilaterally imposing arbitration agreements on unwilling employees, the effect of compulsory arbitration on the enforcement of important public policies such as nondiscrimination, and the possibility that employers will abuse employment arbitration by using it to vitiate employees' substantive employment rights. Finally, this chapter offers some concluding remarks concerning the future of compulsory employment arbitration.

Arbitration has several significant advantages over litigation. A principal advantage is that because it is less expensive than litigation it gives low-income employees who cannot afford litigation an opportunity to enforce their employment rights. A principal disadvantage is that because it is a private dispute resolution system and the arbitration agreement is almost always drafted by the employer there is an unsettling opportunity for employers to use arbitration to destroy, rather than enforce, employees' employment rights. Implemented properly, arbitration could revolutionize in a positive way how workplace disputes are settled in this country. Implemented improperly, arbitration could return us to the early part of this century when employees had virtually no legal protection at all.

Two

The Emergence of
Compulsory Arbitration

ALTHOUGH THE USE OF COMPULSORY ARBITRA-
tion in the nonunion employment setting is a relatively
recent phenomenon, its use in other settings has an
extensive legal pedigree, all of which is relevant to ascertaining the scope
and enforceability of compulsory employment arbitration today. This
chapter details that pedigree, beginning with the enforcement of arbitration agreements at English common law, and concluding with the United
States Supreme Court's 1991 *Gilmer* decision.

A. Arbitration at Common Law

At both English and American common law, an agreement to arbitrate was revocable by either party at any time before an award was rendered.[1] The breach of an arbitration agreement would give rise to an
action for nominal damages arising from the breach, but would not bar a
proceeding at law; neither courts at law nor courts in equity would de-
cree specific performance.[2] This rule had its genesis "in the contests of
the courts of ancient times for extension of jurisdiction—all of them being
opposed to anything that would altogether deprive every one of them of
jurisdiction."[3]

In 1889, the English Parliament passed the Arbitration Act of 1889,[4]
which validated arbitration agreements and required courts specifically to
enforce them.[5] American courts, however, continued to adhere to the
principle that an agreement to arbitrate operated to divest courts of legis-
latively-granted jurisdiction and, therefore, was illegal and void.[6] Around
the turn of the century, judicial attitudes began to change in favor of
arbitration, but the laws invalidating arbitration agreements remained in-
tact. For example, in *United States Asphalt Refining Co. v. Trinidad Lake
Petroleum Co.*,[7] a 1915 case decided by the United States District Court

for the Southern District of New York, an obviously reluctant court refused to issue a stay of litigation pending arbitration. In its opinion, the court noted that "[t]here has long been a great variety of available reasons for refusing to give effect to the agreements of men of mature age, and presumably sound judgment, when the intended effect of the agreements was to prevent proceedings in any and all courts and substitute therefore the decision of arbitrators." These reasons, the court stated, generally revolved around the outdated[8] and ill-reasoned[9] reluctance of judges to "permit any other body of men to even partially perform judicial work."[10]

B. The Federal Arbitration Act

In 1920, the American Bar Association (ABA) Committee on Commerce, Trade and Commercial Law began to ponder the "further extension of the principle of commercial arbitration."[11] Five years later, a bill drafted by the Committee was introduced in Congress[12] to reverse the common law rule barring specific performance of arbitration agreements.[13] This bill was enacted as the United States Arbitration Act.[14] In 1947, Congress reenacted and codified the USAA in the Federal Arbitration Act (FAA).[15]

The FAA creates a body of federal substantive law permitting judicial enforcement of agreements to arbitrate in connection with commerce and maritime transactions. Section 2 of the FAA provides that a

written provision in any maritime transaction or a contract evidencing a transaction involving commerce to settle by arbitration a controversy thereafter arising out of such contract or transaction, or the refusal to perform the whole or any part thereof, or an agreement in writing to submit to arbitration an existing controversy arising out of such a contract, transaction, or refusal, shall be valid, irrevocable and enforceable, save upon such grounds as exist at law or in equity for the revocation of any contract.[16]

Sections 3 and 4 define the FAA's enforcement procedures. Section 3 permits a party to an arbitration agreement to obtain a stay of proceedings in federal court when an issue is referable to arbitration. Section 4 permits such a party to obtain an order compelling arbitration when another party has failed, neglected, or refused to comply with an arbitration agreement, and allows for judicial enforcement of any award rendered.

The FAA covers all written arbitration agreements involving maritime transactions and interstate commerce. It excludes, however, "contracts of employment of seamen, railroad employees, or any other class of workers engaged in foreign or interstate commerce." The meaning of this "contracts of employment" exclusion is discussed in chapter 3.

The FAA does not create an independent basis for federal subject matter jurisdiction.[17] It does not, therefore, guarantee that a person who is a party to an arbitration agreement will be able to enforce the agreement in *federal* court. To get to federal court, either a federal question must be at issue (federal statutory employment discrimination claims provide such a federal question), or the parties to the lawsuit must be citizens of different states and the amount in controversy must exceed $75,000. Even if neither of these conditions are met and the case cannot be brought in federal court, this does not mean that the arbitration agreement is unenforceable. Under such circumstances, suit may be brought in state court to compel arbitration pursuant to the requirements of the FAA. If state law is inconsistent with the FAA, the FAA "trumps" the inconsistent state law. In this regard, two United States Supreme Court decisions[18] and innumerable lower court decisions have made it clear that the FAA preempts state law on the issue of whether courts may compel arbitration.[19]

C. *Wilko* and the FAA's Initial Confinement to Nonstatutory Claims

Aside from upholding the constitutionality of the FAA in 1932, the Supreme Court remained silent on the subject of the FAA until nearly thirty years after the FAA's original enactment. This silence was broken in the 1953 decision of *Wilko v. Swan*.[20] In *Wilko*, a buyer of securities claimed that the seller had procured the transaction through fraudulent misrepresentations, and brought suit under Section 12(2) of the Securities Act of 1933.[21] The sales contract, however, contained an arbitration clause, and the seller, pursuant to Section 3 of the FAA, moved for a stay of the suit pending arbitration. The Supreme Court found that the purpose of the Securities Act was to protect investors, and that investors would be best protected if they were not bound to arbitration agreements in the sale of securities. Based on these findings, the Court concluded that Congress must have intended the Securities Act provisions to override the general enforceability of arbitration agreements under the FAA. The Court held that a party could not waive a claim under Section 12(2) of the Securities Act through a predispute arbitration agreement, and declared the arbitration clause void.[22]

In its decision, the Court emphasized Section 14 of the Securities Act, which provided that "[a]ny condition, stipulation, or provision binding any person acquiring any security to waive compliance with any provision of this sub-chapter or of the rules and regulations of the Commission shall be void." [23] The Court reasoned that an agreement to arbitrate is necessarily a waiver of substantive law, and was "the kind of 'provision' that cannot be waived under Section 14 of the Securities Act." [24]

Lower federal courts subsequently interpreted *Wilko* as creating a "public policy" defense to the enforcement of arbitration agreements under the FAA when statutory claims were at issue. This defense was premised on the assumptions that: (1) a judicial forum was superior to arbitration for enforcing statutory rights; (2) compulsory arbitration constituted a waiver of the statutory right to a judicial forum, which contravened public policy; and (3) the informality of arbitration made it difficult for courts to correct errors in statutory interpretation. [25]

D. The *Steelworkers* Trilogy

In three cases decided in 1960, known collectively as the *Steelworkers* Trilogy, [26] the Supreme Court strongly endorsed arbitration as a mechanism for resolving industrial disputes arising under collective bargaining agreements. In doing so, the Court relied not on the pro-arbitration policy of the FAA, but instead (as it had three years earlier in another case [27]) on Section 301 of the Labor-Management Relations Act of 1947. [28] Despite the different source of authority, the Court's strong endorsement of arbitration in the *Steelworkers* cases has had a profound effect on the Court's treatment of cases arising under the FAA.

The holdings of the Trilogy were that arbitrators, and not the courts, are to decide the arbitrability of grievances, [29] that courts should not refuse to order arbitration unless the parties' arbitration clause "is not susceptible of an interpretation that covers the asserted dispute"; [30] and that so long as an arbitrator's award "draws its essence" from the collective bargaining agreement, courts should not review the merits of the award. [31] The significance of the Trilogy, however, is far broader than the sum of its holdings, for in it the Supreme Court erected a system of industrial self-government and a policy of judicial noninterference with that self-government. Under this system, known as industrial pluralism, [32] the National Labor Relations Act (NLRA) [33] established a framework through which employees could organize to acquire the bargaining power necessary to significantly influence wages, working conditions, and other terms and conditions of employment. [34] Employers and employees, roughly co-equal [35] in bargaining power following employees' organization into a union, could jointly negotiate and enforce[36] a collective bargaining agreement establishing the terms and conditions of employment. Sovereignty over labor-management issues, under this notion of industrial pluralism, was shifted from employers and the courts to employers and unions.[37]

Establishing an internal mechanism for resolving disputes between employers and employees was critical to maintaining this shift in sovereignty.[38] As a result of the *Steelworkers* Trilogy, arbitration became this mechanism.[39] In the metaphor of industrial democracy, the workplace "legislature" promulgated the law of the shop through collective bargaining negotiations.[40] Arbitration, as an analog to the judiciary,[41] provided the mechanism by which that law was interpreted and applied. Not only did it serve the instrumental function of interpreting and applying the law, it also fit the theoretical model of an autonomous system.[42] The arbitrator was chosen by, and served at the whim of, the two parties, and the arbitrator's authority was derived exclusively from the terms of the collective bargaining agreement that the parties had negotiated.[43] Arbitration thus completed the metaphor of industrial organization as a self-contained mini-democracy—"an island of self-rule whose self-regulating mechanisms must not be disrupted by judicial intervention or other scrutiny by outsiders."[44]

The *Steelworkers* Trilogy did not overrule the *Wilko* line of cases denying enforcement of agreements to arbitrate statutory claims. Instead, the Court distinguished *Wilko* by pointing out that the *Steelworkers* cases arose in the unique context of industrial self-government. Whereas the alternative to arbitrating statutory claims was judicial resolution of those claims "with established procedures or even special statutory safeguards," the alternative to arbitrating claims arising out of a collective bargaining relationship was perceived by the Court to be "industrial strife."[45] The *Steelworkers* cases thus were predicated, to a large extent, on the Court's fear of labor unrest, a fear not applicable to the statutory cases which did not arise in the labor/employment context until 1974. The Court thus established the twin products of the *Steelworkers* Trilogy—a virtually irrebuttable presumption of arbitrability and a sharply limited role for the courts—as unique to the particular institution of the unionized workplace.[46] After the *Steelworkers* Trilogy, lower federal courts continued to apply *Wilko* to counter attempts to arbitrate statutory claims,[47] creating a rigid divide between arbitrable collective bargaining issues and nonarbitrable statutory issues. This divide was challenged by the 1974 case of *Alexander v. Gardner-Denver Co.*[48]

E. *Alexander v. Gardner-Denver*

Alexander v. Gardner-Denver involved a statutory claim—seemingly nonarbitrable under *Wilko*—that an employer argued was arbitrable pursuant to the terms of a collective bargaining agreement and the *Steelworkers* Trilogy presumption of arbitrability. In *Gardner-Denver,* the Gardner-Denver Company discharged Harrell Alexander, an African-American drill operator, for producing too many defective or unusable parts that had to be scrapped. Alexander, who was a member of Local No. 3029 of the United Steel Workers of America, filed a grievance pursuant to his collective bargaining agreement seeking reinstatement, full seniority, and back pay. He did not specifically allege race discrimination in his grievance, but alleged it for the first time when he filed a charge of race discrimination with the state civil rights commission. At his subsequent arbitration hearing, Alexander testified that his discharge had been caused by race discrimination. The arbitrator ruled that Alexander had been discharged for just cause, making no reference in the arbitration opinion to Alexander's discrimination claim.[49]

Alexander then filed a Title VII race discrimination suit in federal district court. The district court granted summary judgment for the employer and dismissed the suit, finding that the discrimination claim had been submitted to and resolved by the arbitrator. The United States Court of Appeals for the Tenth Circuit affirmed, holding that Alexander voluntarily had elected to pursue his grievance to final arbitration under the collective bargaining agreement nondiscrimination clause, and that Alexander was bound by the arbitrator's decision.[50]

The Supreme Court reversed, holding that an employee does not forfeit his Title VII discrimination claim by first pursuing a grievance to final arbitration under the nondiscrimination clause of a collective bargaining agreement.[51] The Court presented four reasons why labor arbitration was inappropriate for the final resolution of Title VII claims.

First, the Court stated that labor arbitrators have neither the experience nor the authority to resolve Title VII claims. The "specialized competence of arbitrators," the Court noted, "pertains primarily to the law of the shop, not the law of the land."[52] Moreover, because the arbitrator's authority stems from the collective bargaining agreement she has no authority to enforce public laws. If she does, she has "exceeded the scope of the submission," and such an award would not be enforceable.[53]

Second, citing the relative informality of arbitration hearings as compared to judicial proceedings the Court concluded that arbitral factfinding procedures were inadequate to protect employees' Title VII rights. "The record of the arbitration proceedings," the Court opined, "is not as complete; the usual rules of evidence do not apply; and rights and procedures common to civil trials, such as discovery, compulsory process, cross-examination, and testimony under oath, are often severely limited or unavailable."[54] Arbitration procedures, while well-suited to the resolution of contractual disputes, "make arbitration a comparatively inappropriate forum for the final resolution of rights created by Title VII."[55]

Third, the Court pointed out that arbitrators were under no obligation to issue written opinions. Finally, the Court noted the union's exclusive control over the manner and extent to which an employee's grievance is presented. The Court was concerned that a union's duty to represent employees *collectively* might lead it to decide not to pursue adequately an *individual* employee's discrimination claim. A union, for example, might be willing to make concessions to the employer on an individual employee's discrimination claim in return for a wage increase that benefited all employees.

Seven years after the *Gardner-Denver* decision, the Court decided *Barrentine v. Arkansas-Best Freight System, Inc.*[56] In *Barrentine,* the Court extended the *Gardner-Denver* holding to claims brought under the Fair Labor Standards Act, holding that arbitration pursuant to a collective bargaining agreement did not preclude subsequent litigation of a FLSA claim. The Court provided two reasons for its holding. First, the Court stated that "a union balancing individual and collective interests might validly permit some employees' statutorily granted wage and hour benefits to be sacrificed if an alternative expenditures of resources would result in increased benefits for workers in the bargaining unit as a whole."[57] Second, the Court questioned the competence of labor arbitrators to hear statutory claims, stating that "[a]lthough an arbitrator may be competent to resolve many preliminary factual questions, such as whether the employee 'punched in' when he said he did, he may lack the competence to decide the ultimate legal issues [of] whether an employee's right to a minimum wage or to overtime pay under the statute has been violated."[58]

Three years later, in 1984, the Court again[59] extended the *Gardner-Denver* rule—this time to claims arising under 42 U.S.C. § 1983. In *McDonald v. City of West Branch,* the Court, relying on *Gardner-Denver,* decided that arbitration was inadequate on the following four grounds: (1) that a labor arbitrator may not be competent to resolve the complex legal questions arising in a Section 1983 action; (2) that an arbitrator's authority is derived from contract and may not include, or may conflict with, the provisions of Section 1983; (3) that because of a union's role as the collective representative of employees, the union may not forcefully arbitrate a particular employee's grievance; and (4) that arbitral factfinding procedures are insufficient to guarantee protection of statutory rights.

The *Steelworkers* Trilogy and the *Gardner-Denver* line of cases appeared to create a rigid division between the "law of the shop," for which final and binding arbitration was appropriate, and the "law of the land," for which arbitration was not. After *Gardner-Denver,* this policy seemed equally premised on the distinction between the union and the nonunion context, and on the assumption that the arbitral process itself was inferior to the judicial process for the resolution of complex statutory employment discrimination claims. Following this line of Supreme Court authority, several circuit courts ruled that compulsory arbitration clauses contained in individual employment contracts (*i.e.,* in the nonunion context) would not preclude subsequent suits under antidiscrimination laws.[60]

F. The *Mitsubishi* Trilogy

Subsequent to *Gardner-Denver,* decisions in the lower courts continued to deny compulsory arbitration of statutory claims in the employment context, but the Supreme Court issued three decisions approving compulsory arbitration of statutory claims arising under antitrust,[61] securities,[62] and racketeering[63] laws. These cases, known as the *"Mitsubishi* Trilogy," were premised on the FAA. The cases were a radical departure from *Wilko* and its progeny which, as discussed above, for more than thirty years had precluded the application of the FAA to statutory claims.

In the *Mitsubishi* Trilogy, the Court interpreted the FAA as creating a presumption of arbitrability: the Court will presume that Congress did not intend to prohibit arbitration of statutory claims unless the language of the statute in question expressly indicates otherwise.[64] Furthermore, the burden of proof is on the party opposing arbitration to show that Congress intended to preclude a waiver of existing remedies.[65] This fact, as several commentators have noted, has made the presumption virtually irrebuttable.[66] Additionally, the Court explicitly rejected arguments questioning the competence of arbitrators and the sufficiency of arbitral procedures.[67]

Mitsubishi Motors Corp. v. Soler Chrysler-Plymouth, Inc.,[68] the first case of the Trilogy, was decided in 1985, only one year after *McDonald v. City of West Branch.* In *Mitsubishi,* the Supreme Court held that claims arising under the Sherman Antitrust Act[69] were arbitrable pursuant to the FAA.

The case involved a dispute between a Japanese auto manufacturer and its Puerto Rican distributor. When sales of Mitsubishi automobiles declined in Puerto Rico, the distributor, Soler, refused to accept shipments of cars it had ordered. Mitsubishi then sued in federal district court to compel arbitration under the FAA, based on a clause in the distributorship agreement providing that all disputes arising under the agreement were to be arbitrated in Japan. Soler counterclaimed that Mitsubishi had violated the Sherman Act and other federal statutes, and asserted that the counterclaims were not arbitrable under the FAA.

Holding that the claims were arbitrable, the Supreme Court found that there was "no warrant in the [FAA] for implying . . . a presumption against arbitration of statutory claims."[70] To the contrary, it found that under the FAA, "as a matter of federal law, any doubts concerning the scope of arbitrable issues should be resolved in favor of arbitration";[71] as a result, a presumption of arbitrability of statutory claims arose:

We must assume that if Congress intended the substantive protection afforded by a given statute to include protection against waiver of the right to a judicial forum, that intention will be deducible from text or legislative history. Having made the bargain to arbitrate, the parties should be held to it unless Congress itself has evinced an intention to preclude a waiver of judicial remedies for the statutory rights at issue.[72]

The *Mitsubishi* Court cited *Wilko* as one instance where Congress had evinced an intention to preclude waiver of the right to a judicial forum.[73] The Court found no such intention, however, in the Sherman Act. Without discussing *Gardner-Denver*,[74] the Court enforced the arbitration agreement.

This new presumption doctrine was predicated on two assumptions, both of which were a marked departure from prior precedent. The first was that an arbitration agreement involves no waiver of substantive rights:

By agreeing to arbitrate a statutory claim, the party does not forego the substantive rights afforded by the statute; it only submits to their resolution in an arbitral, rather than a judicial forum. It trades the procedures and opportunity for review of the courtroom for the simplicity, informality, and expedition of arbitration.[75]

However, as discussed in chapter 9, an arbitrant waives several very important *procedural* rights, including the right to an Article III trial in federal district court, to a trial by jury, and to appeal an adverse verdict except on very narrow grounds.

The *Mitsubishi* Court's second major assumption was that arbitrators are capable of deciding complex statutory issues. Noting that the parties may appoint arbitrators with particular statutory expertise and that the arbitrator (or the parties) may employ experts, the Court concluded that "we are well past the time when judicial suspicion of the desirability of arbitration and of the competence of arbitral tribunals inhibited the development of arbitration as an alternative means of dispute resolution."[76] The "well past" language seems hyperbolic, given that just one year before, in *McDonald*, the Court had stated that an arbitrator may lack the competence required to resolve complex legal issues in a Section 1983 action.

In the second case of the *Mitsubishi* Trilogy, *Shearson/American Express, Inc. v. McMahon*,[77] the Supreme Court extended the *Mitsubishi* presumption to statutory claims arising under Rocketeer Influenced Corrupt Organizations Act (RICO)[78] and Section 10b of the Securities Exchange Act of 1934.[79] This case involved a claim of fraud against a brokerage firm by a customer. When the customer sued in federal court, the brokerage firm moved to compel arbitration pursuant to Section 3 of the FAA. The customer argued that the dispute was not arbitrable pursuant to the public policy defense against compelled arbitration of statutory claims. The Court, interpreting this defense in light of *Mitsubishi*, held that the defense did not apply unless waivers of substantive rights were involved. Since the rationale of *Mitsubishi* was that an agreement to arbitrate statutory claims did not constitute a waiver of statutory rights, the Court held that the public policy defense was inapplicable, and enforced the arbitration agreement.[80]

The Court also reemphasized the language in *Mitsubishi*, stressing the competence of arbitrators to decide statutory issues:

In *Mitsubishi*, for example, we recognized that arbitral tribunals are readily capable of handling the factual and legal complexities of antitrust claims, notwithstanding the absence of judicial instruction and supervision. Likewise, we have concluded that the streamlined procedures of arbitration do not entail any consequential restriction on substantive rights. Finally, we have indicated that there is no reason to assume at the outset that arbitrators will not follow the law; although judicial scrutiny of arbitration awards necessarily is limited, such review is sufficient to ensure that arbitrators comply with the requirements of the statute.[81]

Rodriguez de Quijas v. Shearson/American Express, Inc.,[82] decided in 1989, was the third case of the *Mitsubishi* Trilogy. In *Rodriguez*, the Court expressly overruled *Wilko* and held that an arbitration agreement precluded litigation of claims arising under the Securities Act of 1933[83] and the Securities Exchange Act of 1934.[84] The Court stated that "[t]o the extent that *Wilko* rested on suspicion of arbitration as a method of weakening the protections afforded in substantive law, it has fallen far out of step with our current strong endorsement of the federal statutes favoring this method of resolving disputes."[85] Accordingly, the Court concluded that *Wilko* was incorrectly decided and was "inconsistent with the prevailing uniform construction of other federal statutes governing arbitration agreements in the setting of business transactions."[86] Four Justices dissented, arguing that the *Wilko* interpretation of the securities statutes evincing Congressional intent to preseve a judicial forum should not be reversed merely because of the majority's preference for arbitration on policy grounds.[87]

The *Mitsubishi* Trilogy represented a transformation of the Supreme Court's attitude toward arbitration outside the union context. Before *Mitsubishi*, statutory claims were not arbitrable; after *Mitsubishi*, they were arbitrable so long as they did not arise in the employment context. In the context of its increasing confidence in arbitral resolution of statutory claims involving business transactions the Court, two years after *Rodriguez*, granted certiorari in a case raising the issue of the arbitrability of statutory *employment* claims.

G. *Gilmer v. Interstate/Johnson Lane Corp.*

In *Gilmer v. Interstate/Johnson Lane Corp.*,[88] Robert Gilmer was discharged by Interstate/Johnson Lane Corp. (Interstate) from his position as manager of financial services. A condition of his employment had been to register with several stock exchanges, including the New York Stock Exchange. The NYSE registration application contained a clause by which the applicant "agreed to arbitrate any dispute, claim, or controversy" between him and his employer "arising out of the employment or termination of employment of" the applicant.

Gilmer, sixty-two when Interstate discharged him, first filed a charge with the Equal Employment Opportunity Commission, and then filed a civil suit, alleging that Interstate had fired him because of his age in violation of the Age Discrimination in Employment Act.[89] Interstate moved to compel arbitration, and the district court, relying on *Gardner-Denver*, denied the motion. The Fourth Circuit reversed, finding "nothing in the text, legislative history, or underlying purposes of the ADEA indicating a congressional intent to preclude enforcement of arbitration agreements."[90]

On appeal, the Supreme Court considered four broad arguments supporting Gilmer's claim that the compulsory arbitration clause should not preclude his ADEA suit. First, Gilmer argued that his case was governed by *Gardner-Denver*, and that the rule of that case was that an individual could not, via an arbitration agreement, waive the right to bring a statutory employment claim in a judicial forum. Second, Gilmer argued that compulsory arbitration was inconsistent with the statutory purposes and framework of the ADEA, and that this inconsistency rebutted the presumption of arbitrability created by the *Mitsubishi* Trilogy. Third, he argued that the arbitral forum was inadequate to protect statutory employment rights. Finally, several amici curiae argued that an FAA provision excluding "contracts of employment" rendered the FAA (and its presumption of arbitrability) inapplicable to Gilmer's case. The Supreme Court rejected all four arguments, holding that the FAA entitled Interstate to compel arbitration of Gilmer's age discrimination claims.[91]

1. Gardner-Denver *Distinguished*

Gilmer argued that *Gardner-Denver* protected his right to litigate rather than arbitrate his ADEA claim. The Court distinguished the *Gardner-Denver* decision from Gilmer's case in three ways.[92]

First, the Court noted that because a labor arbitrator's authority is limited to interpreting the collective bargaining agreement at issue, the labor arbitrator—such as the one that decided the plaintiff's case in *Gardner-Denver*—lacked the authority to resolve statutory claims. Gilmer, on the other hand, was not covered by a collective bargaining agreement, and the arbitrator who would decide his case would be given explicit authority to resolve "any dispute, claim or controversy" arising out of Gilmer's employment.

The Court's second basis for distinguishing *Gardner-Denver* was that Gilmer—unlike the plaintiff in *Gardner-Denver*—was not dependent on a union to enforce his statutory claims. Gilmer was not covered by a collective bargaining agreement, hence he did not depend on a union's goodwill to provide adequate representation at the arbitration hearing. Thus, the Court concluded that the tension in *Gardner-Denver* between collective representation and individual rights did not apply to Gilmer's case.

Third, the Court noted that *Gardner-Denver* was not decided under the FAA. Citing *Mitsubishi*, the Court imported the presumption of arbitrability from the commercial arbitration context of the *Mitsubishi* Trilogy to the noncollective bargaining agreement context of *Gilmer*. Because

Gardner-Denver was thus distinguished, it was not explicitly overruled. However, it is unclear how *Gardner-Denver* would be decided today if an employer were to argue the applicability of the reasoning in *Gilmer* to the collective bargaining context.[93]

2. Arbitral Consistency with Individual Rights Statutes

Gilmer next asserted that compulsory arbitration is inconsistent with the statutory framework and the purposes of the ADEA. This inconsistency, he claimed, rebutted the *Mitsubishi* Trilogy's presumption of arbitrability. Gilmer advanced four reasons why compulsory arbitration defeated the congressional purposes underlying the ADEA.

First, he argued that compulsory arbitration subverted the congressional goal of furthering important social policies, such as the that of eliminating invidious discrimination from the workplace. The Court rejected this argument, finding that the arbitral forum was adequate to protect these social policies.

Second, Gilmer argued that compulsory arbitration would undermine the role of the EEOC in enforcing the ADEA. If the Court held that the arbitrator's decision was binding, grieving employees would not be forced to file an EEOC charge before proceeding to arbitration, as the ADEA now requires them to do prior to filing suit. Arbitration, thus, would effectively shut the EEOC out of the enforcement process, in violation of a strong congressional policy to encourage voluntary conciliation of disputes between employer and employee with the EEOC as intermediator.[94] The Court rejected Gilmer's argument, reasoning that an arbitration agreement would not preclude an employee from filing an EEOC charge, and, therefore did not shut the EEOC out of the dispute resolution process.[95] The Court further noted that the EEOC's role in fighting discrimination did not depend on individual employees filing charges, because the EEOC can investigate claims even when a charge is not filed. The Court also asserted that "nothing in the ADEA indicates that Congress intended that the EEOC be involved in all employment disputes."[96] Finally, the Court, citing the Securities Exchange Commission's involvement in enforcing securities statutes and the *McMahon* decision holding that securities disputes were arbitrable, stated that the mere involvement of an administrative agency in the enforcement of a statute does not preclude compulsory arbitration.

Third, Gilmer argued that compulsory arbitration denied employees the judicial forum provided by the ADEA. The Court disagreed with Gilmer's assertion that this denial was contrary to congressional intent.[97] First, the Court pointed out that the ADEA never explicitly precluded compulsory arbitration and that Gilmer, hence, had failed to overcome the *Mitsubishi* presumption of arbitrability. The Court next stated that the congressional directive to the EEOC to pursue " 'informal methods of conciliation, conference, and persuasion' " indicated that Congress would not preclude out-of-court dispute resolution methods such as arbitration.[98] The Court also asserted that arbitration is consistent with Congress' grant of concurrent jurisdiction over ADEA claims to state and federal courts because arbitration agreements further an objective of permitting parties to choose a forum, whether judicial or otherwise, for dispute resolution in much the same way as the provision for concurrent jurisdiction.[99]

Finally, Gilmer argued that compulsory arbitration agreements should not be enforced because they often are the product of employer coercion, the result of unequal bargaining power between employers and employees.[100] The Court flatly rejected this argument, stating that "[m]ere inequality in bargaining power . . . is not a sufficient reason to hold that arbitration agreements are never enforceable in the employment context."[101] Instead, the Court held that such agreements would be enforced absent "the sort of fraud or overwhelming economic power that would provide grounds 'for the revocation of any contract,' "[102] and that "claim[s] of unequal bargaining power [are] best left for resolution in specific cases."[103]

3. Arbitral Adequacy

Another argument advanced by Gilmer was that arbitration was inadequate to protect statutory employment rights because of its informality. The Court, first observing that the *Mitsubishi* trilogy had rejected this argument as " 'far out of step with our current strong endorsement' " of arbitration,[104] then cited the relatively formal NYSE arbitration rules to rebut Gilmer's specific challenges.[105] Further, the Court indicated that the FAA, by providing that courts may overturn arbitration decisions "[w]here there was evident partiality or corruption in the arbitrators," also protects employees from biased arbitrators.[106]

Gilmer also complained that arbitral discovery was more limited than that available through federal courts, thereby limiting an employee's ability to prove discrimination. After noting that NYSE rules permitted "document production, information requests, depositions, and subpoenas," the Court declared that "by agreeing to arbitrate, a party 'trades the procedures and opportunity for review of the courtroom for the simplicity, informality, and expedition of arbitration.' "[107]

Gilmer further attacked arbitral adequacy on the ground that arbitrators were not required to issue written opinions.[108] As a result, the public would be unaware of employers' discrimination policies, effective appellate review would be hampered, and the development of the law would be stifled. The Court countered Gilmer's attack with three responses. First, the Court pointed out that the NYSE arbitration rules require arbitrators to issue written, detailed opinions, and to make those opinions publicly available. Second, the Court reasoned that courts would continue to issue judicial opinions because not all employers and employees are likely to sign binding arbitration agreements. Third, the Court attacked the uniqueness of Gilmer's argument, noting that settlement agreements, which are encouraged by the ADEA, similarly fail to produce written opinions.[109]

As a separate attack on arbitral adequacy, Gilmer argued that judicial review of arbitral decisions was too limited. The Court, responding in a footnote and citing a case from the *Mitsubishi* trilogy, stated that " 'although judicial scrutiny of arbitration awards necessarily is limited, such review is sufficient to ensure that arbitrators comply with the requirements of the statute' at issue."[110]

Gilmer's final attack on arbitral adequacy concerned the arbitrators' limited power to award relief. In rejecting this argument, the Court indicated that NYSE rules granted NYSE arbitrators the authority to award equitable relief and hear class actions. The Court further opined that even if the lack of such authority would not justify concluding that arbitral procedures were inadequate to protect employees' statutory rights.[111]

The Court, therefore, rejected all of Gilmer's complaints concerning arbitral adequacy. Because the NYSE rules created a relatively formal arbitral setting, it was possible that the courts could interpret *Gilmer* as requiring a such a setting for the judicial grant of an order compelling arbitration. If courts interpreted *Gilmer* this way, they would refuse to compel arbitration of any claim where the arbitration procedures were less formal than the procedures created by the NYSE arbitration rules. However, because the *Gilmer* Court did not rely exclusively on NYSE formality to reject Gilmer's arguments against enforcement of his arbitration agreement, such an interpretation was, though possible, not inevitable. This is discussed further in Chapter 9.

4. The FAA "Contracts of Employment" Exclusion

In addition to Gilmer's arguments, the Court received briefs from several amici curiae contending that an FAA provision excluding "contracts of employment" rendered the FAA—and its presumption of arbitrability—inapplicable to this case. Section 1 of the FAA, the definitional section, states that "nothing herein contained shall apply to contracts of employment of seamen, railroad employees, or any other class of workers engaged in interstate commerce."[112] The Court noted that Gilmer had not presented, and the courts below had not considered, the effect of this provision on Gilmer's case.[113] Nevertheless, the Court concluded that because the arbitration agreement was contained in Gilmer's registration application with the NYSE, it was not part of his "contract of employment" with Interstate.

Some commentators have argued that both the "plain meaning"[114] and the legislative history[115] of the FAA compel courts to construe the "contracts of employment" exception to exclude all employment contracts. If courts accept this argument, *Gilmer* becomes a very narrow decision, applicable only to employees in the security industry whose arbitration agreement is contained not in their formal employment contract, but rather in their registration application with the NYSE.[116] However, nearly every court that has considered the issue has interpreted the clause to exclude only those workers directly involved in interstate commerce, such as truck drivers.[117] A complete analysis of the "contracts of employment" exception is found in the next chapter.

The legal status of arbitration agreements has undergone tremendous change in the last hundred years. Although the strongly proarbitration tenor of the Supreme Court's recent decisions indicates a substantial likelihood that arbitration may become the preeminent method for resolving employment disputes, there is ample opportunity for either the Court or Congress to decide that the current experiment with compulsory employment arbitration is a mistake that should be ended. One legal issue providing this opportunity is discussed in chapter 3.

Three

The FAA "Contracts of Employment" Exclusion

T HE *GILMER* DECISION DISCUSSED IN CHAPTER 2 strongly endorsed compulsory arbitration as a means of resolving employment disputes. One might think that, given a fervent desire by most employers to avoid the seven-digit amounts that juries award in employment cases almost daily,[1] employers would have wasted no time in requiring their employees to sign arbitration agreements. As discussed in chapter 1, however, only a small number of employers have implemented such a requirement, though many are considering doing so. This hesitation stems from the fact that *Gilmer*, while enforcing arbitration of an age discrimination claim pursuant to the arbitration agreement used in the securities industry, did not resolve conclusively whether other types of claims were similarly arbitrable, or whether other types of arbitration agreements would be enforced. There is little advantage to arbitration if a prerequisite to arbitration is litigating arbitrability and enforcement issues up through the circuit courts.

Gilmer left three important issues unanswered. The first is whether a clause in the Federal Arbitration Act (FAA) excluding certain "contracts of employment" will be interpreted to preclude courts from enforcing employment arbitration agreements. The second is whether the FAA, which the *Gilmer* Court used to compel arbitration of an age discrimination claim, applies equally to other types of claims, such as race discrimination claims and sexual harassment claims and claims based on state tort law. The third issue is whether the NLRA prohibits, and whether the Equal Employment Opportunity Commission can prohibit, compulsory employment arbitration. This chapter examines the first issue; issues two and three are discussed in chapter 4, 5, and 6.

These "open issues" give courts and Congress the opportunity to wait and see how the experiment with employment arbitration works before irrevocably committing to it. If compulsory arbitration lives up to its potential as a fast, inexpensive, accessible, and ecumenical method of resolving employment disputes, the courts and/or Congress can confirm its preeminent status by resolving these open issues in favor of arbitration. If, however, the experiment fails and compulsory arbitration is used by employers as a vehicle for eviscerating employees' individual employment rights, the experiment can quickly be ended.

As discussed in Chapter 2, the *Gilmer* decision, permitting an employer to compel an employee to arbitrate statutory employment claims, was based on the FAA, which creates a body of federal substantive law enforcing agreements to arbitrate in transactions involving commerce.[2] Section 1 of the FAA contains an exclusionary clause providing that "nothing contained herein shall apply to contracts of employment of seamen, railroad employees, or any other class of workers engaged in foreign or interstate commerce."[3] The *Gilmer* Court avoided the issue of whether this "contract of employment" exclusion applied to Gilmer on the grounds that the issue had not been argued in the lower courts and that Gilmer's arbitration agreement was not part of his "contract of employment" with his employer since it was contained in his registration application with the New York Stock Exchange. The Supreme Court's failure to interpret this exclusion has created uncertainty regarding the enforceability of employment arbitration agreements. If the exclusion is interpreted broadly to exclude *all* employment contracts, *Gilmer* becomes a very narrow decision applicable only to employees in the securities industry whose arbitration agreements are contained not in their formal employment contract, but rather in their registration application with the NYSE. If, on the other hand, this exclusion is interpreted only to apply to employees in the transportation industry *such as* seamen and railroad employees, *Gilmer* becomes an extremely broad decision that permits the vast majority of American employers to require their employees to arbitrate their employment claims.

A. Legislative History

Most attempts to interpret this "contracts of employment" exclusion begin with the legislative history of the United States Arbitration Act (USAA), later recodified as the FAA. The first draft of the proposed arbitration act, prepared by the ABA Committee on Commerce, Trade, and Commercial Law, was created in 1921 and introduced in the Senate[4] and the House[5] in December 1922. It was one of three proposals, including a uniform state law and an international treaty, designed to encourage commercial arbitration:[6]

> In the opinion of your committee, the adoption of the international treaty, the federal statute and the uniform state statute will put the United States in the forefront in this procedural reform. It will raise the standards of commercial ethics. It will reduce litigation. It will enable business men to settle their disputes expeditiously and economically, and will reduce the congestion in the federal and state courts. In pressing forward this improvement in the law, the [American Bar] Association will align itself with the best economic and commercial thought of the country and will do much to overcome the criticism of the law's delays.[7]

This bill did not contain the exclusionary language now in Section 1.

Andrew Furuseth, president of the International Seamen's Union of America and a long-time leader of the American Federation of Labor,[8] objected to the bill vigorously, claiming that it constituted a "compulsory labor" bill.[9] Both he and the AFL, which also protested the bill,[10] clearly believed that workers would be forced to sign arbitration clauses[11] and that arbitrators would be biased in favor of employers to an even greater degree than injunction-prone judges.[12] However, it is less clear whether Furuseth's concern was directed primarily at seamen or at all workers generally. Furuseth's intention in this regard is crucial because the purported parochialism of his interests has led many courts to infer a Congressional intent identical to Furuseth's purported intent and to interpret the "contracts of employment" clause accordingly—that is, as excluding only the seamen and similarly situated transportation workers that Furuseth apparently had in mind when he lobbied for the exclusion.

The most common view of Furuseth's concern, and the view universally adopted by the courts which have considered the issue, is that Furuseth was concerned primarily if not exclusively with the way the proposed legislation would affect his particular constituency, seamen. By this view, Furuseth feared that arbitration would eviscerate the protective statutory laws that seamen has fought to secure: the "seamen's right to wages [under contract and under the Seamen's Act of 1915],[13] to food [under maritime law], to damages under the Jones Act [of 1920],[14] together with his present right to quit work in harbor [without being detained and forcibly returned to work—again, under the Seaman's Act]. . . . With the seamen, the machinery is there"[15] to, by inserting boilerplate arbitration clauses into the seaman's standard form contracts, abate these protections by eliminating the role of the courts in enforcing them.[16] Furuseth therefore, according to this view, argued to the ABA Committee that seamen should be exempted from the Arbitration Act because Congress already had provided a statutorily-based procedure for arbitration of their concerns.[17]

Another view, recently advanced by Professor Matthew Finkin, is that Furuseth was concerned with the effect of the USAA not only on seamen, but on all workers.[18] Finkin points out that the arbitration clauses which Furuseth feared could have been used by *any* employer—not just employers of seamen—to compel arbitration.[19] Finkin also assembles several statements made by Furuseth indicating the broader scope of his concern. For example, in Furuseth's 1923 analysis of the USAA contained in an appendix of the proceedings of the Seamen's Union Annual Convention of that year, Furuseth states that although it is "presumed that the arbitrator will do justice, but he must primarily see that the contract is carried out, whether it has reference to the labor of procuring, making, transporting or delivering commodities, or the labor of repairing, building, or erecting any structure, or in the work performed to those ends by individual workmen or mechanics." [20] In that same analysis, Furuseth states: "So much for the seamen. (Was it the Protective and Indemnity Insurance lawyers that drew this bill?) Hardly. There were others. The bill applies to all workers in interstate and foreign commerce and to others, that are not necessarily workers—to shippers and travelers." [21] And, in referring to the unbalanced bargaining power that would compel workers to accept arbitration provisions: "Will such contracts be signed? Esau agreed, because he was hungry. It was the desire to live that caused slavery to begin and continue. With the growing hunger in modern society, there will be but few that will be able to resist. The personal hunger of the seamen, and the hunger of the wife and children of the railroad man will surely tempt them to sign, *and so with sundry other workers in 'Interstate and Foreign Commerce.'* "[22]

Moreover, when the 1924 Seamen's Union Annual Convention again endorsed Furuseth's analysis, it resolved to continue its cooperation with the AFL "in preventing the enactment of any measure designed to fasten any species of compulsory arbitration *upon any group of workers in America.*"[23]

Furuseth did not testify in the December 1923 Congressional hearings on the bill before the Judiciary Committee. However, W. H. H. Piatt, the chair of the ABA Committee, referred to Furuseth's objection and attempted to reassure labor representatives:

[Mr. Furuseth of the Seamen's Union] has objected to [the federal bill], and criticized it on the ground that the bill in its present form would affect, in fact compel, arbitration of the matters of agreement between the stevedores and their employers. Now, it was not the intention of this bill to make an industrial arbitration in any sense; and so I suggest that . . . if your honorable committee should feel that there is any danger of that, they should add to the bill the following language, "but nothing herein contained shall apply to seamen or any class of workers in interstate commerce or foreign commerce." It is not intended that this shall be an Act referring to labor disputes at all. It is purely an Act to give merchants the right or the privilege of sitting down and agreeing with each other as to what their damages are, if they want to do it. Now, that is all there is in this.[24]

Senator Walsh of Montana responded:

The trouble . . . is that a great many of these contracts that are entered into are really not voluntarily [*sic*] things at all. Take an insurance policy; there is a blank in it. You can take that or you can leave it. The agent has no power at all to decide it. Either you can make that contract or you cannot make any contract. It is the same with a good many contracts of employment. A man says "There are our terms. All right, take it or leave it." Well, there is nothing for the man to do except to sign it; and then he surrenders his right to have his cased tried by the court, and has to have it tried before a tribunal in which he has no confidence at all.[25]

The exchange continued, and Mr. Piatt allayed Senator Walsh's fears by indicating that the bill was not intended to apply to such situations. Senator Walsh then stated: "And then [carriers] have the regular bill of lading contract, but they have a further provision that any controversy arising under the contract shall be submitted to arbitration; and the fellow says 'Well, I haven't any confidence in it. If I have a controversy[,] I would like to have it tried before a court, where I feel I can get justice.' "[26] Mr. Piatt responded: "I would not favor any kind of legislation that would permit the forcing [*sic*] a man to sign that kind of a contract."[27]

The report of these same hearings also reproduces a January 21, 1923 letter from Secretary of Commerce Herbert Hoover to Senator Thomas Sterling, the Chair of the subcommittee considering the bill. Hoover, who had actively supported the bill,[28] stated:

The clogging of our courts is such that the delays amount to a virtual denial of justice. I append an excerpt of the American Bar Association report which would seem to support that statement. I believe the emergency exists for prompt action and I sincerely hope that this Congress may be able to relieve the serious situation. If objection appears to the inclusion of *workers' contracts* in the law's scheme, it might be well amended by stating "but nothing herein contained shall apply to contracts of employment of seamen, railroad employees, or any other class of workers engaged in interstate or foreign commerce.[29]

The subcommittee then amended the bill to incorporate this exclusion:

Objections to the bill were urged by Mr. Andrew Furuseth as representing the seamen's union. Mr. Furuseth, taking the position that seamen's wages came within admiralty jurisdiction and should not be subject to an agreement to arbitrate. In order to eliminate this opposition, the Committee consented to an amendment to Section I as follows: but nothing herein contained shall apply to contracts of employment of seamen, railroad employees, or any other class of workers engaged in foreign or interstate commerce. Various suggestions were made by the Committee on the Judiciary, and to meet these suggestions, but without changing the substantial form of the bill, it was amended . . .[30]

The 1922 bill was not enacted. In December 1923, a new bill was introduced in the House and Senate that contained the exclusionary clause now found in Section 1.[31] At the ensuing hearings and floor debates, several persons testified that the bill was intended to apply to commercial arbitration only, and not to organized labor. Apparently, organized labor was satisfied because it did not attend the hearings.[32]

Shortly after the bill passed in 1924, the AFL claimed that its intervention and protests had resulted in the adoption of the Section 1 exclusion, which "exempts labor from the provisions of the law."[33] A year later, the ABA Commerce Committee proposed a bill to require arbitration of disputes arising out of collective bargaining agreements.[34] Once again, the AFL opposed such a bill.[35] The ABA committee abandoned the proposal, concluding that "public opinion is not yet ready for this legislation," and that "it would be a mistake to press it actively at the present time."[36]

The legislative history of the exclusionary clause does not conclusively indicate how the clause should be interpreted. The fact that the clause was added at the behest of the Seamen's Union and the AFL may suggest the clause should be interpreted to exclude unions and collective bargaining agreements from the scope of the arbitration act. The Seamen's Union's particularized fears about the arbitration act infringing upon the statutorily-based arbitration procedure already in place for transportation workers (such as seamen) might indicate that the act should be interpreted to exclude only those classes of workers. The discussion between Mr. Piatt and Senator Walsh can be taken to indicate that Congress intended to exclude take-it-or-leave-it standard form contracts in which the contracting party seeking to include an arbitration clause has more bargaining power than the other party. Finally, statements throughout the legislative history can be interpreted to evince Congressional intention that the Act apply only to commercial contracts, and not in the labor and/or employment context. The fact that it is possible to find support in the legislative history for each of these interpretations makes it extremely difficult to provide a definitive answer to the issue increasingly before courts today: whether the exclusionary clause puts nonunion *employment* contracts outside the scope of the FAA.

Courts were not faced with this issue with great frequency until the late 1980s and early 1990s, when securities employers began attempting to enforce the arbitration clauses such as the one at issue in *Gilmer*. Prior to that, judicial attempts to interpret the exclusionary clause focused on the issue of whether the clause excluded from the scope of the FAA collective bargaining agreements negotiated by unions and employers. These decisions are important because they form the basis by which the exclusionary clause is interpreted in today's nonunion context.

B. Pre-*Lincoln Mills* Interpretation

In the 1957 decision of *Textile Workers Union v. Lincoln Mills*,[37] the United States Supreme Court held that in enacting Section 301 of the Labor-Management Relations Act of 1947 (LMRA),[38] which authorized federal suits for violation of contracts between employers and unions, Congress granted federal courts the authority to order specific performance of an arbitration agreement contained in a collective bargaining agreement. Prior to this decision, the lower federal courts were split on the issue of whether, and if so under what authority, a court could compel arbitration of a dispute arising under a collective bargaining agreement.

Before the enactment of the LMRA in 1947, state law supplied the substantive law applied to suits for violation of collective bargaining agreements.[39] After the enactment of Section 301, however, parties seeking to compel arbitration pursuant to arbitration clauses contained in collective bargaining agreements increasingly began looking to federal law, both to avoid the common law rule existing in most state jurisprudence that arbitration agreements were revocable and unenforceable,[40] and in the hope that either the attitude of the federal judiciary or the provisions of the FAA would permit enforcement.[41]

A party seeking to compel arbitration pursuant to the FAA prior to *Lincoln Mills* ran headlong into the "contracts of employment" exclusion of Section 1 of the FAA. Before *Lincoln Mills* mooted the issue by declaring that such a suit could be brought under Section 301 without need for the authority of the FAA,[42] the issues for parties facing the exclusion revolved around attempts to avoid the exclusion. Parties seeking to compel arbitration relied on three major arguments: first, that the exclusionary clause did not apply to the entire FAA; second, that a collective bargaining agreement was not a "contract of employment"; and third, that the exclusionary clause only applied to workers engaged directly in interstate commerce.[43] A party seeking to compel arbitration only had to convince the court that one of these arguments was valid to obtain a stay of judicial proceedings.

1. Does the Exclusionary Clause Apply to the Entire FAA?

The first method by which parties sought to avoid the exclusionary clause was to limit the effect of the clause on the rest of the statute. The issue was whether the phrase "nothing herein contained" meant "nothing in this statute," "nothing in this section," or "nothing in the foregoing definition of commerce."

If the phrase were given the first meaning, then the exclusionary clause would be given the broadest application and would not support a motion to stay. If given the second meaning, the exclusion would be, for all practical purposes, interpreted out of existence. This was so because Section 1 of the statute contained no substantive provisions; it contained merely definitions and exceptions to the operation of the statute.[44] Since courts were reluctant to interpret the clause in a way that made the clause itself meaningless, most cases focused on whether the phrase "nothing herein contained" could be interpreted to mean "nothing in the foregoing definition of commerce."

The essential argument was that the exclusionary clause of Section 1 created an exception only to those sections whose application depended on a showing that the promise to arbitrate was written in a "maritime transaction" or a "contract evidencing a transaction involving commerce." Section 2, which makes arbitration agreements enforceable, is such a section, being operative only when the agreement is found "in any maritime transaction or a contract evidencing a transaction involving commerce." Section 3, on the other hand, permits a party to obtain a stay of judicial proceedings when an issue is referable to arbitration, and does not contain a "transaction involving commerce" requirement. The argument goes that Congress included the "transaction involving commerce" requirement in Section 2 because those were the only kinds of agreements that it believed it had the power to regulate under the Constitutional theories prevailing in 1925 when the Arbitration Act was enacted;[45] Section 3 is based on Congress' much broader power to regulate procedure in the federal courts, and contains no such requirement.[46] The Section 1 definitions of "maritime transactions" and "commerce" therefore relate to Section 2, and have no application to the motions for a stay pending arbitration authorized by Section 3. The exclusionary clause in Section 1 was interpreted as serving the same limited purpose; the phrase "nothing herein contained" was interpreted to refer to the rest of Section 1 and through it to the provisions affected by the definitions (such as Section 2), but not to the entire statute (such as Section 3). In effect, the exclusionary clause of Section 1 is interpreted much more narrowly than the enforceability clause of Section 2, despite the fact that the clauses contain virtually identical language.[47] This results in the broadest possible reading of the scope of the FAA.

Although the Third Circuit adhered to this interpretation for six years,[48] it repudiated this view in the 1951 decision of *Amalgamated Association of Street, Electric Railway Motor Coach Employees of America, Local Div. 1210 v. Pennsylvania Greyhound Lines.*[49] This decision, which interpreted the words "nothing herein contained" to mean "nothing contained in the statute," relied on the inclusion of the catchline "Exemptions to Operation of Title" in the 1947 recodification of the Arbitration Act to establish Congressional intent that the exclusion should be applied to the entire statute.[50] This reliance was misplaced; it ignored the fact that the recodification was entirely ministerial and was not intended to change existing law,[51] and the fact that the catchline originated not with Congress but with the editors of West Publishing Company, who put it in the United States Code.[52] Several other courts similarly interpreted the exclusion to apply to the entire Arbitration Act, though not all of them relied on the catchline for authority.[53] This controversy was finally settled by the United States Supreme Court in *Bernhardt v. Polygraphic Co.*,[54] which interpreted Sections 1, 2, and 3 as interrelated parts of the statute.

2. Is a Collective Bargaining Agreement a "Contract of Employment?"

The second major argument for avoiding the "contracts of employment" exclusion was that a collective bargaining agreement was not a "contract of employment," and therefore not excluded.[55] Proponents of this argument generally relied on Justice Jackson's dicta in *J.I. Case Co. v. NLRB:* "Collective bargaining between employer and the representatives of a unit, usually a union, results in an accord as to terms which will govern hiring and work and pay in that unit. The result is not, however, a contract of employment except in rare cases; no one has a job by reason of it and no obligation to any individual ordinarily comes into existence from it alone. The negotiations between union and management result in what often has been called a trade agreement, rather than in a contract of employment."[56] Several federal judges relied on this statement to hold that collective bargaining agreements were not "contracts of employment" within the meaning of the Arbitration Act.[57]

This interpretation was not widely adopted, for two reasons.[58] First, the courts pointed to the legislative history of the USAA. The exception for contracts of employment was introduced into the USAA to meet the objections of the Seafarers' International Union, which feared that the application of the statute to maritime transactions would force upon seamen a form of "compulsory arbitration." Since it appeared to these courts that the seamen's undertakings to submit disputes to arbitration were contained in collective bargaining agreements, Congressional intent in enacting the exclusionary clause must have been, by this argument, to exclude arbitration agreements contained in collective bargaining agreements.[59]

Second, courts held that Justice Jackson's extremely technical distinction between collective bargaining agreements and employment contracts was inconsistent both with judicial usage and common understanding of the terms.[60] One court explained: "a collective bargaining agreement entered into by a union for the benefit of employees (present or future) is a prospective contract of employment which becomes absolute at the time of hiring. The hiring merges with and becomes a part of the contract of employment, the terms and conditions of which have been determined in advance. To hold that the bargaining agreement at that time does not constitute a contract of employment is to ignore realities."[61]

Thus, most courts considering the issue concluded that collective bargaining agreements were contracts of employment and rejected Justice Jackson's approach to limiting the scope of the exclusionary clause.[62]

3. Does the Exclusionary Clause Apply Only to Workers Directly Engaged in Interstate Commerce?

Because neither of the first two approaches to limiting the effects of the Section 1 exclusionary clause were widely adopted, parties seeking to compel arbitration pursuant to collective bargaining agreements often were forced to resort to the argument that Congress, by exempting the employment contracts of "seamen, railroad employees, or any other class of workers engaged in foreign or interstate commerce," intended that the exclusion apply only to employees engaged directly in interstate commerce *such as* seamen and railroad employees. This argument, which is the most important legacy of the pre-*Lincoln Mills* line of cases interpreting the FAA, is developed most forcefully in the Third Circuit *en banc* decision of *Tenney Engineering, Inc. v. United Electrical Workers Local 437.*[63]

In *Tenney*, an employer brought an action under Section 301 of the

LMRA to recover damages for breach of a no-strike clause in a collective bargaining agreement. The union argued that the alleged violation gave rise to a dispute cognizable under the arbitration clause of the agreement. Therefore, it moved for a stay pending arbitration pursuant to the FAA. The district court denied the stay, and the union appealed.

On appeal, the Third Circuit initially noted and approved its earlier decisions which had held that the Section 1 exclusionary clause applies to the entire FAA, and that the "contracts of employment" to which this clause refers include collective bargaining agreements.[64] The court framed the issue as whether the employees, who the parties had stipulated were engaged in the manufacture of goods for interstate commerce and in incidental plant maintenance, were a "class of workers engaged in foreign or interstate commerce" within the meaning of the exclusionary clause.[65]

The court began its analysis of this issue by reviewing the legislative history of the clause. After citing references to Furuseth's objections on behalf of the Seamen's Union, the court concluded:

It thus appears that the draftsmen of the Act were presented with the problem of exempting seamen's contracts. Seamen constitute a class of workers as to whom Congress had long provided machinery for arbitration. In exempting them the draftsmen excluded also railroad employees, another class of workers as to whom special procedure for the adjustment of disputes had previously been provided. Both these classes of workers were engaged directly in interstate or foreign commerce. To these the draftsmen of the Act added "any other class of workers engaged in foreign or interstate commerce." We think that the intent of the latter language was, under the rule of ejusdem generis, to include only those other classes of workers who are . . . actually engaged in the movement of interstate or foreign commerce or in work so closely related thereto as to be in practical effect part of it. The draftsmen had in mind the two groups of transportation workers as to which special arbitration legislation already existed and they rounded out the exclusionary clause by excluding all other similar classes of workers.[66]

Thus, the court held that the Section 1 exclusion of workers "engaged in" interstate commerce applied only to workers engaged "directly" in interstate commerce, and not to those whose work merely "affected" interstate commerce.[67]

This interpretation of the phrase "engaged in . . . interstate commerce" is at least arguably consistent with the distinctions which the Supreme Court had drawn—by the 1950s—among the phrases "affecting commerce," "engaged in the production of goods for commerce," and engaged "in commerce." As Professor Archibald Cox stated in 1954: "The first phrase is probably co-extensive with the power of Congress under the Commerce Clause; the second covers most activities prior to an interstate shipment but little else; in some contexts, the last is so narrow that it does not even cover the cook of a track maintenance gang on an interstate railroad."[68] However, it is doubtful whether Congress understood these distinctions in 1924, long before they were drawn by the Court. At that time, the concept of federal jurisdiction under the Commerce Clause was far narrower than it was in the 1950s, and the phrase "any other class of workers engaged in interstate or foreign commerce" might legitimately have been understood as broad enough to reach every employment contract subject to federal regulation.[69] Consequently, Cox concludes, "it would seem equally accurate historically and equally permissible textually to read the words either as co-extensive with the Constitutional power of Congress however defined or else as limited to the few types of employment believed subject to federal regulation in 1924."[70]

The problem with *Tenney*'s interpretation of "engaged in interstate commerce," however, is that it is difficult to reconcile with the Section 2 "transaction involving commerce" clause. Recall that Section 2 makes arbitration agreements enforceable only when they are found "in any maritime transaction or a contract evidencing a transaction involving commerce." If the Section 2 clause were interpreted in the same way that the *Tenney* court interpreted the exclusionary clause, the FAA itself would reach only contracts linked directly with foreign or interstate commerce. A party wishing to enforce an arbitration clause contained in an employment contract, therefore, would be put in the difficult position of demonstrating that the employees are part of a transaction "involving commerce" for purposes of Section 1, but at the same time are not "engaged in commerce" for purposes of Section 2. This dilemma can only be avoided if "involving commerce" is interpreted broadly to mean "affecting commerce" and "engaged in commerce" is given its most narrow, technical reading.[71]

The Supreme Court's *Lincoln Mills* decision mooted *Tenney*'s authority holding that courts could compel arbitration pursuant to arbitration clauses found in collective bargaining agreements. The analysis by which the *Tenney* court reached that conclusion, however, survives. Since the *Gilmer* case opened the door—at least partway—to the enforcement of employment arbitration agreements outside the collective bargaining context, courts once again are grappling with the contracts of employment exclusion. *Tenney*'s legacy is that it provides an interpretation of the FAA exclusionary clause which permits courts to compel arbitration of employment disputes. Although the vast majority of courts have followed *Tenney* and enforced such arbitration agreements, several courts and many scholars[72] have suggested that the Section 1 exclusion should be construed differently. The next section describes the various constructions of the exclusion that courts and scholars recently have adopted or proposed.

C. Modern Interpretations

1. Exclude Only Workers "Directly Engaged in Interstate Commerce"

Nearly every circuit court which has construed the FAA "contracts of employment" exclusionary clause since *Tenney* has followed *Tenney* and held that the clause excludes only those workers directly involved in interstate commerce, such as transportation workers.[73] Most have done so by citing to *Tenney* and its analysis of the legislative history of the FAA. For example, in *Erving v. Virginia Squires Basketball Club,*[74] Julius "Dr. J" Erving sued to set aside his contract with the Virginia Squires after he signed a contract with the Atlanta Hawks. The Squires moved to compel arbitration pursuant to an arbitration clause in the contract Erving had signed with the Squires. The Second Circuit, following *Tenney* and holding that the contract was not within the scope of the FAA exclusionary clause, required Erving to arbitrate.[75]

Other courts have obtained the same result by interpreting the FAA anew. For example, in *DiCrisci v. Lyndon Guaranty Bank,*[76] the court looked to the "plain meaning" of the FAA to justify its conclusion that the FAA exclusion only reaches workers directly engaged in interstate commerce. The Court explained:

Although at first glance it might seem likely that Congress would have intended "commerce" to have the same meaning throughout the Act, the reference to "workers engaged in foreign or interstate commerce in section 1 would be surplusage if it were simply coextensive with Congress's powers under the commerce clause. Under *Southland Corp.,* [Section 2] gives the Act as a whole the same reach as Congress's commerce clause power. Therefore, if Congress had wanted to excluded [sic] *all* employment contracts from the Act, it could simply have said "employment contracts" and left it at that. Any workers beyond the reach of the commerce clause would not be covered by the Act in the first place.[77]

Cases such as *Erving* and *DiCrisci,* which restrict the scope of the FAA exclusion to workers directly engaged in interstate commerce, give the FAA extremely broad reach, and permit compulsory arbitration its fullest effect. Other courts and scholars, whether relying on different interpretations of the FAA and its legislative history or on the perceived unfairness of compulsory arbitration, have come to the opposite conclusion.

2. Exclude All Employment Contracts

Only two circuit courts that have construed the FAA "contracts of employment" exclusion since *Tenney* have held that the exclusionary clause should be broadly construed; one of those circuits has since reversed itself and adopted the *Tenney* interpretation. The sole circuit apparently adhering to a broad construction of the exclusion is the Fourth Circuit, which reached its conclusion in *United Electrical, Radio & Machine Workers v. Miller Metal Products, Inc.*[78] In that case, the Fourth Circuit rejected *Tenney*'s position that the exclusionary clause should be construed as not applying to employees engaged in the production of goods for interstate commerce, as distinguished from workers engaged in transportation in interstate commerce.[79] However, the court went on to limit expressly its holding to the issue of whether the FAA is applicable to collective bargaining agreements:

[W]e do not decide that workers and employers may not agree to arbitrate their differences. Nor do we decide that such agreements to arbitrate may not be specifically enforced. What we decide, and all we decide, is . . . that the provisions of the United States Arbitration Act may not be relied on to state proceedings in a suit brought on a collective bargaining agreement entered into by workers engaged in interstate commerce as those here were engaged.[80]

It is questionable, however, whether *Miller Metal Products* is still good law even in the Fourth Circuit. In *Kropfelder v. Snap-On Tools Corp.*,[81] a district court in the Fourth Circuit declined to follow *Miller Metal Products*, stating:

In light of the time which has passed since the *Miller Metal* decision [footnote omitted] the strong federal policy in favor of arbitration, and the great weight of circuit court authority, this Court is of the view that the Fourth Circuit would not, as of this date, apply the words used in *Miller Metal* so as to exclude Section 1's application in all non-collective bargaining contexts, and would instead apply the views expressed by majority of the courts that as to non-collective bargaining contracts the FAA excludes only those workers involved in the interstate transportation of goods.[82]

The Sixth Circuit briefly adopted (in dicta) a broad interpretation of the exclusionary clause in *Willis v. Dean Witter Reynolds, Inc.*[83] In that case, Willis sued in state court on state law claims of sexual harassment and breach of contract. Dean Witter removed the case to federal court based on diversity and moved to compel arbitration based on the arbitration clause in Willis' securities registration form. Because, as in *Gilmer,* Willis' agreement to arbitrate was found in her registration form rather than in a contract with her employer, the Sixth Circuit held that the "contracts of employment" exclusion was irrelevant.[84] Before doing so, however, it considered at length the legislative history of the exclusion, and concluded in dicta that the clause should be interpreted to exclude *all* employment contracts.

The *Willis* court found unpersuasive *Tenney*'s justification for interpreting the "engaged in interstate commerce" clause of Section 1 differently than the "involving commerce" clause of Section 2. Instead, the court stated, "the same meaning for 'commerce' was meant to apply throughout the entire Act," and that meaning was intended to be coextensive with Congress' power under the Commerce Clause.[85] According to the court, this interpretation was consistent with its interpretation of the exclusion's legislative history and congressional intent that the FAA apply exclusively to *commercial* contracts.[86]

However, in *Asplundh Tree Expert Co. v. Bates*,[87] the Sixth Circuit expressly repudiated its interpretation of the FAA exclusionary clause as announced in *Willis,* and held that the exclusionary clause "should be narrowly construed to apply to employment contracts of seamen, railroad workers, and any other class of workers actually engaged in the movement of goods in interstate commerce in the same way that seamen and railroad workers are." The court concluded that (1) the legislative history of the FAA indicated Congress was concerned specifically with seamen and railroad workers, implying a lack of any intent to exclude others; (2) the language of the exclusionary clause used narrower terms than the scope provisions of Section 2; and (3) the FAA's underlying purpose, to favor arbitration, supports the narrow construction of the exclusionary clause.[88]

A broad reading of the exclusionary clause, such as that adopted in *Miller Metal Products* and *Willis,* would effectively preclude compulsory arbitration of most employment disputes. *Gilmer* would become a very narrow decision applicable only to employees in the securities industry whose arbitration agreements are contained in their securities registration form, not in their formal employment contract. Although the lower courts have been virtually unanimous in rejecting this interpretation, there is ample support for it in the text of the FAA and the Act's legislative history. It remains a significant possibility, therefore, that the Supreme Court will in future reconsider the proarbitration tenor of *Gilmer* and interpret the FAA restrictively.

3. Exclude Only "Workers"

Some commentators have suggested that the Section 1 exclusion of "workers engaged in foreign or interstate commerce" should be interpreted to focus on the word "workers." [89] Under this interpretation, the exclusion would apply to owners and supervisors, against whom the law would permit enforcement of arbitration agreements. "Workers," however defined, could not be compelled to submit their employment disputes to arbitration.

This approach finds support in the Second Circuit's 1955 decision of *Bernhardt v. Polygraphic Co. of America*,[90] where the issue was whether a contract between a plant superintendent and his employer was governed by the FAA. The Court concluded that it was not, stating: "The words "any other class of workers," read in connection with the immediately preceding words, show an intention to exclude contracts of employment of a 'class' of 'workers' like 'seamen' or 'railroad employees.' Plaintiff was not hired as a 'worker' but as a plant superintendent, at a salary of $15,000 a year, with managerial duties fundamentally different from those of 'workers.' " [91]

This approach at least is arguably consistent with the legislative history of the FAA, assuming such history is read to suggest that Congress excluded contracts of employment from the FAA to prevent employers from forcing arbitration on employees not powerful enough to stop them. It would help allay commentators' fears that compulsory arbitration currently is being used by employers for just such a purpose. It would be consistent with the notion, implied in *Gilmer*, that "professional" employees are sufficiently astute and possess sufficient bargaining power to look out for themselves, while "workers" are in need of special protection.[92] Finally, this approach allows *Gilmer*, in which the plaintiff was a manager of financial services, to be reconciled with *Alexander v. Gardner-Denver Co.*[93] (as discussed in Chapter 2, the Supreme Court held in *Gardner-Denver* that an employee does not forfeit his Title VII discrimination claim by first pursuing a grievance to final arbitration under the nondiscrimination clause of a collective bargaining agreement), in which the plaintiff was a drill press operator, albeit on grounds not advanced in either decision.

4. Exclude Only Those Workers Whose Claims Are Subject to Arbitration under the Terms of a Collective Bargaining Agreement

A final approach to the FAA exclusion is to interpret it as excluding only those workers whose statutory claims are subject to arbitration under the terms of a collective bargaining agreement. This approach is consistent with, though not compelled by, the *Gilmer* and *Gardner-Denver* decisions.[94] It also is consistent with the FAA's legislative history, at least assuming that the exclusionary clause was added specifically for the benefit of unions such as the Seafarer's Union and the AFL.[95] Most commentators advocating this approach to interpreting the exclusionary clause have assumed that interpretation is an either/or proposition: *either* the clause should be read broadly to exclude *all* employment contracts, *or* the clause should be construed narrowly to exclude *only* collective bargaining agreements.[96] This assumption runs into two problems. The first, as several pre-*Lincoln Mills* courts noted, is that collective bargaining agreements are both popularly and judicially considered to be a subset of employment contracts.[97] Therefore, it is difficult to exclude collective bargaining agreements without also excluding all other employment contracts.

Second, the legislative history indicating that the Seafarers' Union and the AFL deserve credit for the exclusionary clause indicates that those unions might have been just as concerned with limiting the FAA's effect on *individual* employment agreements as with limiting its application to collective bargaining agreements. For example, at the Seamen's Union convention in 1923, at a time when the proposed USAA contained no exemptions, Furuseth submitted an analysis of the arbitration act. In that analysis, he condemned the prospect of employers inserting arbitration clauses in individual employment contracts and collective bargaining agreements.[98] Furuseth had good reason to be equally concerned with both types of employment agreements: a large percentage, if not a majority, of the seamen who made up his constituency were employed pursuant to individual contracts of hire for personal service, and not under collective bargaining agreements.[99] Although courts and commentators have assumed that Furuseth's objections were directed primarily, if not exclusively, at the arbitration of collective bargaining agreements, Furuseth seems to have been as concerned with the arbitration of individual employment agreements.[100]

It is certain from the legislative history of the FAA contracts of employment exclusion that this history can be molded to fit whatever interpretation a court or commentator prefers.[101] Until the Supreme Court provides definitive guidance on the exclusion's meaning, the law will be unsettled as to the FAA's applicability to arbitration agreements contained in standard employment contracts. In addressing this issue the Court can either confirm that compulsory arbitration is the employment dispute resolution mechanism of the future, or impose such severe restrictions that arbitration becomes inapplicable to virtually the entire American workforce.

Four

Applicability of the FAA to Other Employment Laws

THIS CHAPTER EXAMINES THE SECOND ISSUE LEFT open by *Gilmer*. Strictly speaking, *Gilmer* only permits the compelled arbitration of age discrimination claims brought pursuant to the federal statute prohibiting age discrimination. Can the reasoning used by the Court in *Gilmer* also be used to support compulsory arbitration of claims raised under other federal statutes (such as Title VII's prohibition of race and sex discrimination), state legislation (such as state antidiscrimination statutes that parallel Title VII), and state common law (such as defamation and intentional infliction of emotional distress)? Does it make any difference if these claims are brought in a state court instead of a federal court?

One way that the Court (or Congress) might significantly restrict compulsory employment arbitration is by confining it to the factual scenario at issue in the *Gilmer* decision—that is, to federal age discrimination claims. If the FAA is construed as not applying to suits arising under state law, or as not applying to other federal statutes such as that prohibiting race and sex discrimination, compulsory arbitration becomes far less useful as a comprehensive method of resolving workplace legal disputes. These issues are discussed in this chapter.

The basic issue is whether the FAA and its presumption of arbitrability is applicable to the broad spectrum of claims employees may bring under federal and state legislation and common law doctrines. The *Gilmer* decision held that the FAA could permit compulsory arbitration of claims brought pursuant to the Age Discrimination in Employment Act.[1] The Court based its decision on the presumption created by *Mitsubishi* that issues arising under a federal statute are assumed arbitrable unless the party seeking to avoid arbitration can show that, in passing the statute, Congress intended otherwise.[2] In *Gilmer*, the Court examined the text and legislative history of the ADEA and found no such intent.[3] This conclusion is hardly surprising, since the Congress that passed the ADEA in 1987—when *Wilko* was still good law—almost certainly never considered the possibility that claims arising under the ADEA could be subject to compulsory arbitration. The issue now is whether courts similarly will find such an absence of contrary congressional intent when parties seek to compel arbitration of causes of action arising under (1) federal legislation other than the ADEA (most importantly, Title VII) and (2) state legislation and state common law doctrines.

A. Title VII and Other Federal Legislation

Courts following *Gilmer* have compelled arbitration of claims arising under the Americans with Disabilities Act,[4] the Fair Labor Standards Act,[5] the Rehabilitation Act of 1973,[6] the Employee Polygraph Protection Act,[7] the Employee Retirement Income Security Act,[8] the Equal Pay Act,[9] the Family and Medical Leave Act,[10] the Jury Systems Improvement Act[11] (forbidding employers from discriminating against employees because they have served on a jury), and 42 U.S.C. § 1981.[12] In addition, the Fourth,[13] Fifth,[14] Sixth,[15] Ninth,[16] and Eleventh[17] Circuits have held that *Gilmer* subjects Title VII claims to compulsory arbitration.[18] Two other circuits, the First and the Eighth, have held that a compulsory arbitration clause does not preclude a judicial remedy.[19] It is doubtful whether the holdings of these two circuits are still good law, however, because both decisions predate *Gilmer.*

The Supreme Court's treatment of *Alford v. Dean Witter Reynolds, Inc.*[20] often is cited to support extending the Court's reasoning of *Gilmer* to Title VII claims.[21] In *Alford,* a stockbroker named Alford had signed an arbitration agreement similar to the one signed by Gilmer. She originally sued Dean Witter Reynolds in federal district court, alleging Title VII violations of sex discrimination and sexual harassment. Dean Witter Reynolds, pointing to the FAA and the *Mitsubishi* trilogy, moved to dismiss the complaint and to compel arbitration. The district court denied the motion, and the Fifth Circuit, relying on *Gardner-Denver,* affirmed.[22] After the Fifth Circuit's original *Alford* decision *(Alford I),* the Supreme Court decided *Gilmer.* On petition for certiorari in *Alford I,* the Supreme Court vacated and remanded the Fifth Circuit's original decision for further consideration in light of *Gilmer.*[23] The Fifth Circuit, in a second decision *(Alford II),* then reversed its first decision, concluding that *"Gilmer* requires us to reverse the district court and compel arbitration of Alford's Title VII claim."[24]

The Supreme Court's vacation of *Alford I* for reconsideration in light of *Gilmer* does not necessarily indicate that the Court approved the extension of *Gilmer* to Title VII claims.[25] However, because post-*Gilmer* federal decisions unanimously have held that *Gilmer* applies to Title VII claims, the current state of the law appears to be that *Gilmer* and the FAA compel courts to enforce compulsory arbitration clauses in Title VII cases. Section 118 of the Civil Rights Act of 1991[26] ("Civil Rights Act") seems to support this conclusion, providing that "[w]here appropriate and to the extent authorized by law, the use of alternative means of dispute resolution, including settlement negotiations, conciliation, facilitation, mediation, factfinding, minitrials, and arbitration, is encouraged to resolve disputes arising under the Acts or provisions of Federal law amended by this title."

This language is very similar to, and is a much stronger endorsement of, arbitration than the ADEA language upon which the *Gilmer* Court relied when it concluded that Congress had not intended to preclude compulsory arbitration.[27] One commentator considering the effect of the Civil Rights Act on *Gilmer* has concluded that the "clear meaning" of the Act was to "recognize[ ] the arbitrability of discrimination claims arising under [Title VII, the ADEA, and the ADA]."[28]

Some portions of the Civil Rights Act's legislative history indicate that Congress intended this result. Interpretive memoranda placed in the record by Senator Robert Dole and Representative Henry Hyde state in identical language their support for compulsory arbitration: "This provision encourages the use of alternative means of dispute resolution, including *binding* arbitration, where the parties knowingly and voluntarily elect to use these methods. In light of the litigation crisis facing this country and the increasing sophistication and reliability of alternatives to litigation, there is no reason to disfavor the use of such forums."[29] Both memoranda cite *Gilmer* with approval.

Other sections of the legislative history indicate, however, that Congress may *not* have intended to permit compulsory arbitration. Using identical language, the House Committee on Education and Labor and the House Committee on the Judiciary, describing the purpose of Section 118, stated that

[t]he Committee emphasizes, however, that the use of alternative dispute resolution mechanisms is intended to supplement, not supplant, the remedies provided by Title VII. Thus, for example, the Committee believes that any agreement to submit disputed issues to arbitration, whether in the context of a collective bargaining agreement or in an employment contract, does not preclude the affected person from seeking relief under the enforcement provisions of Title VII. This

view is consistent with the Supreme Court's interpretation of Title VII in *Alexander v. Gardner-Denver Co.*, 415 U.S. 36 (1974). The Committee does not intend for the inclusion of this section [*sic*] be used to preclude rights and remedies that would otherwise be available.[30]

In fact, the Republican version of the Civil Rights Act, proposed by President Bush and introduced as an amendment in the nature of a substitute,[31] would have encouraged the use of arbitration " 'in place of judicial resolution.' "[32] Noting that this proposal would allow employers to "refuse to hire workers unless they signed a binding statement waiving all rights to file Title VII complaints," the House Committee on Education and Labor rejected this proposal, stating that "[s]uch a rule would fly in the face of Supreme Court decisions holding that workers have the right to go to court, rather than being forced into compulsory arbitration, to resolve important statutory and constitutional rights, including employment opportunity rights. American workers should not be forced to choose between their jobs and their civil rights."[33]

This legislative history suggests that *Gilmer*'s post-1991 progeny were wrongly decided—that Congress did *not* intend for statutory employment claims to be subject to compulsory arbitration. If this is true, however, the statutory language of the Civil Rights Act is hard to explain. Why would Congress, if it wished to preclude compulsory arbitration, endorse arbitration using virtually the same language that the Court previously had construed to prove congressional approval of compulsory arbitration? Because *Gilmer* was decided six months before the Civil Rights Act was passed and signed, Congress had plenty of time to amend the proposed Act to express clearly its intent regarding compulsory arbitration. Perhaps its failure to do so, and its reliance on the legislative history of *Gardner-Denver*, indicates its agreement with the Court's analysis distinguishing *Gilmer* from *Gardner-Denver*.[34] Moreover, post-*Gilmer* congressional attempts to overrule legislatively *Gilmer*, or to restrict *Gilmer* to the ADEA, have failed.[35]

Even assuming that Congress intended in 1991 to preclude compulsory arbitration on the facts of *Gilmer*, it is unclear how broadly Congress intended that preclusion to be interpreted. The legislative history of the Civil Rights Act indicates that Congress' main concern was that unequal bargaining power would allow an employer to coerce an otherwise-unwilling employee to sign a compulsory arbitration agreement as a condition of employment.[36] An employer that gives its employees a bona fide choice of whether or not to agree to compulsory arbitration, rather than merely presenting the employee with a take-it-or-leave-it contractual offer of employment, avoids the issue with which Congress appeared to be primarily concerned.

Like the FAA "contracts of employment" exclusion, the legislative history of the 1991 Civil Rights Act pertaining to the arbitrability of federal employment discrimination claims is sufficiently ambiguous to permit courts and commentators to draw whatever conclusion they like.[37] As with interpretation of the FAA, the overwhelming current trend seems to favor interpreting the Civil Rights Act in a way that will permit broad enforcement of employment arbitration agreements. However, again like the FAA, the Supreme Court has not definitely ruled on the issue, leaving open the possibility that a contrary future ruling could significantly restrict the applicability of compulsory arbitration.

B. State Legislation and Common Law

The FAA neither clearly demarcates its impact on state statutory and common law nor provides a basis for independent federal question jurisdiction, so its enforcement is left in large part to the state courts.[38] This creates a host of federalism questions, such as whether and to what extent the FAA preempts contrary state law, whether causes of action based on state law are subject to compulsory arbitration under the FAA, and whether the FAA is applicable to state courts applying state substantive law. A series of Supreme Court decisions has resolved much of this ambiguity in favor of arbitration.

The first major case was *Bernhardt v. Polygraphic Co.*[39] In *Bernhardt,* a supervisor of a lithography plant sued his employer in Vermont state court for damages resulting from his discharge. After the employer removed the case to federal district court, the employer relied on an arbitration agreement signed by the employee to move for a stay pending arbitration. The district court denied the motion pursuant to a Vermont law making arbitration agreements revocable. The Second Circuit reversed on the ground that Section 3 of the FAA (permitting stays pending arbitration) was a mandatory procedural rule applicable in all federal proceedings.[40] The Second Circuit further held that Section 3 did not violate the federalism doctrine previously announced by the United States Supreme Court in *Erie Railroad Co. v. Tompkins,*[41] because Section 3 merely created a change in forum and did not implicate substantive rights.[42]

Until the Supreme Court's 1938 *Erie* decision, Congress had broad legislative power over the rules governing federal courts, derived presumably from congressional power to control the courts' jurisdiction. In *Erie,* the Court expressed its concern that rules governing the federal courts were affecting the outcome of state law cases that were being decided by federal courts because of diversity jurisdiction.[43] It was unthinkable, the Court opined, that two otherwise identical cases, predicated on precisely the same state law, could be decided differently merely because one was brought in state court and the other was brought in federal court.[44] To eliminate this problem, the Court fashioned the rule that in diversity cases, federal courts are required to follow state rules of decision in matters that are "substantive" rather than "procedural," or where the matter is "outcome determinative."[45]

In *Bernhardt,* the Supreme Court faced the issue of whether the FAA was an unconstitutional intrusion by Congress into state law. Assuming that legislative authority for passing the FAA derived from congressional power over federal court jurisdiction, the FAA could only pass constitutional muster if it could be characterized as procedural rather than substantive. Borrowing heavily from the then-extant decision of *Wilko v. Swan,*[46] the Court found that the FAA was substantive, because "[t]he change from a court of law to an arbitration panel may make a radical difference in ultimate result."[47] Citing *Wilko,* the Court noted that this outcome determinacy resulted from the wide-ranging inadequacies of arbitration compared to litigation—including the lack of written opinions, the inability of arbitrators to accurately decide issues of law, and limited judicial review.[48] The *Bernhardt* court avoided this potential *Erie* problem by holding that the FAA was inapplicable because the contract between a lithography company and its supervisor was not a contract "in commerce" as required by the FAA.[49] The Court thus significantly narrowed the scope of the FAA specifically to avoid the federalism issue.

Although *Bernhardt*'s narrow reading of the FAA and suspicion of the arbitral forum was repudiated in later decisions,[50] the notion of the FAA as "substantive" survived. For example, in *Prima Paint Corp. v. Flood & Conklin Manufacturing Co.,*[51] the Court held that a defense of fraud in the making of a contract containing an arbitration agreement was arbitrable under the FAA. Prima Paint had agreed—in a contract containing an arbitration clause—to acquire Flood & Conklin's paint business. Prima Paint later sued in federal court to rescind the contract, on the ground that Flood & Conklin had committed fraud in the inducement of the contract (although not in the inducement of the arbitration clause in particular). The Court held that, notwithstanding a contrary state rule, consideration of a claim of fraud in the inducement of a contract "is for the arbitrators and not for the courts."[52] In doing so, it adopted the "severability doctrine" divorcing arbitration clauses from the underlying agreement: "Accordingly, if the claim is fraud in the inducement of the arbitration clause itself—an issue which goes to the 'making' of the agreement to arbitrate—the federal court may proceed to adjudicate it. But the statutory language does not permit the federal court to consider claims of fraud in the inducement of the contract generally."[53]

This severability doctrine has been roundly criticized as "problematic" and illogical because it is improbable that fraud tainting the contract generally would not also affect the arbitration agreement.[54] However, the doctrine announced by *Prima Paint* is less important for present purposes than the process by which the Court arrived at its conclusion. The Court based the authority to fashion a federal rule in the face of conflicting state authority on the theory that Congress passed the FAA pursuant to its commerce and admiralty powers, rather than pursuant to its power to regulate federal courts as assumed in *Bernhardt*.[55] Because congressional power pursuant to the commerce clause is not restricted by *Erie*, this eliminated the *Erie* problem articulated in *Bernhardt*, and made it clear that federal courts could apply the FAA in diversity cases predicated on state law.

The Court further expanded the reach of the FAA into state law in the 1983 case of *Moses H. Cone Memorial Hospital v. Mercury Construction Corp.*[56] In that case, a dispute over the performance of a construction contract (which contained an arbitration clause) had led to a hospital's filing a declaratory and injunctive lawsuit in state court to avoid arbitration. The contractor subsequently filed a suit in federal court for an order compelling arbitration under the FAA. The federal district court stayed the federal court action pending resolution of the state litigation. The United States Supreme Court held that the district court had abused its discretion in issuing the stay, noting that the FAA "is a congressional declaration of a liberal federal policy favoring arbitration agreements, notwithstanding any state substantive or procedural policy to the contrary. The effect of the section is to create a body of federal substantive law of arbitrability, applicable to any arbitration agreement within the coverage of the Act."[57] Whereas in *Bernhardt* the notion of the FAA as "substantive" was used to restrict the scope of the FAA, in *Moses H. Cone* it was used to expand the scope of the FAA. The federal substantive law created by the FAA, the Court stated, provides that "any doubts concerning the scope of arbitrable issues should be resolved in favor of arbitration," whether the issues arise in state or federal court.[58]

A year later in *Southland Corp. v. Keating*,[59] the Court again decided in favor of arbitration in another issue involving federalism. In *Southland*, several franchisees sued a franchisor claiming that the franchisor had violated disclosure requirements of the California Franchise Investment Law. The California Supreme Court held that the claims were not arbitrable, despite an arbitration clause in the franchise agreements. The California court based its decision on a provision in the California Franchise Investment Law that it construed as requiring judicial rather than arbitral consideration of claims brought under the statute.

The United States Supreme Court reversed, holding that the California Franchise Investment Law violated the Supremacy Clause of the United States Constitution insofar as it conflicted with the FAA. The Court concluded that "[i]n enacting [Section] 2 of the federal Act, Congress declared a national policy favoring arbitration and withdrew the power of the states to require a traditional forum for the resolution of claims which the contracting parties agreed to resolve by arbitration."[60] Therefore, the Court held that the FAA preempts all state law which conflicts with the FAA's broad policy favoring arbitration.[61]

In the 1995 case of *Allied-Bruce Terminix Cos. v. Dobson*,[62] the Court enforced an arbitration clause in a home extermination contract on the basis that the contract "turn[ed] out, in fact, to have involved interstate commerce." In so doing, it reversed a judgment of the Alabama Supreme Court, which had held the FAA inapplicable because the parties had not considered that interstate commerce would be involved when they entered into the agreement. The Court held that the FAA's reach is coextensive with its broad delegation of power under the commerce clause.[63] As a result, the Court expressly overruled *Bernhardt*'s restrictive interpretation of the scope of the FAA, and reaffirmed that the FAA is preemptive and applies equally in both federal and state courts.

Most, recently, in *Doctor's Associates, Inc. v. Casarotto*,[64] the Supreme Court invalidated a Montana statute requiring that an arbitration clause be "typed in underlined capital letters on the first page of the contract."[65] The Court rejected the Montana Supreme Court's finding that the notice provision was consistent with, and thus not preempted by, the FAA. The Montana Supreme Court had concluded that the goal of the FAA was not to promote arbitration at any cost, but rather to promote arbitration that was knowingly agreed to by the parties.[66] The United States Supreme Court reversed, holding that any state law targeted specifically to void arbitration agreements, not contracts in general, was preempted by the FAA, even if the purpose of the state law was to promote the knowing choice of arbitration.[67] The effect of *Doctor's Associates* was to significantly restrict the circumstances under which state legislatures are permitted to impose additional requirements beyond those imposed by the FAA as a precondition for enforcement of the arbitration agreement.[68]

It is now black-letter law that the FAA governs in state courts as well as federal courts;[69] that causes of action are subject to the FAA whether they arise from antidiscrimination or commercial law,[70] statutory[71] or common law;[72] that the FAA preempts any state law contrary to the broad presumption of arbitrability created by the FAA;[73] and that FAA preemption forbids states from conditioning enforcement of compliance with procedural requirements beyond those imposed by the FAA or by the states on other contracts generally.[74] As discussed in the section of this chapter dealing with the application of the FAA to Title VII, however, the presumption of arbitrability is only a presumption, which may be rebutted upon a showing of conflicting Congressional intent. The impossibility of ascertaining such intent in the context of state law causes of action has made courts resort to methods of reasoning that are little short of bizarre.

The presumption of arbitrability, first articulated in *Mitsubishi* and later applied in *Gilmer*, puts the burden on the party seeking to avoid arbitration to prove that Congress, when enacting the statute creating the cause of action, intended to preclude waiving a judicial forum for claims arising under the statute. This formulation was workable in *Gilmer*, where the Court examined the legislative history of the ADEA to search for indications of whether Congress intended to forbid employees from agreeing to arbitrate future claims. However, the presumption is nonsensical for causes of action arising under state law, because the United States Congress had nothing to do with the creation of those causes of action. It makes little sense, for example, to ask whether Congress intended to preclude a waiver of a judicial forum by the New York legislature's passage of an antidiscrimination statute, or by the Texas Supreme Court's adoption of the tort of intentional infliction of emotional distress. Courts have developed four approaches to resolving this problem.[75]

The first and most common approach is to examine congressional intent in creating a "parallel" federal cause of action. For example, *Fletcher v. Kidder, Peabody & Co.*[76] involved a race discrimination action brought in a New York state court under the New York Human Rights Act.[77] The chief court for the State of New York held that because the cause of action was based on state rather than federal law, "the courts are obliged to draw analogy to the equivalent Federal law, where possible, and to consider Congress' intentions with regard to the rights created by that law."[78]

Because the analogous federal statute (Title VII) did not evince congressional intention to preclude prospective arbitration agreements, the court held that this intention should be imputed to the state statute, and so the court compelled arbitration.[79] This approach, while yielding predictable results in statutory employment discrimination cases, provides no guidance when no analogous federal cause of action exists, as is often the case when claims are based on state common law doctrines.

The second approach is to make the "presumption" of arbitrability irrebuttable, and to enforce arbitration of *all* state causes of action. This was the approach a Missouri appellate court adopted in *Boogher v. Stifel, Nicolaus & Co.*[80] Although simple and determinate, this approach is inconsistent with the Supreme Court's rebuttable presumption test.

The third approach, adopted by a California district court in *Bakri v. Continental Airlines, Inc.,*[81] is to examine whether the *state's* legislature intended to preclude arbitration. The problem with this approach is that it is inconsistent with the Supreme Court's *Southland* decision, which invalidated a state statute that the California Supreme Court had interpreted to preclude arbitration. This approach also provides little guidance for causes of action predicated on state common law, since judges are even less likely than legislatures to venture an opinion on arbitrability when creating a new cause of action.

The final approach involves an ad hoc balancing of competing interests. In *Singer v. Salomon Bros.,*[82] a New York state court balanced the "strong public policy [promoted by arbitration] favoring a decrease in the courts' burdensome caseload" against the "public interest in [the] adjudication of delicate claims such as discrimination cases," and concluded that the former outweighed the latter. This approach does not suggest a principled basis for distinguishing cases and, as such, suffers from indeterminacy.

Although these four cases differ markedly in their approach to determining whether a given state law negates the *Mitsubishi* presumption of arbitrability, the result is relatively constant: Courts almost always find the claim to be arbitrable. When these cases are juxtaposed with the cases discussed in the first half of this chapter, it becomes clear that virtually every conceivable employment claim is arbitrable, whether based on federal law, state law, statutory law, common law, or any permutation of these. This is important because employers are unlikely to adopt compulsory arbitration policies if they simultaneously must maintain a litigative response system for dealing with nonarbitrable claims.

• • •

It has become black-letter law that the FAA preempts contrary state law, that causes of action based on state law are subject to compulsory arbitration under the FAA, and that the FAA applies to state courts applying state substantive law. The settled state of these federalism issues contrasts sharply with the FAA contracts of employment exclusion and the applicability of the FAA to federal legislation other than the ADEA. The unsettled state of these issues demonstrates the ease with which the current experiment with compulsory employment arbitration might abruptly be terminated.

This might happen in either of two ways. First, the Supreme Court might interpret the FAA contracts of employment exclusion broadly, or decide that the FAA presumption of arbitrability does not apply to federal legislation other than the ADEA. This effectively would narrow the applicability of the FAA so significantly as to make it virtually irrelevant in the American workplace. Although the Court has given no indication that it intends to proceed in this direction, both its declination to address the contracts of employment issue in *Gilmer* and its perfunctory remand of *Alford* leave this a distinct possibility.

Second, Congress might amend the FAA to provide that it is wholly inapplicable in the employment context, or it might amend the 1991 Civil Rights Act or other federal employment laws to expressly rebut the presumption of arbitrability. Several bills have been proposed in the last several years that would accomplish either or both results.[83] Although none of these bills has passed to date, these options remains open to Congress should arbitration go awry.

There is yet a third possible way that Congress or the courts might restrict the scope of compulsory employment arbitration. This is discussed in the next chapter.

Five

Employment Arbitration and the National Labor Relations Act

A S DISCUSSED IN CHAPTER 2, THE NATIONAL
Labor Relations Act[1] (NLRA or Act) was enacted in
1935 to give American employees sufficient bargaining
power to negotiate meaningfully with employers the terms and conditions
of employment.[2] The Act gave employees three basic rights which the
drafters considered essential to etablishing a balance of bargaining power
between employers and employees: the right to organize into unions;
the right to bargain collectively with employees over certain terms and
conditions of employment; and the right to engage in strikes, picketing,
and other concerted activities.[3] To enforce these substantive rights, the
NLRA created the National Labor Relations Board (NLRB or Board)
and gave it adjudicatory powers to determine employee representation
questions and unfair labor practices (practices made illegal by the Act).[4]
Formal hearings on unfair labor practice complaints initially are conducted
by administrative law judges (ALJs), who are appointed by the Board.[5]
The ALJ's decision may be appealed to the Board, which has independent
authority to adopt or reverse the ALJ's decision.[6] The Board's decision
and orders are not self-enforcing, meaning that if the party or parties
against whom an order has been issued refuse to obey, the Board must
apply to the United States Court of Appeals jurisdiction where the unfair
labor practice arose.[7] Board decisions and orders are appealable to these
courts,[8] and the Courts of Appeals' orders in turn are appealable to the
United States Supreme Court.

Although the NLRA was not designed with compulsory employment
arbitration in mind, it is at least possible that two NLRA provisions could
be interpreted as making some or all employment arbitration agreements
illegal. First, requiring employees to waive their right to litigate statutory
claims could be an interference with concerted activities for mutual aid
and protection, in violation of Section 8(a)(1) of the Act. Second, an

employment arbitration system, depending on its structure, might be an employer-dominated labor organization in violation of Section 8(a)(2) of the NLRA. This chapter discusses these issues.

As of early 1997, neither the Board nor any court has ever considered the impact of the NLRA on compulsory employment arbitration agreements. It is unclear, therefore, whether and to what extent courts will interpret Section 8(a)(1) and 8(a)(2) as applied to employment arbitration. This section relies on NLRA precedent in other contexts to predict how the courts and the Board eventually will rule on these issues.

A. Whether Compulsory Arbitration Agreements Violate § 8(a)(1)

Section 7 of the NLRA guarantees employees "the right to self organization, to form, join, or assist labor organizations, to bargain collectively through representatives of their own choosing, *and to engage in other concerted activities for* the purpose of collective bargaining or *other mutual aid or protection. . . .*"[9] Section 8(a)(1) makes it an unfair (and therefore illegal) labor practice for an employer "to interfere with, restrain, or coerce" employees in the exercise of Section 7 rights.[10]

As indicated by the italicized language above, the legal protection extended to employees by Section 7 is not limited to the right to engage in union activity. It also includes activity that is not specifically union-oriented, and has been interpreted as protecting concerted employee activity that is wholly unrelated to union activity. Compulsory employment arbitration agreements might conceivably violate Section 8(a)(1) in two ways. First, requiring employees to sign the agreements, which have the effect of forbidding employees to file employment discrimination lawsuits, might be considered a "restraint" on "concerted activities for the purpose of . . . mutual aid or protection." Second, if employees jointly refuse to sign an arbitration agreement, and the employer takes action against them for their refusal to sign (by, for example, firing them), the employer might be considered to be interfering with or restraining the employee's Section 7 rights. Although neither the courts nor the Board have ever considered whether, or under what circumstances, a compulsory employment arbitration agreement might violate Section 8(a)(1), after reviewing the pertinent law regarding Section 8(a)(1) this section concludes that an employment arbitration agreement probably does not.

The statutory language above indicates that three requirements must be met before the Board or a court will find a Section 8(a)(1) violation. First, the employees' activity must be "concerted." Second, the employees' activity must have been taken for the purpose of "mutual aid or protection." Third, the employer must have acted "to interfere with, restrain or coerce" the complaining employees. These requirements will be addressed in turn. However, even if all three of these requirements are met, employee activity will not be protected if it is unlawful,[11] violent,[12] disloyal,[13] or disruptive.[14]

1. Concerted

To be protected under Section 7, employee activity must be "concerted." This requirement has been broadly construed by the Board and the courts.[15] The Board, in the 1966 case of *Interboro Contractors*,[16] found that an employee acting alone to enforce a collective bargaining agreement was protected by Section 7. In that case, Interboro discharged John Landers because he had complained that certain working conditions violated a clause in the collective bargaining agreement requiring the employer to maintain a safe work place. Landers then filed unfair labor practice charges against Interboro, alleging that Interboro had violated Section 8(a)(1) of the NLRA by discharging him. The administrative law judge found that because Landers had acted alone and for his own benefit, his actions were not protected by Section 7. The Board disagreed, finding evidence that Landers had acted in concert with two other employees. The Board also, however, stated that even if Landers had acted alone, his activity nonetheless would have been concerted because his complaints were attempts to enforce the collective bargaining agreement affecting the rights of all employees. On appeal, the United States Court of Appeals for the Second Circuit affirmed, stating that activities of an individual employee involving attempts to enforce a collective bargaining agreement are concerted activities, even if fellow employees do not join in the complaint.[17]

The *Interboro* rule—that concerted activity exists when an individual employee asserts a right contained in a collective bargaining agreement[18] —was endorsed by the United States Supreme Court in the 1984 case of *NLRB v. City Disposal Systems*.[19] In *City Disposal*, employee James Brown was fired when he refused to drive a truck he thought was unsafe because of faulty brakes. Neither did he discuss his complaint with fellow employees, nor did his fellow employees join Brown to complain about the condition of company trucks. The collective bargaining agreement under which Brown worked provided that the employer could not require employees to operate any vehicle in an unsafe operating condition. The Supreme Court held that when an employee invokes a right rooted in a collective bargaining agreement, he is acting not merely for himself but also on behalf of other employees to whom the agreement applies. The Court therefore held that Brown's refusal to drive a truck was protected by Section 7 because the refusal was an attempt to enforce the collective bargaining agreement.

Until 1975, the *Interboro* rule was applied exclusively to situations where a collective bargaining agreement existed. Courts and the Board long had recognized that Section 7 protects concerted activities outside the union context,[20] but had not addressed the issue of whether, outside the context of a collective bargaining agreement, an individual employee's actions could be considered concerted activity. In the 1975 case of *Alleluia Cushion Co.*,[21] however, the Board extended the *Interboro* rule to situations where the protesting employee was neither unionized nor covered by a collective bargaining agreement.

Alleluia involved an employee, Jack Henley, who was fired after he wrote a letter to the California Occupational Safety and Health Administration complaining about the lack of both safety equipment and supervisor concern in the workplace. The ALJ concluded that Alleluia had not violated Section 8(a)(1) because Henley's action had not been "concerted." Noting that Henley had not sought the aid or approval of his fellow employees in complaining about Alleluia's alleged safety violations, the ALJ found that Henley had acted solely out of his individual concern for safety. The ALJ therefore held that his acts were not concerted under Section 7.

The Board disagreed, and reversed. It first noted that the lack of apparent support from other employees was not significant, since safe working conditions are important to all employees. It next noted that the ALJ's decision was inconsistent with public policy favoring safe workplaces. Finally, the Board held that "where an employee speaks up and seeks to enforce statutory provisions relating to occupational safety designed for the benefit of all employees, in the absence of any evidence that fellow employees disavow such representation, we will find an implied consent thereto and deem such activity to be concerted."[22] The Board thus implied that whenever a single employee complains about statutory rights affecting all employees, the Board will find that complaint to be protected concerted activity under Section 7 of the NLRA.[23]

After *Alleluia*, the Board applied this rationale to other situations where individual employees, not represented by a union or protected by a collective bargaining agreement, resorted to administrative agencies or complained to their employer about working conditions. For example, the Board deemed an individual employee's actions to constitute protected concerted activity where the employee: filed a claim for unemployment compensation benefits;[24] enquired at the employer's bank as to whether there were sufficient funds on deposit to meet the upcoming payroll;[25] asked for a salary increase;[26] protested a change in working conditions that resulted in lower wages;[27] expressed an intention to file a claim for workers' compensation benefits;[28] filed a claim with a governmental agency for back overtime wages;[29] wrote a letter complaining about racism, sexism, favoritism, and denial of a wage increase;[30] refused a work assignment unless paid the same as male employees doing the same job;[31] filed a discrimination complaint with a government equal employment opportunity agency (such as the Equal Employment Opportunity Commission);[32] complained to the local media about discriminatory working conditions;[33] met with and complained to an equal employment opportunity investigator regarding the employer's alleged discriminatory employment practices;[34] participated in a United States Department of Labor investigation of working conditions;[35] complained to the Department of Transportation about a truck's safety;[36] filed a complaint with the Department of Labor;[37] and participated in a compliance investigation of the employer's administration of a contract covered by a federal statute governing wages, hours, and conditions of employment.[38]

The Board adhered for nine years to *Alleluia's* extension of the *Interboro* rule to nonunion and noncollective bargaining situations. During that time, the *Alleluia* doctrine was rejected by the Second,[39] Fourth,[40] Fifth,[41] Sixth,[42] Seventh,[43] Eighth,[44] and Ninth[45] Circuits. In 1984, however, in *Meyers Industries (Meyers I)*, the Board overruled *Alleluia*.[46]

Meyers involved a complaint by Kenneth Prill, a truck driver, to his employer, Meyers Industries, Inc., about brake malfunctions in the company trucks. Prill also complained about these malfunctions to Ohio state inspection authorities. Later, while driving a truck for Meyers, Prill was involved in an accident caused by the truck's faulty brakes. Immediately after the accident, Meyers ordered Prill to drive the company truck back to the company office. Prill refused. Meyers then fired Prill for defying its direct order to drive the truck, and for having complained to state inspection authorities.

The ALJ, relying on *Alleluia*, concluded that Meyers had violated Section 8(a)(1) of the NLRA. The Board, however, reversed the ALJ's conclusion and overruled *Alleluia*, holding that, absent union activity or a collective bargaining agreement, concerted activity exists only when an employee acts in conjunction with, or on behalf of, fellow employees, and not solely on behalf of himself. On appeal, the Court of Appeals for the

District of Columbia set aside the Board's order, and returned the case to the Board for reconsideration in light of the Supreme Court's decision in *City Disposal*, which had just been published.[47]

On remand, the Board in *Meyers II* reaffirmed its holding in *Meyers I* that concerted activity exists only when an employee acts with, or on the authority of, fellow employees.[48] The Board distinguished *City Disposal* because it involved a collective bargaining agreement, and held that a nonunion employee's decision to assert a statutory right is not an extension of collective action in the same way as an employee's attempt to enforce a provision in a collective bargaining agreement. According to the Board, *City Disposal* stood for the propositions that concerted activity can include some, but not all, individual activity by employees; that an essential component of concerted activity is its collective nature; and that the Section 7 definition of concerted activity is separate from the concept of "mutual aid and protection."

Concluding that the Board's decision in *Meyers I* was consistent with the Supreme Court's decision in *City Disposal*, the Board next discussed the meaning of concerted activity. Whereas in *Meyers I* the Board had concluded that an employee only engages in concerted activity when acting in conjunction with or on behalf of other employees, the Board in *Meyers II* concluded that the *Meyers I* definition of concerted activity does not always leave individual employee activity unprotected. The *Meyers I* definition of concerted activity, explained the Board in *Meyers II*, fully embraces individual employee activity, but only if its purpose is to initiate, induce, or prepare for collective employee action.

Prill appealed *Meyers II* to the D.C. Circuit Court of Appeals. The D.C. Circuit held that the Board adequately had distinguished *City Disposal*, and found that in *Meyers II* the Board had "adopted a reasonable—but by no means the only reasonable—interpretation of Section 7."[49]

Following *Meyers*, actions taken by individual employees on their own behalf generally have not been found to be "concerted."[50] For example, in *ABF Freight Systems*,[51] the Board held that an employee who acted alone when he complained of a tractor-trailer's safety and refused to drive it was not engaged in concerted activity. Similarly, in *Bearden & Co.*,[52] the Board held that an employee who filed an individual unemployment compensation claim was not engaged in concerted activity.

Although it now is clear that, in the absence of a collective bargaining agreement, an individual acting alone does not engage in "concerted" activity, the Board has been very liberal in deciding whether an employee is acting independently or with other employees. For example, in *Con-*

sumer Power Co.,[53] the Board held that an employee's individual complaint to a supervisor regarding the employer's failure to provide protection to another employee who had received a threat of violence from a customer was concerted, because that activity was a continuation of safety complaints voiced by all employees at weekly meetings with their employer. In *Every Woman's Place,*[54] the Board held that an employee who, without first having received instructions from other employees, called the Department of Labor to complain about insufficient wages she and her fellow employees were receiving, engaged in a concerted activity because that phone call was a "logical outgrowth" of protests the employee had made along with other employees on prior occasions. Finally, in *NLRB v. Jasper Seating Co.,*[55] two employees walked out to protest cold working conditions caused by a door left open near their workplace. Other employees had complained of the heat when the door was shut. Even though no other employees agreed with the protesting employees' demand to close the door, the Seventh Circuit upheld the Board's decision that the protest was concerted because it focused on a continuing dispute over working conditions.

If a nonunion employee challenges a compulsory employment arbitration agreement under Section 8(a)(1), the employee must demonstrate some "concerted" action against the employer. She will not satisfy this requirement merely by protesting to the employer or filing an administrative equal employment opportunity charge on her own behalf, but will do so if she protests or files such a charge on behalf of herself and others, if the protest or charge relates to the subject of previous complaints by other employees to the employer, or if she and other employees individually protest or file separate charges that relate to a working condition that they had discussed before taking action.[56] The "concerted" requirement, therefore, will be met in many challenges to employment arbitration agreements.

2. Mutual Aid and Protection

The second requirement that must be satisfied to successfully bring a claim under Section 8(a)(1) is that the employees' concerted action must have been taken for their "mutual aid and protection." Courts and the Board have construed "mutual aid or protection" so broadly that virtually any activity relating to conditions of employment satisfies this requirement.[57] For example, in *Kaiser Engineers v. NLRB,*[58] The Ninth Circuit approved the Board's holding that a group of engineers acted for their mutual aid and protection when they wrote to several legislators a series of letters in which they opposed any relaxation of immigration laws that would allow foreign-educated engineers to immigrate to the United States. The employees' activity, which their employer, who was heavily engaged in overseas engineering projects, opposed, did not concern a matter over which the employer had any control, and was wholly outside the confines of the employer's relationship with its domestic engineer employees. Nonetheless, the Board concluded that the engineers acted for their mutual aid and protection. Similarly, in *Frank Briscoe, Inc. v. NLRB*,[59] the Third Circuit approved the Board's holding that five employees' filing of separate charges with the Equal Employment Opportunity Commission constituted activity for their mutual aid or protection because it sought to end the employer's alleged discriminatory practices.

About the only thing that will not satisfy the mutual aid and protection requirement is "individual griping and complaining."[60] Examples include an employee who makes demands for special treatment,[61] who attempts to gain more favorable contract terms for himself, or[62] who complains about his personal share of overtime work.[63] Of course, this kind of activity also fails to satisfy the requirement that the action be "concerted."[64]

Employee activity, therefore, will satisfy the "mutual aid and protection" requirement first, if it meets the "concerted" requirement, and second, if it somehow concerns conditions of employment. Because any legal challenge to an employer's employment practices invariably will concern a condition of employment (at least as that phrase is broadly construed by the Board), this requirement will be satisfied, in challenges to compulsory employment arbitration agreements, any time the "concerted" requirement is satisfied.

3. Interfere with, Restrain, or Coerce

The third requirement for bringing a successful challenge under Section 8(a)(1) is that the employer have interfered with, restrained, or coerced employees regarding their protected activities. Most cases interpreting this requirement involve employer attempts to frustrate union organizational efforts by, for example, issuing threats,[65] making promises or grants of benefits,[66] interrogating or polling employees under coercive circumstances,[67] or using or threatening violence.[68] In other contexts more germaine to challenges to compulsory employment arbitration agreements, this requirement almost always is satisfied easily because the employer's challenged activities were designed overtly to punish an employee's actions. Most of these cases involve employer attempts to discharge an employee for having engaged in what the employee considers protected activity. Resolution of the case, therefore, usually turns on whether the activity was concerted and taken for employees' mutual aid and protection, or whether the employer's conduct constituted interference, restraint, or coercion.

As discussed earlier in this section, compulsory arbitration agreements are likely to be challenged on 8(a)(1) grounds in two ways. The first is by asserting that an employer violates 8(a)(1) by requiring its employees to sign the arbitration agreement. There are two reasons why this requirement, in and of itself, probably will not constitute interference, restraint or coercion. First, the agreement itself will not in any way affect employees' ability to act collectively. As the Supreme Court noted in *Gilmer v. Interstate Johnson/Lane Corp.*,[69] an employee who has signed a compulsory arbitration agreement neither waives the right to file (either individually or jointly) an administrative charge with a federal or state equal employment opportunity agency; nor loses the right to bring a class action or to seek class-wide injunctive relief from the arbitrator. An arbitration agreement, therefore, does not affect employees' opportunities to act concertedly for their mutual aid and protection. Furthermore, such an agreement does not substantively affect the employee's rights because, as the *Gilmer* Court stated, arbitration agreements do not affect the parties' underlying substantive rights; the agreements simply transfer their resolution to an arbitral, rather than a judicial, forum.[70]

Say, however, that an employer implements an across-the-board compulsory employment arbitration policy, and requires all employees, as a condition of their continued employment, to sign an arbitration agreement. Say, further, that a group of employees discusses the new policy over lunch one day and decides collectively that they will refuse to sign this agreement. If the employer later fires these employees for failing to sign the agreement, has the employer violated Section 8(a)(1)?

A strict application of the three-part test discussed in this section would indicate that the employer has done so. The employees' conduct is "concerted" because they jointly decided to refuse to sign the arbitration agreement. The conduct is for their "mutual aid and protection" because it is concerted, and affects the terms and conditions of the employees' employment. Thus, the employer "interfered" with their protected activity by firing them.

Notwithstanding the above analysis, it is doubtful whether a court would conclude that the employer has violated Section 8(a)(1). For one, it would allow employees to avoid virtually any new term or condition of employment as long as they acted together in refusing to comply with it.

This would all but end the at-will nature of employment in this country. Second, courts are likely to look to the Federal Arbitration Act's (the FAA is discussed in detail in chapters 2 and 3) strong policy in favor of arbitration, and conclude that this interpretation of the NLRA is inconsistent with that policy.'

At one point, the NLRB took the position that it was an unfair labor practice to require an employee to agree to mandatory arbitration of all claims.[71] Recently, however, Board officials appear to have tempered their position and have suggested that the NLRB will find an unfair labor practice only if a mandatory arbitration agreement inhibits employees' ability to file charges with the NLRB.[72] The administrative cases the Board has pursued thus far indicate the Board's apparent adherence to this latter policy.[73]

B. Whether Compulsory Arbitration Agreements Violate § 8(a)(2)

As discussed at the beginning of this chapter, one of the primary purposes of the NLRA was to facilitate the process by which workers organized themselves into unions and thereby gained sufficient power to enable them to bargain meaningfully with employers over the terms and conditions of employment.[74] The sponsors and drafters of the Act believed that this purpose would be frustrated if employers were allowed to create "sham" unions (often called "company" unions) that gave employees the false impression that their chosen representatives would bargain on their behalf.[75] Company unions became widespread in the 1920s and were even more common in the early 1930s.[76]

Company unions invariably were poor step-cousins to independent unions.[77] Many of the plans adopted by employers to create company unions retained management's absolute authority over policy formation, and relegated the company union to discussing issues of policy implementation.[78] The company unions seldom had any real authority; final decisions almost always required management approval.[79] Topics that company unions were permitted to consider often were restricted to grievance and personnel matters, housekeeping and safety issues, and improvements in productivity; they seldom were permitted to consider issues concerning wages and working conditions.[80] Because the company unions rarely required employees to pay dues, they generally could not finance strikes or other activities opposing the employer.[81] As a result, although in theory company unions acted as workers' bargaining representatives, in reality the unions had little actual bargaining power, and few ever successfully negotiated written agreements with management on wages, hours or working conditions.[82]

It was with good reason, therefore, that in introducing the proposed NLRA to Congress the Act's chief sponsor, Senator Robert Wagner, declared that "the greatest obstacles to collective bargaining are employer-dominated unions, which have multiplied with amazing rapidity since the enactment of the [National Industrial Recovery Act of 1933]. Such a union makes a sham of equal bargaining power. . . ."[83] To eliminate this obstacle, Section 8(a)(2) of the NLRA contains a prohibition making it an unfair (and therefore illegal) labor practice[84] "(2) [t]o dominate or interfere with the formation or administration of any labor organization or contribute financial or other support to it."[85] The NLRA also contains an extremely broad definition of "labor organization" in Section 2(5): "(5) The term 'labor organization' means any organization of any kind, or any agency or employee representation committee or plan, in which employees participate and which exists for the purpose, in whole or in part, of dealing with employers concerning grievances, labor disputes, wages, rates of pay, hours of employment, or conditions of work."[86] A proviso in Section 9(a) of the NLRA, however, states: "[a]ny individual employee or a group of employees shall have the right at any time to present grievances to their employer and to have such grievances adjusted, without the intervention of the bargaining representative, as long as the adjustment is not inconsistent with the terms of a collective-bargaining contract or agreement then in effect: Provided further, That the bargaining representative has been given opportunity to be present at such adjustment."[87]

To summarize: An employer violates Section 8(a)(2) of the NLRA (by, for example, adopting a compulsory employment arbitration program) only if the employer meets each of the three following statutory criteria. First, the employer must create a "labor organization" within the meaning of § 2(5). Second, if such a labor organization is created, it must be "dominated" by the employer. Third, the organization must not fall within the § 9(a) proviso, which permits employers to allow employees to present their grievances to the employer for decision. Each of these criteria will be addressed in turn.

1. Is a Compulsory Employment Arbitration Program a "Labor Organization"?

As indicated above, Section 2(5) of the NLRA defines "labor organization" as not only an organization, but also "any agency or employee representation committee or plan." Courts and the Board have interpreted this section broadly, and have held that a group of individuals may comprise a labor organization even though the group lacks a constitution or by-laws, elected officials, formal meetings, dues, or other formal structure.[88]

However, not all "plans" or employee committees are "labor organizations" within the meaning of Section 2(5). Section 2(5) further requires the plan or committee to be an *employee representation* plan or committee, and it must exist for the purpose of "dealing with" employers concerning the terms and conditions of employment. Some courts have interpreted the first of these requirements—"representation"—as requiring that the structure of employee participation be representational in nature.[89] Thus, the Board has held that a labor organization is not created by semiautonomous work teams in which all employees participate.[90] Similarly, the Sixth Circuit has ruled that committees on which employees serve by rotation are not labor organizations because they are not representational.[91] In the Board's more recent decisions, however, it has expressly declined to decide whether a planned organization that does not act as a representative of other employees is automatically disqualified from the definition of "labor organization" under Section 2(5).[92]

An organization or plan, in order to qualify as a labor organization under Section 2(5), also must exist for the purpose of "dealing with" the employer. The Supreme Court considered the "dealing with" requirement in *Cabot Carbon Co.*[93] In that case, the employer established employee committees, consisting of elected employer representatives, to discuss grievances and working conditions with management.[94] The Fifth Circuit found that these committees were not labor organizations within the meaning of the NLRA. The court held that the phrase "dealing with" in Section 2(5) meant "bargaining with," and that since the committees served only as a forum for discussion and had never negotiated or bargained with the employer, they had not "dealt with" the employer and therefore were not labor organizations under the NLRA.[95]

Reversing the Fifth Circuit's decision, the Supreme Court held that the employee committees were labor organizations within the meaning of Section 2(5). After reviewing the legislative history of Section 2(5), the Court concluded that "dealing with" should be interpreted more broadly than "bargaining with." The Court also rejected the company's argument that the committees' proposals and recommendations did not amount to "dealing with" because the company retained final decisional authority. The Court noted that this equally would be true if the employer had been dealing with an independent labor organization, the only difference being that an autonomous organization would have greater bargaining power.[96]

Following *Cabot Carbon,* the Board and most courts of appeals have continued to interpret the "dealing with" requirement broadly. The Board, for example, has stated that presentations of employee views unaccompanied by specific recommendations constitute impermissible "dealing with," as do "discussions" between an employee advisory committee and an employer.[97] The Seventh Circuit, in *NLRB v. Ampex,* held that an employee committee designed to serve as a channel of communication, characterized by the employer as "a suggestion box made less impersonal," similarly constituted impermissible "dealing with."[98] And in *NLRB v. Stowe Manufacturing Co.,* the Second Circuit held that a question and answer session between management and employees constituted impermissible "dealing with."[99]

One exception to the general rule of interpreting the "dealing with" requirement broadly involves situations where an employer has delegated to employee groups managerial authority to adjudicate grievances. In *Spark's Nugget, Inc.,*[100] the employer created an Employees' Council which consisted of an employee-elected representative, the employer's Director of Employee Relations, and a third member selected by the first two. The committee convened on an *ad hoc* basis whenever an employee who had filed a grievance failed to resolve it through discussions with his supervisor and department head. The committee only heard cases filed by individual employees; it did not initiate grievances, recommend changes in the terms and conditions of employment, or act as an advocate of employee interests. The Board concluded that: "The Employees' Council performs a purely adjudicatory function and does not interact with management for any purpose or in any manner other than to render a final decision on the grievance. Therefore, it cannot be said that the Employees' Council herein 'deals with' management. Rather, it appears to perform a function for management; i.e., resolving employee grievances."[101] Because the Council did not "deal with" management, the Board concluded that it was not a labor organization under Section 2(5).

In *Mercury-Memorial Hospital,*[102] the Board considered an employer-sponsored grievance committee whose powers significantly exceeded those of the Council in *Sparks Nugget.* In *Mercury-Memorial Hospital,* the committee had the power not only to decide grievances, but also to propose to the director of personnel, and through him to all administrative heads of the company, any changes in work "rules, regulations, and standards."[103] The Board nonetheless held that this did not constitute "bargaining with" the employer, and therefore held that the grievance committee was not an impermissible labor organization within the meaning of Section 2(5).[104]

To fall within the *Sports Nugget* exception to the "dealing with" requirement, however, real management authority must be delegated to the employee organization. The boundary of the exception is illustrated by the Board's decision in *Keeler Brass Automotive Group*.[105] In *Keeler Brass,* the employer established a grievance committee that did not have full decisional authority over the grievances it heard; its only authority consisted of making recommendations to management. In practice, the committee would make a recommendation to management, management would respond with a counterproposal, and the committee and company would continue to go "back and forth explaining themselves until an acceptable result was achieved."[106] The Board concluded that this constituted impermissible "dealing with" and therefore held that the grievance committee was a labor organization.

The vast majority of compulsory employment arbitration policies, at least in the form that most employers currently have adopted them, probably do not constitute "labor organizations" within the meaning of Section 2(5). All articulated definitions of the term, and all its Board and judicial constructions, assume that inherent in the definition of "labor organization" is the notion of a group, collective or aggregational action of employees. This simply is not present in most arbitration policies, which typically consist of nothing more than a series of arbitration contracts individually signed by the employer's employees. Even in instances where the employer implements a multi-step grievance procedure culminating in binding arbitration, there is no "organization" of "labor" beyond the fact that all employees are required, individually, to follow specified dispute resolution procedures.

An exception might exist where the arbitration agreement is part of a much broader dispute resolution program. If that program creates a grievance committee to hear employment disputes before they are referred to arbitration, the committee itself might be a labor organization as that phrase is commonly understood. This type of committee probably would constitute a "labor organization" under Section 2(5) if it were elected by employees (or were otherwise representational in nature) and if its decisions were not adopted as the company's position on underlying disputes.

2. Is It "Dominated"?

The second question to ask when determining whether a compulsory employment arbitration program is impermissible under Section 8(a)(2) is whether it is dominated by the employer. The Supreme Court established the basic framework for determining whether an employer "dominates" a labor organization in *Newport News Ship Building & Dry Dock Co. v. NLRB.*[107] In that case, the Court upheld a Board order disestablishing an employer-assisted representation plan that gave the employer the power to veto the organization's proposed actions, even though the challenged plan had prevented serious labor disputes and was strongly supported by the company's employees. The Board and the Court found that the employer possessed such "control of the form and structure of an employee organization" as to deprive its employees of the "complete freedom of action guaranteed to them by the [NLRA]."[108]

Since *Newport News,* the Board has interpreted "domination" broadly, finding Section 8(a)(2) violations where an employer assisted a labor organization in electing its representatives,[109] supplied a venue[110] or refreshments[111] for the organization's meetings, or provided financial[112] or material[113] assistance. The courts have taken a more flexible approach, and generally decide domination cases by weighing a long list of factors.[114] The Sixth Circuit, for example, has stated that these factors include:

The lack of any written governing instrument and lack of any independent means of financial support on the part of the labor organization, the fact that its meetings were held only on company property, the attendance at these meetings of high management representatives, the taking and distribution of minutes by a management official, the fact that meetings could be called by a management official, the fact that employees were paid for the time spent at meetings, management participation in the elections, management preparation and distribution of ballots, management determination of employee electoral units, management determination of time of election, managerial prerogatives which may affect the status of an employee for election purposes (such as promotion, transfer and discharge), absence of independent legal advice on part of labor organizations and general reliance on the advice of management for its functioning and activities.[115]

As discussed before, most employment arbitration policies do not qualify as labor organizations. In these cases, probably neither courts nor the Board will ever determine whether employer domination exists. In instances where a broad dispute resolution program does create something resembling a labor organization, such as where it creates an elected grievance committee, that organization probably will be considered to be "dominated" by the employer. In *Keeler Brass,* discussed above, the Board held that an elected grievance committee epitomized a dominated labor organization, since its structure and function were determined by management, and its continued existence depended on the whim of management.[116]

3. Is It a 9(a) Grievance Procedure?

The final issue in determining whether an employment arbitration program violates Section 3(a)(2) is whether that program falls within the § 9(a) proviso. This proviso states that employers may allow employees to present their grievances to management for decision, and was considered by the Supreme Court in *Cabot Carbon* along with the "dealing with" provision in § 2(5). The Fifth Circuit had held that the Board's broad interpretation of "dealing with" conflicted with Section 9(a). The Supreme Court disagreed. According to the Court, Section 9(a) merely allows employees to present their grievances personally to their employer; but does not permit an employer to form or maintain an employee committee expressly to deal with the employer concerning grievances. Therefore, the Court held, the proviso did not limit the Section 8(a)(2) proscriptions of employer-dominated labor organizations.[117]

As a result of the Court's narrow interpretation of Section 9(a), it is likely that any compulsory arbitration program found to be an employer-dominated labor organization also will be found to be unprotected by Section 9(a).

Putting together the three requirements for an 8(a)(2) violation, it appears fairly certain that most employment arbitration policies will not violate this provision of the NLRA. An exception to this is where an employer creates an elected employee grievance committee that does not have final authority to decide the company's position on employee grievances. Employers therefore should be careful to avoid creating this kind of committee when they develop employment arbitration programs.

Because neither the Board nor the courts have yet considered whether, and if so under what circumstances, compulsory employment arbitration agreements might violate the NLRA, this issue is extremely unsettled. A review of the case law regarding the application of the NLRA in other contexts reveals that if employees jointly refuse to sign an arbitration agreement, and the employer takes action against them for this refusal, the employer's action might constitute a violation of Section 8(a)(1) of the Act. It is unlikely that the NLRA would be interpreted this way, however, because that would extend American employment law far beyond what the framers of the Act intended. A review of Section 8(a)(2) caselaw reveals that courts or the Board are unlikely to find that compulsory employment arbitration agreements violate that section of the Act.

Another potential threat to compulsory arbitration comes from the

Equal Employment Opportunity Commission, which recently has become extremely vocal in its opposition to compulsory arbitration and has begun litigating cases against employers that have implemented compulsory arbitration policies. The role of the EEOC in the future of compulsory employment arbitration is discussed in the next chapter.

Six

The Role of the EEOC

THE EQUAL EMPLOYMENT OPPORTUNITY COMMIS-
sion (EEOC) is the administrative agency created by
Congress to administer Title VII,[1] the Age Discrimination in Employment Act (ADEA),[2] and the Americans with Disabilities
Act (ADA).[3] In the last several years, the EEOC has indicated its acceptance of "voluntary" forms of alternative dispute resolution (including
arbitration), by which the EEOC means agreements between employers
and employees to arbitrate or mediate employment disputes that already
have arisen. The EEOC does not, however, consider prospective agreements to arbitrate to be voluntary, particularly when such agreements are
presented by the employer as condition of employment. Instead, the
EEOC apparently believes that such agreements are by their very nature
the product of employer coercion. This has led the EEOC to oppose
employers' attempts to introduce compulsory arbitration programs into
the workplace.

The EEOC has opposed compulsory employment arbitration in two
ways. The first is by asserting, accurately, that the signing of an arbitration
agreement by an employer and employee does not affect the employee's
right to file a charge of discrimination with the EEOC, or the EEOC's
right to investigate that charge and file suit in its own name on behalf
of the aggrieved employee and other similarly situated employees. This
approach essentially seeks to circumvent the arbitration agreement by
litigating through the EEOC what the employee contractually has agreed
not to litigate on her own. The second approach constitutes a more direct
attack on compulsory arbitration agreements. The EEOC has attacked
compulsory arbitration agreements directly by issuing regulation-like policy statements confirming its opposition to compulsory arbitration, and
litigating cases against employers that have implemented compulsory arbitration agreements.

This chapter initially provides a brief history of the EEOC,[4] focusing on the specific powers Congress has given or denied it to enforce the federal antidiscrimination laws. The chapter then discusses each of the ways the EEOC has opposed compulsory arbitration, and considers the likely effect each form of opposition will have on the future of compulsory arbitration.

A. History and Overview of the EEOC

The EEOC was created by Congress in Title VII of the Civil Rights Act of 1964.[5] Proponents of Title VII, as it originally was proposed, envisioned an agency with broad powers to investigate alleged violations of workplace discrimination and enforce Title VII requirements against employers that refused to comply voluntarily with those requirements. These powers would include the authority to: (1) promulgate rules and regulations to eliminate ambiguities in the statute and provide for the enforcement of the statute's requirements; (2) receive and investigate allegations of employment discrimination; (3) attempt to mediate conflicts between employers and employees regarding allegations of discrimination; (4) issue "cease-and-desist" orders, upon finding that a statutory violation has occurred, to compel employers to stop their discriminatory practices; and (5) file a lawsuit in federal court on behalf of aggrieved employees.

The first proposed power was to promulgate rules and regulations. When Congress passed Title VII, it allowed several important policy questions to go unanswered, often in the interest of avoiding contentious debate that might sideline passage of the larger civil rights package of which Title VII was a part. Proponents of the original bill envisioned the EEOC as having the authority to resolve those unanswered policy questions by issuing "suitable regulations" for the enforcement of Title VII.[6] The EEOC's proposed rulemaking powers received scant attention in the long congressional debate over passage of Title VII, because legislators doubted whether the EEOC would exercise the full extent of the rulemaking power delegated to it. This doubt arose in large part because the EEOC was modeled on the National Labor Relations Board, the administrative agency created by Congress to administer the law governing unions. The NLRB, which has full rulemaking authority,[7] traditionally has chosen to exercise its authority through the adjudication of cases rather than by substantive rulemaking.[8] Legislators opposed to creating a strong antidiscrimination enforcement agency therefore had no reason to believe that the EEOC's rulemaking authority was particularly threatening.[9]

Nonetheless, the EEOC's authority to issue substantive regulations did not survive the passage of Title VII. Two days before the bill was passed by the House, the bill was amended to provide that the EEOC's rulemaking authority would be limited to "procedural regulations."[10] This amendment was adopted without debate, thereby removing the EEOC's authority for substantive rulemaking.[11]

The EEOC's second proposed power was the authority to receive and investigate allegations of discrimination in employment. Title VII set up an elaborate procedure (one commentator has called it "an administrative obstacle course"[12]) that employees must follow before they are permitted to file a lawsuit against an employer for an alleged violation of Title VII. One of these procedures—filing a charge of discrimination—involves notifying the EEOC in a sworn written statement alleging that employment discrimination has occurred.[13] To preserve their right to bring a lawsuit, employees must file charges within three hundred days of an alleged discrimination.[14] After receiving a charge of discrimination, the EEOC has the power to investigate it by issuing subpoenas to compel the attendance and testimony of witnesses or the production of documents;[15] interviewing the charging party (the employee), one or more representatives of the employer, and relevant witnesses;[16] and conducting on-site inspections.[17] The EEOC's power to receive and investigate charges survived the passage of Title VII.

Following an EEOC investigation of an employment discrimination charge, one of two things may occur: Either the charge may be dismissed as unfounded, or it may be resolved informally through "conference, conciliation, and persuasion" if the EEOC finds reasonable cause to believe the charge is true.[18] The latter constitutes the third power initially proposed for the EEOC. Congress apparently believed that when confronted with an EEOC finding of discrimination employers willingly would meet the aggrieved employee at a negotiating table presided over by the EEOC, and the parties amicably and voluntarily would resolve their disputes with the EEOC as conciliator. The EEOC, therefore, was given the power to attempt "through conciliation and persuasion to resolve disputes involving employment discrimination charges."[19] This reflects Congress' vision of a system where, following investigation, the EEOC would be able to dispose of most charges without resort to litigation. Although the system has not functioned this way for a variety of reasons, the EEOC's mandate to try to achieve voluntary compliance with Title VII through conciliation and persuasion is still cited by courts as the reason for the statutory requirement that employees timely notify the EEOC as a prerequisite to filing suit.[20]

Assuming that the EEOC's efforts to achieve voluntary compliance with Title VII prove ineffectual, the issue arises as to how an aggrieved employee's Title VII rights may be enforced. The most common method[21] is for an employee to sue the employer on her own behalf. Title VII explicitly permits employees to enforce Title VII in this way after they have received a "right-to-sue" letter[22] from the EEOC informing them that the EEOC has exhausted both its investigation and its efforts to achieve voluntary compliance.[23]

As originally drafted, Title VII would have given the EEOC two enforcement powers in addition to the enforcement power created by the individual employee's right to file suit. Both of these powers would have arisen only after the EEOC found "reasonable cause" to believe that a statutory violation had occurred. First, the EEOC would have been permitted to issue a "cease-and-desist" order to compel an employer to stop its discriminatory practices. Second, the EEOC would have been given the authority to file a lawsuit in federal court on behalf of the aggrieved employee.

The first enforcement power—the power to issue cease-and-desist orders—was hotly contested in the congressional debates preceding the passage of Title VII. Opponents of the bill, fearful of creating a civil rights enforcement agency that could investigate and prosecute as well as adjudicate employers' liability, fought hard to limit what they viewed as the potentially unchecked power of the EEOC.[24] As a result, the House rejected the proposal of the House Education & Labor Committee to provide the EEOC with direct enforcement power in the form of cease-and-desist orders,[25] but retained the EEOC's power to prosecute violations by bringing suit on behalf of aggrieved employees.[26] The version of the bill that became law did not authorize the EEOC to issue cease-and-desist orders. In 1972, an unsuccessful attempt was made to give the EEOC the authority to issue such orders.[27]

The EEOC's second proposed enforcement power—the prosecution power—was removed from the bill shortly before passage as part of a last-minute compromise.[28] As the Senate was debating the bill, a bipartisan group of its supporters worked with the Department of Justice and key House members to draft a pair of substitute amendments that would help ensure passage of the omnibus civil rights bill.[29] These amendments limited the EEOC's enforcement power to seeking conciliation.[30]

Because of the absence of any real enforcement authority, the EEOC, for most of the first decade of its existence, was perceived as "toothless,"[31] a "poor-enfeebled thing"[32] as compared to other administrative agencies.[33] To correct this situation,[34] the EEOC's prosecutorial power was reinstated as part of the 1972 Equal Employment Opportunity Act amendments to Title VII.[35] This power theoretically is a potent weapon in the EEOC's arsenal, because it puts the powers of the federal government—with its presumptively large purse and the expertise of its EEOC staff—behind the aggrieved employee. This power is significantly less potent in practice, however, because the EEOC's backlog of cases and chronic staff shortage permits it to file suit in only one-half of one percent of the cases it considers.[36]

B. Whether the EEOC May Sue on Behalf of an Employee Who Has Signed a Compulsory Arbitration Agreement

In *Gilmer v. Interstate/Johnson Lane Corp.*,[37] the plaintiff argued that compulsory arbitration would undermine the EEOC's role in enforcing federal antidiscrimination laws. Gilmer's argument was that if the Supreme Court approved the use of compulsory arbitration, aggrieved employees would not be required to file an EEOC charge before proceeding to arbitration, as they must before filing suit. This effectively would shut the EEOC out of the enforcement process, in violation of the strong congressional policy of encouraging voluntary conciliation of disputes between employer and employee with the EEOC as intermediator.

The Supreme Court rejected Gilmer's argument, noting that "[a]n individual ADEA claimant subject to an arbitration agreement will still be free to file a charge with the EEOC, even though the claimant is not able to institute a private judicial action."[38] The Court further noted that the EEOC's role in fighting discrimination was not dependent on individual employees filing a charge because the EEOC can investigate claims even when a charge is not filed.[39] The Court explained that "arbitration agreements will not preclude the EEOC from bringing actions seeking class-wide and equitable relief."[40]

The Supreme Court's discussion of the EEOC has been interpreted as confirming that the agency has independent authority to investigate and conciliate an EEOC charge and to file suit should its conciliation efforts fail.[41] This interpretation is consistent with other judicial decisions holding that such authority is independent of an aggrieved employee's claim.[42] For example, in *General Telephone Co. v. EEOC*,[43] after receiving complaints of sexual discrimination from four General Telephone employees the EEOC sued the company, seeking injunctive relief and back pay for all women affected by General Telephone's alleged discriminatory practices.

General Telephone moved to dismiss the suit based on the EEOC's failure to certify the class (that is, to specify the employees) for which it was seeking relief pursuant to Federal Rule of Civil Procedure 23.[44] The Supreme Court held that certification was unnecessary because the EEOC was proceeding in its own name and pursuant to its own statutory authority to file suit, and not on behalf of the employees.[45] Securing relief for a group of aggrieved individuals was a paramount purpose of the EEOC's statutory authority to file suit, but not the sole purpose; rather, it was one goal "among others."[46] Among such other goals, the Court stated, was to "implement the public interest" in obliterating all traces of employment discrimination.[47] This case illustrates that the EEOC has the authority to litigate employment discrimination claims on its own, and that this authority is independent of the right that employees have to file suit on their own behalf.

Courts also have confirmed the EEOC's independent authority to sue in situations where the aggrieved employee has settled her complaints against the employer. For example, in *EEOC v. McLean Trucking Co.*,[48] Allen Brown, Jr., an African American truck driver employed by McLean, filed an EEOC charge, alleging that McLean's "no transfer rule" discriminated against him and other African American drivers. While his EEOC charge was pending, Brown filed a grievance pursuant to a collective bargaining agreement between McLean and his own union. Before Brown's grievance was arbitrated, he asked the EEOC to withdraw his charge. The EEOC, however, refused to grant its consent to withdraw.[49] In July 1971, Brown's grievance was arbitrated, and he was awarded part of the relief he had requested.

In March 1972, the EEOC entered a decision finding reasonable cause to believe that McLean's transfer policies violated Title VII and that the company was maintaining racially segregated job classifications. In July 1972, Brown filed a Title VII lawsuit against McLean based on essentially the same allegations. Two months later, the EEOC filed an additional suit against McLean, again alleging racial discrimination in its transfer policies and job classifications.

In October 1973, Brown voluntarily dismissed his lawsuit against McLean pursuant to a compromise settlement between him and the company. McLean then moved to dismiss the EEOC's lawsuit, arguing among other things that Brown's acceptance of the arbitration award and settlement of his Title VII claims against McLean precluded the EEOC's right to bring suit. The district court agreed and dismissed the EEOC's suit.

On appeal, the EEOC argued that neither Brown's acceptance of the arbitration award nor the settlement of his suit precluded the EEOC's right to bring an action in the public interest to eliminate discriminatory practices uncovered during the EEOC's investigation of Brown's discrimination charge. The Sixth Circuit agreed, concluding that the "EEOC sues to vindicate the public interest, which is broader than the interests of the charging parties," and that the "EEOC is not barred by the doctrine of *res judicata* from basing its complaint on charges of discrimination which it never agreed to settle."[50]

The Ninth Circuit reached the same conclusion in *EEOC v. Goodyear Aerospace Corp.*[51] In that case, Marshaline Pettigrew filed a charge with the EEOC, alleging that Goodyear had failed to promote her because of her race. After the EEOC had sued Goodyear, Pettigrew and Goodyear signed a settlement agreement in which Goodyear promoted her in return for her signing a release and requesting that the EEOC dismiss its lawsuit against the company. When she did so, the EEOC refused to dismiss the lawsuit. Goodyear then requested that the trial court dismiss the lawsuit, arguing that the settlement mooted the EEOC's suit. The trial court agreed and dismissed the EEOC's case. The Ninth Circuit reversed, holding that Pettigrew's settlement did not moot the EEOC's right to seek injunctive relief to protect employees as a class and to deter Goodyear from discrimination.[52] The court explained: "Goodyear's argument erroneously assumes that the EEOC's [lawsuit] is merely a representative suit, and not one to vindicate public interests."[53]

Finally, in *EEOC v. United Parcel Service*,[54] Jerome Patterson, a package delivery driver for UPS, challenged UPS' policy that employees with beards could not hold jobs in public contact positions. Patterson suffered from a skin condition which affects approximately 25 percent of the African American male population; the sole treatment for this condition is to refrain from shaving. When UPS informed Patterson that he would be transferred to a lower-paying, nonpublic contact position if he did not shave, Patterson filed a charge with the EEOC. After conducting an investigation, the EEOC brought suit against UPS on behalf of Patterson and other similarly situated African American males. After Patterson settled with UPS, the district court granted summary judgment in favor of UPS on the EEOC suit, concluding that the EEOC lacked standing because it could not present an actual injured party to the court. The Tenth Circuit reversed, holding that the EEOC's right to proceed with its suit was not dependent on its producing an injured party; this right "endure[d] until the alleged discrimination [w]as eradicated."[55]

Other courts similarly have held that the EEOC's right to sue an employer for violation of Title VII is independent of an aggrieved employee's right to bring such a suit.[56] These cases, together with the Supreme Court's discussion of the issue in *Gilmer*,[57] strongly suggest that a worker's signing a compulsory arbitration agreement will not affect that employee's right to file a charge with the EEOC, or the EEOC's right to investigate the charge and, upon a finding of discrimination, to sue the employer.

The existence of a compulsory arbitration agreement, however, may limit the types of relief that the EEOC is entitled to seek, particularly if such an agreement results in an arbitration award being rendered before an EEOC lawsuit is resolved. In both *McLean* and *Goodyear*, in which the aggrieved employees had settled their claims against the company before the conclusion of the EEOC's litigation, the courts held that the prior private settlements limited the scope of relief the EEOC could seek on behalf of the settling employees. These courts held that the EEOC suit did not entitle settling employees to recover any "private benefits," such as back pay, not granted to them in their settlements.[58] The EEOC thus was restricted to seeking class-wide and injunctive relief.

The same argument can be applied in the context of compulsory arbitration agreements. Just as an employee who has settled a case with an employer should not be given the opportunity to relitigate a personal claim through the EEOC, an employee who has signed a compulsory arbitration agreement should not be given the opportunity to arbitrate first, then achieve through the EEOC what could not be gained through arbitration. This limitation to the EEOC's authority to seek relief is consistent with the Supreme Court's dicta in *Gilmer* that compulsory arbitration agreements will not preclude the EEOC from seeking class-wide and equitable relief.

C. Whether the EEOC May Prohibit Compulsory Arbitration Agreements

The EEOC, perhaps fearful that compulsory arbitration makes its role in the resolution of Title VII claims obsolete, recently has become extremely vocal about its policy opposing "mandatory programs that make agreement to binding arbitration of employment discrimination claims a precondition for getting or keeping a job, or that attempt to preclude an individual's right to have the EEOC process [his or her] charge."[59] The EEOC also has begun litigating, and publicizing, several cases seeking to overturn employers' requirements that employees sign compulsory arbitration agreements.[60]

For example, in *EEOC v. River Oaks Imaging and Diagnostic*,[61] the EEOC sued an outpatient medical testing facility (ROID) in Houston,

Texas, that had implemented a compulsory employment arbitration policy. ROID's policy required employees to pay half the cost of arbitration up front. It provided that employees could inform ROID of their claims and initiate arbitration any time within one year of the occurrence of alleged wrongs; this provision had the potential to lull employees into inaction and mislead them with respect to the EEOC's 300-day filing deadline. Although the policy's signature page stated that it was a "Voluntary Agreement," a separate "Acknowledgment" page provided: "I acknowledge that I have been provided with a copy of ROID's policy on Mandatory Arbitration. I understand that my continued employment with ROID shall be deemed as evidence of my consent to abide by this policy. I further understand that my refusal to sign this agreement shall be deemed a voluntary termination initiated by the employee."[62]

ROID implemented its compulsory arbitration policy *after* two employees had filed discrimination charges with the EEOC.[63] These two employees were fired "on the spot" when they each refused to sign a compulsory arbitration agreement until after they had consulted lawyers. The employees were fired even though a cover letter accompanying the agreement recommended that employees consult a lawyer before signing.

After a hearing, the court concluded that ROID's arbitration policy was "misleading and against the principles of Title VII" and "might constitute retaliation against [the two] employees for making complaints to the EEOC."[64] The Court, therefore, enjoined ROID's operation of the policy.[65] The *ROID* case represents a court's justified revocation of a compulsory arbitration policy that was misleading both on its face and as implemented, and that appeared to have been enacted specifically in retaliation against employees who already had filed discrimination charges with the EEOC. As such, this case probably does not foreshadow any future judicial trend toward the nonenforcement of compulsory arbitration agreements.

The EEOC's policy pronouncements opposing compulsory arbitration are a different matter. Although it thus far has stopped short of issuing a formal rule or regulation resisting compulsory arbitration, the EEOC has been extremely vocal in the popular and trade press about its opposition to compulsory arbitration, and its Office of Legal Counsel has issued a notice to this effect.[66] Whether the EEOC's informal pronouncements—and any formal ones should they be forthcoming—will be used as the basis for judicial nonenforcement of compulsory arbitration agreements depends on the degree to which courts are willing to defer to its opinion on the subject.

As many commentators have noted, judicial deference to rules and policy promulgations by administrative agencies come in all shapes and sizes.[67] At one extreme, the reviewing court treats the agencies' opinions with only as much deference as it would the opinions of an expert or litigant.[68] At the other extreme, the reviewing court adopts and applies a reasonable agency opinion with which it disagrees.[69]

The Supreme Court's inconsistency on the subject makes it unclear to what extent courts will defer to the EEOC. In *Griggs v. Duke Power Co.*,[70] the Supreme Court gave "great deference" to the EEOC's guidelines permitting only "job-related tests" to serve as employment prerequisites; as a result, the Court invalidated an employer's practice of requiring intelligence tests and a high school diploma that bore no relationship to the job but caused fewer African Americans to be hired and promoted. The Court adhered to this "great deference" policy in *Albemarle Paper Co. v. Moody*,[71] though in that case it noted that EEOC's guidelines were not "administrative 'regulations' promulgated pursuant to formal procedures established by Congress." By this, the Court meant that the EEOC had neither issued formal notice of the proposed guidelines nor provided an opportunity for the public to comment on the guidelines before they took effect, as is required of rules issued by agencies under the Administrative Procedure Act.[72] Justice Burger, concurring and dissenting in *Albemarle,* stated that for this reason the EEOC guidelines deserved less deference from the courts than formal regulations promulgated by other agencies.[73]

In *General Electric Co. v. Gilbert*,[74] the Court reversed its "great deference" policy. In *Gilbert,* the issue was whether Title VII's prohibition against sex discrimination also prohibited discrimination on the basis of pregnancy. The EEOC had issued interpretive guidelines asserting that it did. The Court not only disagreed, but belittled the guidelines. According to the Court, since Congress had given the EEOC the authority to issue procedural but not substantive rules, its substantive guidelines were merely interpretive rules entitled to "less weight" from the reviewing court.[75] The Court's distinction between substantive rules (which create, regulate, and define the rights and duties of persons affected by the statute) and procedural rules (which prescribe the method of enforcing the substantive rights or obtaining redress for their violation)[76] indicates that EEOC rules falling within the former category are more likely to be enforced by courts than rules falling within the latter category.

Consistent with this approach, the Court deferred to the EEOC in *EEOC v. Commercial Office Products Co.*,[77] in which the issue, a procedural one, was whether a state's waiver of its exclusive sixty-day period for processing discrimination charges "terminated" the state agency's proceedings. The EEOC had assumed, in various "worksharing" agreements with state equal employment opportunity agencies, that the state agency's waiver of the sixty-day period did terminate that agency's proceedings, and thus permitted the EEOC immediately to begin to process the charge filed with the EEOC.[78] The Supreme Court, deferring to the EEOC's interpretation, agreed.[79]

Three years later, however, in *EEOC v. Arabian American Oil Co.*[80] *("Aramco")*, the Court refused to defer to the EEOC's policy permitting extraterritorial application of Title VII. As in *Gilbert*, the Court gave only persuasive weight to the EEOC's statutory interpretation of this substantive issue.[81] Unlike the EEOC's interpretation before the Court in *Gilbert*, however, the interpretation at issue in *Aramco* did not derive from an "interpretive guideline." Instead, it was expressed in a series of less formal documents, including a policy statement, a decision by the EEOC, a letter from the EEOC's General Counsel, and testimony by the EEOC's Chair.[82]

Not surprisingly, lower court decisions concerning the degree of deference due to the EEOC are in substantial disarray.[83] Although it is tempting to say that the Supreme Court defers to the EEOC only to the extent that the agency's opinions coincide with those held by a majority of justices, it probably is more apposite to note that, with the exception of *Griggs*, the Court has tended to give greater deference to the EEOC's opinions on procedural, as opposed to substantive, matters. This is consistent with Congress' decision, when it passed Title VII, to give the EEOC only procedural rulemaking authority. It also appears from *Aramco* that the Court will give less deference to the EEOC's informal types of policy pronouncements, such as those which to date the agency has issued on the subject of compulsory arbitration.

The Supreme Court's substantive-procedural distinction would appear to give the EEOC's opinion on compulsory arbitration a fair amount of deference, especially if the EEOC were to promulgate its opinion in a more formal guideline or regulation. In *Mitsubishi Motors Corp. v. Soler Chrysler-Plymouth, Inc.*,[84] the Supreme Court held that compulsory arbitration agreements did not affect a party's statutory rights; rather, they merely changed the procedures and forum by which those rights are decided. As such, the EEOC's opinion on the issue of compulsory arbitration probably would be given the deference afforded the procedural rule in the *Commercial Office Products* case.

This assumes, however, that the EEOC has any authority at all to issue policy pronouncements on the subject of compulsory arbitration. *Gilmer* and the other leading compulsory arbitration cases were primarily concerned with applying the Federal Arbitration Act[85] to various causes of action, such as those created by the federal antidiscrimination laws (e.g., Title VII, the ADEA, and the ADA) arising out of the employment context. While the EEOC has statutory authority to interpret these laws, it has no such power to interpret the FAA. This means, for example, that the EEOC cannot issue a regulation providing that the FAA's "contracts of employment" exclusion be interpreted broadly to exclude all employment contracts. The EEOC's inability to issue an opinion on the proper scope of the FAA has reduced it to issuing vague policy pronouncements stating that compulsory arbitration is inconsistent with the policies underlying the antidiscrimination statutes, a position that the Supreme Court emphatically rejected in *Gilmer.* The most that the EEOC can do is to venture an opinion that the legislative histories of the antidiscrimination statutes rebut the *Mitsubishi/Gilmer* presumption of arbitrability[86]—to argue, in effect, that there is some indication in the legislative history that Congress did not intend to permit compulsory arbitration. Such an effort by the EEOC would seem to be pointless, however, given (as discussed in chapters 2 and 4) that the Supreme Court already has found to the contrary regarding the ADEA, and given that no circuit court that has considered the issue to date has found preclusive legislative intent in Title VII.

The EEOC's public huffing and puffing against compulsory employment arbitration seems to be all smoke and no fire. The EEOC simply does not have the authority to issue an outright ban on compulsory arbitration, and the arguments it might advance to limit compulsory arbitration already have been decided by the Supreme Court in favor of arbitration. The EEOC still can file suit against employers that have implemented compulsory arbitration programs, but the law as it stands now strongly favors arbitration, and the EEOC's limited and ever-dwindling budget make it impossible for it to sue more than a small percentage of employers that adopt compulsory arbitration programs.[87] The EEOC thus is reduced to issuing vague and meaningless policy declarations and suing employers, such as ROID, who have instituted particularly egregious and unfair arbitration agreements. The EEOC, at least insofar as its power to oppose compulsory arbitration is concerned, is still toothless.

Seven

Compulsory Employment Arbitration in the Securities Industry

THE ERA OF COMPULSORY EMPLOYMENT ARBITRA-
tion began with the Supreme Court decision of *Gilmer v.
Interstate/Johnson Lane Corp.*[1] Gilmer was the manager
of financial services for Interstate. A condition of his employment was
to register with several stock exchanges, including the New York Stock
Exchange. Gilmer's NYSE registration application contained a clause by
which he agreed to arbitrate "any dispute, claim or controversy" between
himself and Interstate arising out of his employment or the termination
of his employment.[2] When Gilmer attempted to litigate his age discrimination claim, the Court dismissed his lawsuit and ordered the parties to
arbitration.[3]

It is hardly surprising that the seminal case on compulsory employment arbitration arose in the context of the securities industry. This industry pioneered the use of compulsory arbitration agreements as a means of
resolving disputes between securities exchanges and investors. In 1872,
the NYSE became the first securities exchange to provide an arbitration
forum to resolve disputes between members and their customers;[4] the
other exchanges followed suit over the next 100 years.[5] The industry
also pioneered the use of compulsory arbitration agreements to resolve
employment disputes by enforcing agreements, such as the one signed by
Gilmer, that are contained in registration agreements between securities
industry employees and the various stock exchanges.[6] While other employers only recently have begun to draft and implement these agreements,
employers in the securities industry had an elaborate arbitral system already in place long before *Gilmer* was issued.

Since the *Gilmer* decision, a large body of case law has developed
around the arbitration of employment disputes in the securities industry.

This case law allows for a comprehensive industry study of the use and implementation of compulsory employment arbitration. Because the use of arbitration agreements by the securities industry has a long and unique history, it first will be necessary to examine more generally the way that all disputes—employment and non-employment alike—are resolved in the securities industry.

A. The Resolution of Disputes in the Securities Industry

The securities industry is organized around self-regulatory organizations (SROs), which are "groups of industry professionals [that] . . . operate and regulate" market facilities.[7] SROs include the nine securities exchanges, such as the American and the New York Stock Exchanges, and the National Association of Securities Dealers (NASD), which regulates the over-the-counter market.[8] The SROs provide market facilities where securities are bought and sold. Securities firms, such as Dean Witter Reynolds and Shearson Lehman/American Express, are known as "member firms" because they are members of, and help to govern, the SROs.[9] Member firms employ "registered representatives" who sell securities and arrange for execution of investors' buy and sell orders by communicating these orders to the markets maintained by the SROs.[10] A prerequisite to communicating buy and sell orders to an SRO market is registration with that particular SRO. Consequently, securities firms frequently require employees to register with one or more stock exchanges, thereby becoming registered representatives of these exchanges.[11]

SROs are essentially self-regulating; they have the authority "to adopt and enforce standards of conduct for their members' securities firms."[12] The Securities and Exchange Commission (the SEC), the government agency that regulates the securities industry, oversees the SROs through its review, approval, or rejection of SROs' rules.[13] These rules, which before they become effective must be approved by the SEC, include procedural rules governing the resolution of disputes between investors and the member firms.[14]

Prior to 1976, the SEC left the task of investor dispute resolution to the SROs and the courts.[15] As a result, most SROs had differing rules for administering securities arbitration disputes.[16] In June 1976, however, the SEC initiated efforts to create a uniform procedure for the SROs' separate arbitration systems and rules for use in resolving such disputes.[17] The SEC felt that a uniform set of procedures would protect consumers and "encourage the individual investor to participate in the securities markets."[18] After conducting public hearings, the SEC issued a report that recommended adopting new procedures for handling investor disputes and creating a new entity to administer the system,[19] and invited further comment on its recommendations.

In response to this request, several SROs proposed establishing a securities industry task force to consider the development of a "uniform arbitration code and the means for establishing a more efficient, economic, and appropriate mechanism for resolving investor disputes involving small sums of money."[20] As a result of this proposal, the securities industry, in collaboration with the SEC, created the Securities Industry Conference on Arbitration (SICA), a group composed of SRO representatives, the securities industry association, and several public representatives.[21] The purpose of SICA was to develop rules for the resolution of disputes involving small claims between customers and member firms.[22]

SICA initially developed a simplified arbitration procedure for resolving customers' small claims ($2,500 or less) and published an informational booklet describing these procedures.[23] Recognizing that the development of a small claims procedure was merely a first step, SICA then began working on a uniform system of arbitration procedures to cover all claims by investors.[24] SICA thus expanded the existing rules of SROs and developed the first version of the Uniform Code of Arbitration (UCA).[25]

The UCA is a set of the securities industry's private rules. By incorporating and harmonizing preexisting individual SRO rules, the UCA provided a uniform system of dispute resolution for small claims in the securities industry. Although neither the SEC nor the SICA mandates SRO adoption of the UCA, the SROs voluntarily adopted the UCA with only minor variations.[26] Thus, the arbitration rules promulgated by the SROs are similar, though not identical.

In 1987, the Supreme Court, in *Shearson/American Express, Inc. v. McMahon*,[27] compelled arbitration—pursuant to the arbitration clause in the investor's agreement with the brokerage firm—of a statutory fraud claim brought by the investor against the brokerage firm. Following the *McMahon* decision, there was a substantial amount of ferment and discussion within the SEC, Congress, the states, and the securities industry regarding compulsory arbitration agreements.[28] The SEC staff recommended that the SEC request Congress to amend securities laws to prohibit brokers from conditioning opening a customer account on the customer's signing a compulsory arbitration agreement; this proposal was rejected by the SEC.[29] At about the same time, a bill was introduced in

Congress that, among other things, would have required that agreements to arbitrate disputes in the securities industry be nonbinding.[30] The bill, which eventually was defeated, was opposed by the SEC, the securities industry, and the SROs.[31]

Against this background, on July 8, 1988, the SEC asked the securities industry and the SROs to consider ways to improve arbitration procedures and disclosures about those procedures.[32] The SROs, through SICA, adopted rule changes to improve the method by which investors were informed about the arbitration agreements they were signing and to prohibit SRO members from limiting the ability of the arbitrators to make any award.[33] The proposed rule changes were submitted to the SEC and approved on May 10, 1989.[34]

The avowed purpose of creating an arbitration system in the securities industry was to resolve commercial claims brought against it by investors, using an arbitrator with a thorough understanding of the industry.[35] It since has been expanded to include not only investor-securities industry disputes but also intraindustry disputes, such as those between two member firms or between a member firm and its employees.[36] For example, the NASD Code of Arbitration Procedure at Part I makes eligible for arbitration "[a]ny dispute, claim or controversy . . . arising out of the employment or termination of employment of associated person(s) with any member [firm]." Part II requires arbitration of "any dispute, claim, or controversy . . . eligible for submission under Part I of this Code between or among members and/or associated persons . . . or arising out of the employment or termination of employment of such associated person(s) with such member. . . ."[37] This language, which was approved by the SEC on August 31, 1993, and became effective on October 1, 1993, was added so there would be no doubt that the arbitration clause covered employment disputes. It effectively requires arbitration of all disputes arising between securities firms and their registered representative employees.[38]

Although the SEC, the federal agency which regulates the securities industry, monitors and oversees the securities industry's arbitration of investor-firm disputes, it exercises virtually no oversight over intraindustry disputes, such as employment discrimination claims.[39] This is because the SEC considers its primary responsibility under its enabling act[40] to be preserving the integrity of the securities markets and protecting investors, not industry employees.[41] The SEC neither reviews employment cases nor compiles information regarding the nature, type, or outcome of such cases.[42]

B. The Process of Selecting an Arbitrator:
Problems of Selection Bias and Lack of Adequate Knowledge

Many commentators believe that the securities industry's arbitration system has done a good job of adjudicating securities disputes,[43] which is the purpose for which it was designed. These commentators emphasize that most arbitrators in the pool have (or at least should have) extensive experience in the securities industry,[44] allowing them to evaluate claims in light of industry customs and practices, and sparing the parties the burden of educating the trier of fact about the complex financial instruments and transactions at issue in most securities disputes.[45] Other commentators, however, have criticized the arbitration system for permitting potentially biased industry representatives to sit on arbitration panels, for inconsistency in the quality of arbitrators, for the lack of written decisions justifying arbitration awards, for the difficulty of obtaining effective judicial review of arbitral awards, and for the lack of investor success when pursuing seemingly meritorious claims.[46]

The efficacy and fairness of the securities industry arbitration system in resolving investor disputes is open to debate. It is much clearer, however, that this arbitration system was originally not designed to handle employment claims,[47] and it has done a poor job of adjudicating such claims. Much of the security industry's handling of employment claims has focused on the process by which arbitrators are selected. Critics have charged that the process of selecting arbitrators—and possibly the arbitrators themselves—is biased in favor of securities industry employers, and that the arbitrators do not have sufficient knowledge of employment law to decide the legal issues arising in complex employment discrimination cases.[48]

To become an arbitrator in the securities industry, a person first must be appointed to the SRO "pool" of arbitrators. Arbitrators may apply directly for inclusion in the pool, but otherwise they are recruited into the pool based on the recommendations of current arbitrators, employees of the SROs, and the NASD Board of Governors or the NYSE Board.[49] This "word of mouth" recruitment process[50] has resulted in a demographically unbalanced pool of arbitrators. The General Accounting Office (GAO), a government agency that engages in audit and oversight activities on direction from Congress,[51] conducted a demographic study of persons in the NYSE pool of arbitrators as of December 31, 1992. Of the 726 arbitrators in the pool, 89 percent were men and 11 percent were women. With regard to the 349 arbitrators whose race was identifiable, 97 percent were white, .9 percent black, .6 percent Asian, and 1 percent other.[52] Some commentators and litigants have suggested that the demographic profile of arbitration panels may make it impossible for employment claimants in the securities industry to obtain fair hearings.[53]

To overturn an arbitral award because of a biased arbitrator, a party to arbitration must prove to a court that "there [existed] evident partiality or corruption by the arbitrator[ ]."[54] An arbitration panel's demographic composition alone is unlikely to justify nonenforcement of an arbitration agreement or vacation of an arbitral award. It is highly doubtful whether the federal judiciary, which itself is no more demographically diverse than the securities arbitration pool,[55] can be persuaded that a lack of demographic diversity proves arbitral bias. Nonetheless, the securities industry would be well advised to intensify its efforts to recruit female and minority arbitrators. Both in the popular press and in the minds of many securities industry employees, the appearance of bias adversely reflects upon the integrity of the arbitral forum.[56]

After arbitrators are appointed to the securities industry arbitration pool, they are divided into two groups: "industry" and "public." An industry arbitrator is a person who (1) "is associated with a member [firm], or broker/dealer, government securities broker, government securities dealer, or registered investment adviser . . ., (2) has been associated with any of the above within the past three . . . years . . ., (3) is retired from any of the above, . . . or (4) is an attorney, accountant, or other professional who devoted twenty . . . percent or more of his or her professional work effort to securities industry clients within the past two years."[57] An industry arbitrator, therefore, is someone with strong ties to the securities industry. Public arbitrators consist of persons not employed by member firms, such as attorneys, accountants, educators, and knowledgeable investors, although such persons are classified as industry arbitrators if they routinely represent industry firms or individuals.[58] This industry public classification system is intended to limit the existence or appearance of industry bias while maintaining a pool of arbitrators purportedly knowledgeable about the securities industry.[59]

The size and composition of the arbitration panel[60] for a given dispute depends upon the amount of money in controversy and the way the dispute is classified. Claims for less than $30,000 are heard by a single arbitrator; claims exceeding $30,000 are heard by a panel of three arbitrators.[61] Arbitrators are chosen primarily according to their "industry" or "public" classification.[62] Disputes between member firms are categorized as industry cases and arbitrated exclusively by industry arbitrators.[63] An investor dispute with a member firm is categorized as a public dispute in which the majority of those empaneled must be public arbitrators.[64] Employment disputes between a member firm and its employees are treated for arbitration purposes as public disputes and thus are heard by a panel with a majority of public arbitrators.[65]

The securities arbitration process is initiated when an aggrieved party —a customer, a securities industry employee, or a member firm—files a Statement of Claim and the required fee with the SRO's Director of Arbitration.[66] The Director of Arbitration then forwards the claim to the defendant, who must respond within twenty business days.[67] The Director of Arbitration next appoints either an arbitrator or a panel of arbitrators.[68] Arbitrator selection is primarily based on the arbitrator's industry or public classification, and secondarily on an arbitrator's education, employment, availability, possible conflicts of interest, frequency of service, ratings, and (for the chair of a panel) status as an attorney.[69] Once notified of appointment, each arbitrator is expected to initiate conflict of interest checks against the parties, their lawyers, and potential witnesses.[70] The Director of Arbitration then notifies the parties of the arbitrators' identities. Such notification includes the arbitrators' ten-year employment history and any of their conflict of interest disclosures.[71] Each party then is given an opportunity to object to members of the panel, as well as one peremptory challenge and unlimited challenges for cause.[72]

The SRO's Director of Arbitration's appointment of arbitrators creates an obvious appearance of potential bias.[73] Those employers accused of discriminatory employment practices are SRO members, and the SRO promulgates rules governing arbitration, picks arbitrators, and oversees the arbitration process. The selection of arbitrators by what is essentially a securities industry employers' association stands in stark contrast to the practice of most neutral arbitration agencies that provide both parties with equal input during the selection process. It also differs from the labor arbitration practice of jointly selecting arbitrators, and resorting to alternative selection methods (such as by independent third parties) only if parties cannot make a joint selection.[74] Moreover, securities industry arbitrators, whether industry or public, always will have some current or former affiliation with a securities firm, because that is how they qualify to join the pool. Added to this are the far better-than-even odds that an entire three-arbitrator panel will be made up of elderly white men, and at least one member of that panel will be an industry arbitrator with strong ties to a securities industry employer. It is not difficult to understand why the system may be perceived as biased. The composition of the panel, and the way it is selected, increases the likelihood that arbitration panels in securities industry employment discrimination cases are subject to the very biases that a plaintiff may seek to remedy.[75]

The way the securities industry selects arbitrators to hear an employment dispute is subject to justified additional criticism because the process fails to ensure that appointed arbitrators have even a minimal knowledge of employment law. Whereas a member firm or public investor bringing suit on a securities issue can be confident that an industry arbitrator will be qualified to resolve the dispute, a securities industry employee bringing an employment claim cannot be certain that the public arbitrator chosen will be even minimally qualified to hear the claim. Knowledge, training, and experience in employment law are not factors in deciding whether to add an arbitrator's name to the securities arbitration pool, nor are they prerequisites to being chosen to sit on an arbitration panel in an employment case. There simply is no requirement that an arbitrator selected to decide an employment case be knowledgeable in employment law.[76]

A year after the Supreme Court issued its *Gilmer* decision, the GAO produced a report critical of the process by which the securities industry chose its arbitrators. The GAO found that the "arbitration forums [*sic*] lacked internal controls to provide a reasonable level of assurance regarding either the independence of the arbitrators or their competence in arbitrating disputes."[77] The GAO concluded that "the forums [*sic*] had no established formal standards to initially qualify individuals as arbitrators, did not verify background information provided by prospective or existing arbitrators, and had no system to ensure that arbitrators were adequately trained to perform their functions fairly and appropriately."[78]

Two years later, in 1994, the GAO issued another report, this time focusing on the securities industry's arbitration of employment discrimination claims.[79] The 1994 report "arose out of a concern that statutory protections designed to safeguard the rights of employees were being systematically denied by the securities industry."[80] While the report did not comment on the fairness of specific discrimination cases, it identified weaknesses and inconsistencies in arbitration procedures that could result in inappropriate selection of arbitrators. For example, the GAO observed that although arbitrators should be "knowledgeable in the areas of controversy," neither the NASD nor the NYSE "necessarily consider[s], as a primary criterion for arbitration panel selection, arbitrators' expertise in the subject matter of the dispute."[81] The report concluded that "[s]ince discrimination cases involving registered representatives raise issues that are different from the securities-related disputes administered by SROs, it may be appropriate to consider whether the panels for these cases should be comprised differently, and include at least one arbitrator with expertise in employment or discrimination law."[82]

The GAO's criticisms of the securities industry's process of selecting arbitrators are well-founded. Although the demographic disparity between the pool of arbitrators and the general population does not necessarily prove the existence of bias in any individual case, a system that creates such disparity is suspect. It is appalling that arbitrators are selected for a given case by an organization with strong ties to an allegedly discriminatory employer. So, too, is the industry's failure to ensure that employment cases are decided by arbitrators with substantive knowledge of employment law. These problems create, at the very least, a strong appearance that the arbitrators deciding employment cases for the securities industry are not as impartial or competent as they should be.

The problems with employment arbitration in the securities industry do not end with the selection of an arbitrator. Two additional problems are discussed in the next section.

C. Other Procedural Problems with Arbitration in the Securities Industry

In addition to the problems already discussed in this chapter, securities industry arbitration also has other procedural problems. One such problem is that parties have limited access to relevant facts prior to arbitration hearings. The Federal Rules of Civil Procedure provide litigants with broad opportunities to discover such facts. Litigants may, for example, take depositions of witnesses and adversaries by oral[83] or written[84] questions, require opposing parties to answer written questions (interrogatories) regarding the facts of the case,[85] and compel opposing parties to release relevant documents.[86]

In securities industry arbitration, however, discovery is far more limited.[87] As in litigation, the parties to securities arbitration have the right to discover the opponents' relevant documents upon proper service of a request for information.[88] Depositions, however, have a far more limited availability;[89] they are permitted only when witnesses are unwilling or unable to attend the hearing, or in other circumstances in which depositions are absolutely necessary to permit a party to develop a case.[90] Interrogatories generally are not available.[91] Disputes regarding discovery are resolved at a prehearing conference, which any party or arbitrator may call.[92] If these cannot be resolved at a prehearing conference, one of the arbitrators may be appointed to rule on them.[93]

In *Gilmer,* the Supreme Court rejected Gilmer's argument that because arbitral discovery in the securities industry was more limited than
that available through federal courts, Gilmer should not be compelled to
arbitrate his claim. The Court, after noting the types of discovery permitted by the NYSE, declared that "by agreeing to arbitrate, a party 'trades
the procedures and opportunity for review of the courtroom for the simplicity, informality, and expedition of arbitration.' "[94]

Discovery is and should be less formal in arbitration than litigation.
Arbitration derives its principal advantages—speed and low cost—largely
from the fact that discovery is more limited and less formal.[95] However,
many commentators have concluded that, at least in the context of employment disputes, the securities industry goes too far, and that by unrea-
sonably restricting employees' access to discovery, arbitration essentially is
depriving them of any opportunity they might have to pursue their
claim.[96] The fact that an employment claim is being arbitrated rather than
litigated does not diminish in any way the need for complete discovery. In
a simple disparate treatment case,[97] for example, an employee must have
access to the employment records of coworkers in order to show that
similarly situated nonclass members were treated differently.[98] In a disparate impact case[99] the plaintiff must have access to employment records
from which can be derived statistics on how different classifications of
employees were impacted by a given employment practice.[100] In either
type of case, it is far more difficult for an employment discrimination
plaintiff to prove a case without a generous allowance of discovery.

The securities industry's arbitration rules, on their face, neither guarantee nor preclude adequate prehearing discovery. Instead, the scope and
form of discovery generally are left to the discretion of the arbitrators. In
practice, it appears that claimants are not always given an opportunity to
conduct sufficient discovery. This may in part be because, as discussed
earlier in this chapter, the arbitrators who control the parties' access to
discovery may be beholden to, or at least have strong ties to, securities
industry employers. To the extent that plaintiffs are denied an opportunity
to discover their case properly, securities industry arbitration has become
less an inexpensive alternative to litigation, and more a device for shielding
industry employers from legitimate employment discrimination claims.

Another problem with securities industry arbitration concerns the arbitrator's duty to apply the law. As discussed above, not only are arbitrators not required to be familiar with employment law before hearing an
employment case, they also are not required to learn the law prior to
rendering a decision. The Arbitrators' Manual given to all NASD and

NYSE arbitrators provides: "Arbitrators are not strictly bound by case precedent or statutory law. Rather, they are guided in their analysis by the underlying policies of the law and are given wide latitude in their interpretation of legal concepts."[101] Instead of being required to follow the law, arbitrators merely are prohibited from "manifestly disregarding" it.[102] This "manifest disregard" standard has been interpreted to justify overturning of an arbitral award only if an arbitrator knew what the law required but consciously chose to disregard it.[103] An arbitrator is required to follow the law as she understands it, but is not required to grasp the meaning of the law. This is inconsistent with the pronouncement by the Supreme Court in *Mitsubishi Motors Corp. v. Soler Chrysler-Plymouth, Inc.* and in *Gilmer*) that by agreeing to arbitrate, a party "does not forego the substantive rights," but "only submits to their resolution in an arbitral, rather than a judicial, forum."[104] As one commentator has noted, "[I]f arbitrators need not follow the law, this certainly bespeaks a potential loss of substantive statutory rights."[105]

An arbitrator's failure to follow the law, whether due to ignorance or to the "wide latitude" that the securities industry allows in applying legal principles, would not be overly problematic if parties were given an opportunity to appeal the decision to a court that either could decide the case anew or remand it to the arbitrator with instructions concerning the proper application of the law. Such an appeal process, however, does not meaningfully exist in the securities industry,[106] where the absence of written arbitration opinions makes it all but impossible to ascertain whether an arbitrator "manifestly disregarded" the law.[107] The Uniform Code on Arbitration requires that the arbitration award be in writing, signed by a majority of the panel, and delivered within thirty business days of the date the record was closed.[108] The award must contain (1) the names of the parties, (2) a summary of the issues in controversy, (3) the damages and other relief requested, (4) the damages and other relief awarded, (5) a statement of any other issues resolved, (6) the names of the arbitrators, and (7) the signatures of the arbitrators concurring in the award.[109] These award summaries, slightly modified, are publicly available and appear periodically in national legal reporting services covering the securities industry.[110] Arbitrators are not, however, required to write opinions giving their reasons for the award.[111]

To show that an arbitrator exhibited "manifest disregard of the law," "[t]he [arbitrator's] error must have been obvious and capable of being readily and instantly perceived by the average person qualified to serve as an arbitrator. Moreover, the term 'disregard' implies that the arbitrator appreciates the existence of a clearly governing legal principle but decides to ignore or pay no attention to it." [112] An error cannot have been "obvious and capable of being readily and instantly perceived" if there is no written arbitration award explaining the legal standard used, or the manner in which the arbitrator applied the law to the facts of the case decided.[113] Moreover, as discussed previously, the requirement that an arbitrator knew of but decided to ignore a legal principle protects decisions made by those knowing nothing of employment law. The absence of written opinions, coupled with an extremely onerous standard for obtaining judicial review, makes securities industry arbitration awards virtually unreviewable.

The problems with the securities industry's arbitration of employment matters are well illustrated by the case of Helen Walters, who was a trading-room secretary at a California brokerage firm.[114] Walters filed a complaint alleging what appeared to be a clear example of sexual harassment. She claimed that her boss called her obscene and degrading names, physically threatened her, and gave her unwelcome gifts of condoms. The New York Stock Exchange oversaw the arbitration proceedings and empaneled three male arbitrators to hear her case, none of whom had any experience or training in employment or sex discrimination law. The arbitrators' questions to the witnesses focused on comparing the boss's behavior to the norm in the securities industry. This, however, was not the proper legal standard; the proper standard was whether a "reasonable person" would have found the work environment "hostile or abusive." [115] The arbitrators ultimately dismissed Walters' case.[116]

If the arbitrators in Walters' case correctly had concluded that Walters was lying about the conduct she claimed to have endured during her employment, the decision to dismiss her case would have been correct. However, the nature of the arbitrators' questions raises the inference that she lost her case not because the arbitrators did not believe her, but because they reached the incorrect legal conclusion that workplace harassment is legal if everyone else in the industry is doing it. The outcome of this case, and the possibility that it was wrongly decided, should not be surprising, given the way the securities industry arbitration system has been established. As previously discussed, the SROs, which essentially are employers' associations, establish the rules of arbitration and select arbitrators for the pool and for individual cases. These arbitrators, all of whom have relatively strong ties to the industry, are overwhelmingly elderly white men, and many have no knowledge of or experience with employment law. Plaintiffs often are given little or no opportunity to develop their case through discovery. Instead, in most cases, they simply show up at the hearing and tell their story. Arbitrators are not required to follow the substantive law or to issue an opinion explaining the reasons for their decision. The arbitration decision is in practice unreviewable.

The *Gilmer* decision, because it was based on a case arising out of the securities industry, often has been regarded as blessing the securities industry's procedures for arbitrating employment as well as investor claims. However, although the *Gilmer* Court rejected the use of "generalized attacks" on the arbitral process, it expressly left open the question of whether compulsory arbitration agreements may be challenged on the grounds of procedural unfairness, stating that "claimed procedural inadequacies [of arbitration] . . . [are] best left for resolution in specific cases."[117] Robert Gilmer failed to develop a strong factual record in the trial court detailing the shortcomings of the securities industry's procedures for arbitrating employment claims. If he had done so, and had presented these issues to the Supreme Court, the *Gilmer* case might have been decided differently. *Gilmer*, therefore, should not be interpreted as approving wholesale the employment arbitration procedures adopted by the securities industry.

A more detailed discussion of specific procedural issues—such as the selection of arbitrators, written opinion requirements, and the scope of judicial review—is found in chapter 9. It should be clear from this chapter, however, that the securities industry's employment arbitration system is not a model that should be emulated by other employers. Many of its procedures are unfair to employees, and such unfairness may later be used by courts as justification for denying enforcement of arbitration agreements or vacating arbitral awards. A better model for employers to follow is the dispute resolution program created by Brown & Root, discussed in the next chapter.

Eight

Compulsory Arbitration as Part of a Broader Employment Dispute Resolution Process: The Brown & Root Example

Bᴿᴼᵂᴺ & ᴿᴼᴼᵀ ᵂᴬˢ ᴼᴺᴱ ᴼᶠ ᵀᴴᴱ ᶠᴵᴿˢᵀ ᴹᴬᴶᴼᴿ companies in the United States to institute an in-house program for the nonjudicial resolution of employment disputes. In addition to being one of the first programs of its kind in the country, Brown & Root's is also one of the most extensive. It combines compulsory arbitration with a comprehensive dispute resolution process that includes employee training in conflict management, in-house dispute resolution techniques such as conferencing and informal mediation, formal mediation, and procedures designed to ensure that employees are treated fairly throughout the process. During the first three years of its existence, the program has been very successful at retaining employees who otherwise might have quit or been discharged because of a conflict, and has significantly reduced the company's outside legal fees. Brown & Root's dispute resolution program demonstrates that compulsory arbitration and employee fairness need not be mutually exclusive.

Brown & Root is a Houston-based company that employs between 25,000 and 30,000 employees,[1] all of whom are nonunion. Its principal products are construction, maintenance, and engineering services.[2] The company's large number of employees, coupled with the traditionally high turnover rate in the construction and maintenance industries, was forcing it to spend far more in legal fees than it believed was necessary.

The company decided to explore alternatives to litigation after a sexual harassment trial in which the company prevailed cost it $450,000 in outside legal fees.[3] During the five years between the alleged harassment and the trial, the litigation profoundly affected the lives and careers of several employees and former employees, including the plaintiff.[4] The financial and human costs associated with such litigation prompted the company to examine alternatives to the litigation system for resolving employment matters.[5]

In the summer of 1992, Brown & Root's general counsel, Jim Wilson, established a series of task forces to study the company's existing procedures for handling employment problems, and to propose alternatives ranging from no change to radical change. The task forces were comprised of senior management; representatives of the company's legal and employee relations departments; outside legal experts; representatives from the American Arbitration Association (AAA); Chorda Conflict Management, consultants in conflict management design; and Sheppards Associates, experts in employee relations communications.[6] The various task forces interviewed approximately 300 Brown & Root employees, both individually and in focus groups, to determine the employees' perceptions of conflicts common to the company, the company's typical responses to these conflicts, the employees' impressions and opinions of the company's then-current programs intended to address these conflicts, and various alternative dispute resolution proposals.[7] They then recommended and began developing a comprehensive dispute resolution program that included compulsory arbitration.

A. An Overview of Brown & Root's Program

Brown & Root finalized its dispute resolution program (the Program)[8] in February 1993, officially announced it to its employees on May 1, 1993, and implemented the Program on June 15, 1993. In a letter to introduce the Program sent by T. E. Knight, Brown & Root's president and chief executive officer, the company made it clear that the Program was to serve as the exclusive means of resolving workplace disputes involving nonunion employees, explaining that "[i]f legal action is instituted, the court will be requested to refer the matter to the Dispute Resolution Program for final resolution."[9] The letter also stated that after the Program's effective date of commencement, an employee's decision to accept employment or continue working for Brown & Root would mean that that worker had agreed to the terms of the Program, and that the Program would continue to bind the employee following termination of employment. The letter was optimistic in tone, pointing out that the purpose of the Program was "to provide for more effective early resolution of ordinary workplace problems, and fair, less expensive and faster ways than lawsuits to resolve legal disputes."[10]

Just as the Program compels employees to use the Program in lieu of litigation, it also creates a contractual obligation on the part of the company, explicitly amending the at-will employment relationship for that limited effect.[11] Brown & Root can cancel the Program only after giving ten days' notice to employees, and such cancellation does not affect any dispute arising prior to cancellation. Similarly, Brown & Root can amend the Program and its rules at any time, but no such amendment affects any dispute of which the company had notice on the date of amendment.

The Program covers all types of employment disputes, including tort, contract and statutory claims, as well as claims for equitable relief. It explicitly lists sex, race, religion, national origin, and disability discrimination; sexual harassment; defamation; intentional infliction of emotional distress; and claims related to employee benefits as types of claims to which the Program applies. The Program excludes claims for workers' compensation benefits or unemployment compensation benefits, but includes claims for workers' compensation retaliation. It makes clear to employees that they are still free to contact the EEOC or their state Human Rights Commission about workplace discrimination if they so desire.

Brown & Root's dispute resolution Program is unique because it goes beyond the standard arbitration agreement used by the securities industry and most other employers that have instituted compulsory arbitration programs. The goal is not simply to avoid litigation, or even to substitute arbitration in its stead, but to design a system that will minimize the use of all types of adjudication and will encourage the early resolution of disputes by mutual agreement. Brown & Root believes that in a company of 30,000 people, some conflict is inevitable, just as it is inevitable that some employees will get injured on the job or will develop medical conditions. In the same way that the company has a structured response to employees' injuries and illness (through its workers' compensation and medical benefits plans), it wants to have a structured response to employment conflicts—a response that would predate the conflict itself. The goal is to establish a dispute resolution system that will encourage employees to seek resolution before both sides become entrenched or the conflict become irrevocable through a termination.

To this end, Brown & Root has developed a four-step process for the resolution of employment disputes. In Step 1, called the "Open Door Policy," the aggrieved employee simply discusses the dispute with her or his supervisor and other persons up the chain of command. If that does not resolve the dispute, the employee is encouraged to go to Step 2: to arrange a conference with a company representative to consider the dispute and choose a process for resolving it. Step 3 is mediation by an independent mediator provided by AAA. Step 4 is binding arbitration. Although employees are not required to follow the four-step process sequentially, the steps are designed in the logical pattern applicable to most disputes.

B. The Four-Step Process

1. Step 1: The Open Door Policy

Brown & Root's "Open Door Policy" represents the company's written, official commitment to allow employees to go up the chain of command as far as necessary to resolve a dispute. It encourages employees to start with their immediate supervisor, but recognizes that sometimes the supervisor is part of the problem. If the employee is dissatisfied with her immediate supervisor's response or feels she needs to speak with someone else, she may take the problem to the next higher level of supervision, and on up the chain of command until the matter is resolved or until the employee feels it is appropriate to move to another step in the dispute resolution process.

The Program provides employees with several tools to aid them in resolving their conflicts. First, the company guarantees that an employee will not be retaliated against for using the dispute resolution program. This guarantee is particularly potent because of the company's contractual obligation to honor it. By making this guarantee part of the Program, thereby modifying the at-will relationship, Brown & Root has essentially created a cause of action for nonstatutory retaliation where none existed before.[12] Moreover, Brown & Root has repeatedly emphasized to its supervisors that retaliating against an employee for using the Program constitutes grounds for immediate discharge. The company has demonstrated its commitment to this policy by discharging at least one retaliator.[13]

Second, the company provides a 1–800 number Employee Hotline, which an employee may call for free expert and confidential advice. The hotline is staffed by "advisors" who are Brown & Root volunteers with at least fifty hours of training in mediation and collaboration skills. Brown & Root's advisors are similar to ombudspersons in other corporations.[14] Their role varies from case to case, depending on the employee's preference. The advisor can simply answer questions about the dispute resolution program, can act as a conduit between the employee and her supervisor, can give advice on how the employee might be able to solve the dispute on her own, or can act as a mediator, fact finder, or both. The employee has the option of remaining anonymous to an advisor. Approximately ninety percent of all of the advisors' training—and all of the advisors' advising—is done on company time.

Third, Brown & Root employs a full-time Program Administrator to run the dispute resolution program. Employees are encouraged to call this administrator with questions or to initiate conferences and other internal dispute resolution processes.

In addition to administration, the Program Administrator has benefited the company by providing "upward feedback" about how company employees are being supervised.[15] The Administrator is in a position to recognize which sections of the company have an unusually large number of employee complaints. This recognition allows the Administrator to recommend proactive action, such as removing or retraining supervisors, addressing concerns important to employees, and helping prevent future disputes from occurring. Brown & Root's associate general counsel, William Bedman, notes that this has had the unintended consequence of helping the company avoid union attempts to organize the company's employees by helping to resolve problems before they induce employees to seek assistance from a union.

Fourth, Brown & Root has instituted an extensive training session required of all of its approximately 2,000 front-line supervisors. This three-hour session is like a mini-course on mediation. Trainers coach supervisors not to suppress conflicts, and ask them instead to encourage their employees to raise issues as early as possible to promote early resolution and reduce the number of disputes progressing to more formal and external levels. The training session explains the Dispute Resolution Program to the supervisors, emphasizes the Company's commitment to the Program, and helps them realize how important it is that employees not fear being retaliated against for participating in the Program.

Brown & Root also has developed a fifty-hour conflict resolution training session for employees who wish to become advisors. The advisors' training session includes such topics as conflict management, effective listening, ethics (advisors become familiar with the Ombudsman Association's "code of ethics"), confidentiality, neutrality, and Brown & Root's Dispute Resolution Program. To date, approximately one hundred advisors have completed the training. Approximately 180 employees have been trained as in-house mediators.

Finally, Brown & Root pays for employees or former employees to consult with and retain attorneys of their choice, provided that their disputes involve legally/protected employee rights. Reimbursements for attorneys' fees are paid like benefits under standard medical plans. The employee pays a deductible of $25.00. After the deductible, the employee pays 10 percent of the balance; Brown & Root reimburses the employee for the remainder, up to a maximum of $2,500 per year. The employee is solely responsible for choosing the attorney.

This Legal Consultation Plan[16] (the Plan) reimburses the employee for attorneys' fees and does not pay the attorney directly. The Director of the Plan, appointed by Brown & Root, is responsible for administering the Plan. The Plan does not permit Brown & Root to require the Director or her staff to reveal information, such as billing records, privileged under applicable law.

The company's Legal Consultation Plan reimburses the employee for attorneys' fees incurred in an initial consultation regarding the employee's dispute with the company; the negotiation of the dispute prior to mediation, or arbitration, or the mediation prior to arbitration; discovery and preparation for mediation or arbitration; and representation in mediation or arbitration itself. The Plan does not reimburse the employee for legal fees incurred after an arbitration award is rendered. An employee is not required to take advantage of the company's legal representation reimbursement. An employee may, without jeopardizing reimbursement, consult with or hire an attorney before initiating any part of the dispute resolution program; this would be considered an initial consultation that would be reimbursed by Brown & Root.

2. Step 2: The Conference

Step 2 of the Brown & Root Dispute Resolution Program, the Conference, is a meeting at Brown & Root at which the employee and a company representative confer with someone from the dispute resolution program to discuss the dispute and to choose a process for resolving it. This step is intended to be used if attempts to resolve a problem by going up the chain of command prove ineffective. The goal of the Conference is to help the employee and the company agree on a way to settle the dispute. Several options are available.

First, the employee may choose to return to the chain of command to try again. The Conference may have identified other individuals or departments the employee can contact through the open door policy in an attempt to resolve the dispute. "Looping back" helps contain the problem within the company and encourages informal, non-confrontational methods of dispute resolution.

Second, the employee can choose to try an in-house resolution process, such as informal mediation. The mediator in this instance would be a Brown & Root employee with experience and training in resolving employment disputes. The mediator would listen while both parties tell their stories, and try to help the parties work out their problems themselves.

Third, the parties might agree to proceed directly from the Conference to an *outside* resolution process such as mediation or arbitration. This option is open only if the dispute is based on a legally protected right, such as when the employee asserts that her Title VII rights have been violated or that the company has made and breached an enforceable employment contract with her. Mediation and arbitration would not be available to an employee who, for example, is merely protesting a shift assignment, absent an allegation that the shift assignment was made in a discriminatory manner, or that it was made in violation of an employment contract, or that it in some other way constituted a violation of the employee's legal rights. If arbitration and mediation are available options, either the employee or the company can file a request for mediation or arbitration at any stage of the dispute resolution process.

3. Step 3: Mediation

Outside mediation in Brown & Root's dispute resolution program is virtually identical to mediation in other contexts. It is a nonbinding meeting between the employee and a company representative (usually the employee's supervisor) in which a neutral third party, the mediator, helps the parties come to an agreement on their own. The purpose of mediation is to resolve the dispute by opening communication and coming up with options.

An employee may initiate mediation by filing a Request for Mediation with AAA and including with that Request a $50.00 processing fee. Brown & Root pays for all costs of mediation that exceed this $50.00 fee.

All mediations are conducted by a mediator chosen by and through AAA. After mediation is requested, AAA assigns a professional mediator located in or near the city of the employee's residence. The mediator then meets with the parties, typically for a full or half day, to discuss the dispute and possible solutions. If mediation does not successfully resolve the dispute, the parties may proceed to binding arbitration.

4. Step 4: Arbitration

Step 4 of Brown & Root's dispute resolution program requires employees who have a legal claim against the company to submit that claim to binding arbitration. Arbitration is conducted pursuant to the Dispute Resolution Plan and Rules drafted and promulgated by Brown & Root. Either the employee or Brown & Root may file a Request for Arbitration at any point in the dispute resolution process. This Request, which is filed with AAA, must describe the nature of the dispute, the amount in controversy, the remedy sought, and the requested location for the arbitration hearing. If the party filing the Request wants the arbitrator to issue with the award a summary of reasons for the decision, the party must ask for this in her Request.

An employee who wishes to initiate arbitration must include a $50.00 processing fee with her Request. If Brown & Root initiates the arbitration, or if the employee already has paid a $50.00 processing fee for mediation, the employee is not responsible for paying the $50.00 arbitration processing fee. Brown & Root pays for all costs of arbitration that exceed this $50.00 processing fee.

As discussed previously, Brown & Root agrees to reimburse its employees for ninety percent of their legal expenses incurred in preparing for and attending arbitration, up to a maximum of $2,500 per year. If an employee elects not to bring a lawyer to arbitration, Brown & Root also will agree not to bring a lawyer to arbitration.[17] This does not, however, preclude a Brown & Root attorney from working "behind the scenes" to prepare witnesses for the hearing or to draft briefs supporting Brown & Root's argument.

After the arbitration process is initiated, AAA notifies the other parties that an arbitration demand has been made. The nonrequesting party then has twenty-one days to file an answering statement, which must include any counterclaims. If the nonrequesting party wants the arbitrator to issue with the award a summary of reasons for the decision, it must include such a request in the answering statement.

Simultaneous with its notification of the parties that a Request for arbitration has been filed, AAA sends each party a list of potential arbitrators. Each party then has fourteen days to strike any names from the list (potential arbitrators may be stricken for any reason), to number the remaining names in order of preference, and to return the list to AAA. A party may strike one list of arbitrators in its entirety, in which case AAA must issue a new list of potential arbitrators. From among the persons who have been approved by the parties on both lists, AAA selects one potential arbitrator based on the parties' mutual preferences and notifies that person of his or her potential selection. Prior to accepting the appointment, the prospective arbitrator must disclose any circumstance likely to prevent a prompt hearing, or which would create a presumption of bias. Upon receipt of such information from the arbitrator or any other source, AAA either must replace that person or communicate the information to the parties for comment. Thereafter, AAA may disqualify that person as a potential arbitrator.

Prior to the arbitration hearing, and on a schedule determined by the arbitrator, each party must produce, both to the arbitrator and to the other parties, the names and addresses of the witnesses it intends to bring to the hearing and any documents it intends to present. The arbitrator has the discretion to determine the form, amount, and frequency of other prehearing discovery. This discovery may take any form permitted by the Federal Rules of Civil Procedure. At the request of a party or on the initiative of the arbitrator, the arbitrator may hold a conference with the parties to discuss discovery, to clarify issues for the hearing, or for any other reason.

The date, time, and place of the hearing is set by the arbitrator with ten days' notice to the parties. The arbitrator is required to "make every effort, without unduly incurring expense, to accommodate the employee in the selection of a hearing location."[18] The arbitrator may postpone the hearing for good cause or upon agreement of the parties.

At the hearing, witnesses are required to testify under oath. The arbitrator may subpoena witnesses or documents at the request of a party or on the arbitrator's own initiative. Strict conformity to the federal or state rules of evidence is not required; as with arbitration in the labor and commercial context,[19] the arbitrator is "the sole judge of the relevance, materiality, and admissibility of evidence offered."[20] A witness may testify by affidavit, but such testimony is only given "such weight as the arbitrator deems it is entitled to after consideration of any objection made to its admission."[21] The award must be in writing and signed by the arbitrator. The arbitrator is required to write a summary of the reasons for the decision if so requested by the parties in either the Request for arbitration or the answering statement.

The arbitrator's authority is limited to the resolution of legal disputes between the parties. The arbitrator is bound by, and is required to apply, all applicable law, including that related to allocation of burdens of proof as well as substantive law. The arbitrator does not have the authority either to abridge or enlarge substantive rights available under existing law. The arbitrator has the authority to order any relief that a party could obtain from court, including injunctive and other equitable relief, and all forms of damages, including punitive damages. However, the arbitrator, at his or her discretion, may allow an employee a reasonable attorneys' fee as part of the award, regardless of the employee's right to request an attorneys' fee under existing law. This award must be reduced by any amounts paid by the Legal Expense Reimbursement Program. There is no provision permitting the arbitrator to award attorneys' fees to Brown & Root under circumstances in which existing law does not give the company the right to request such fees.

C. Result and Analysis

The Brown & Root Dispute Resolution Program has been in operation since June 15, 1993. Through September 15, 1996, it handled approximately 1,529 employment disputes. Nearly half involved the termination of an employee's employment. Of the disputes that did not involve termination, approximately 10 percent concerned wage and benefits issues. Fewer than 10 percent involved an allegation that the employee had been discriminated against or harassed because of his or her membership in a class protected by federal civil rights laws. The remainder involved conflicts with supervisors and coworkers; morale; job assignments; retaliation; health, safety, and injury issues; and complaints about the hiring process.

The median amount of time taken to resolve each dispute is slightly less than three weeks; the mean is a little more than six and one-half weeks. Forty-one percent of the disputes were resolved within one week of the employee's initial complaint; approximately 65 percent were resolved within four weeks. The longest any dispute took was slightly more than two years; only twenty-one took more than one year. This represents a marked contrast to litigation, which easily can take half a decade or more.

Of the 1,529 disputes filed thus far, approximately 45 percent have been resolved by Program staff, approximately 20 percent have been resolved by an Advisor, 2.5 percent have been resolved through in-house mediation, and only approximately 6 percent had to be referred to outside mediation or arbitration (several of these, however, settled before mediation/arbitration). Approximately 8.5 percent have been resolved in some other manner and approximately 7.5 percent remain pending. In the remaining 10.5 percent of disputes, the employee decided not to pursue the matter further.

In the first two years (the only period for which these particular statistics are available), only eighty employees have requested reimbursement for legal expenses. During this time, Brown & Root paid approximately $85,000 in employees' legal fees. The relatively low number of employees requesting reimbursement reflects the fact that employees seldom decided to hire an attorney to represent them in their disputes. Employees elected to proceed without the use of legal counsel in two-thirds of the arbitrations that have occurred.

When Brown & Root announced its Dispute Resolution Program, the only rank-and-file employee complaint received was that the company was spending too much money on mailouts soliciting employee opinion about the Program. The only serious opposition to the Program came from middle managers and front line supervisors who felt that the Program threatened their authority over their supervisees. Brown & Root's training program directed at supervisors and mid-level managers was essential in convincing them that the Program would help them fulfill, not hinder, their management responsibilities.

Not surprisingly, Brown & Root has had far fewer employment lawsuits filed against it than it did prior to implementing the Program. Before implementation, the company averaged approximately fifteen to twenty lawsuits per year; in the first three and one-half years following implementation, Brown & Root was sued in court a total of fifteen times. In twelve of those suits, the employee voluntarily elected to dismiss the suit and to submit the claim to arbitration. Brown & Root filed Motions to Compel compliance with the Program in each of the remaining three suits. Of these, two suits have been dismissed and referred to mediation; one motion has been denied, and Brown & Root is appealing that decision. Given the prevailing state of the law on compulsory arbitration (discussed in chapters 2 and 3), it is likely that the company will be successful in its efforts to dismiss its employment lawsuits and have the disputes ordered to arbitration.

The number of disputes filed by Brown & Root's employees after the Program was implemented—approximately five hundred per year—is commensurate with the number of annual complaints that Brown & Root received through its internal channels before implementation of the Program. Similarly, the company's settlement rate and its annual budget for those settlements did not change significantly after implementing the Program. Neither did its budget for paying arbitration/litigation awards. The company's adjudicatory winning percentage has actually decreased slightly since arbitration was substituted for litigation.

What has changed dramatically is the company's legal budget. Over the three years that the Program has been in place, the company's outside legal fees, plus the costs of administering the Program (including arbitrator and mediator fees, the salaries of the Program's three administrators, the reimbursement program for employees' legal expenses, and the company's outside legal fees in arbitrations where the employee is represented by counsel) is less than half—approximately forty-seven percent—of what the company spent on outside legal fees before the Program was put in place. While this savings does not take into account the opportunity costs of the company's extensive training programs (*i.e.,* the work that employees would have been performing had they not been receiving training), it also does not reflect the company's substantial savings in human capital. A Brown & Root official who works extensively with the Program estimates that approximately "300 people are still working for us who would not have been without the dispute resolution system."[22] The reduction in turnover and retention of skilled human assets may be the Program's most valuable achievement.

Brown & Root appears to have developed a model dispute resolution system. Procedurally, the company has gone the extra mile to ensure that its Program is scrupulously fair to employees. Its attorney fee reimbursement program, its contractual promise of no retaliation, its commitment to mediation, and its extensive advisor program all are instances in which the company has gone far beyond what is legally required of a compulsory employment arbitration system. These examples illustrate Brown & Root's use of arbitration, not just as a litigation avoidance strategy but as a true dispute resolution strategy.

The fact that the company's settlement rate, settlement budget, and award budget have remained constant would seem to indicate that the Program is at least as fair to employees as litigating the company's employment disputes would be. The increased success rate for employees in arbitration (as compared to litigation) means that more employees are receiving adjudicatory awards, although the awards of victorious employees are likely to be smaller than in litigation. Though empirically unverifiable, this may mean that employees with meritorious claims, who before could not obtain redress because they were unable to hire a lawyer, or because they ran afoul of the convoluted procedural requirements of the federal antidiscrimination statutes, now are obtaining the redress they deserve. The smaller awards indicate a departure from the "jackpot" litigation system. This means that instead of a very few employees receiving very large awards, awards are distributed more equitably among a larger number of aggrieved employees.

Another change, at least from the perspective of Brown & Root's associate general counsel for employment matters, William Bedman, is that adjudication decisions and awards have become much more predictable. Bedman believes that litigating employment disputes was often like flipping a coin: regardless of the underlying merits or the claim for damages, it was virtually impossible to predict whether a jury would find liability and, if so, how much it would award. Although not every arbitration has been decided exactly as Bedman expected, he reports being less surprised by arbitration than by litigation decisions.

The Brown & Root Program is one example of how a company can implement a compulsory arbitration system. However, not all companies prefer—or have the resources—to implement a dispute resolution system as extensive as Brown & Root's. Chapter 9 examines alternative ways a company can implement arbitration, and discusses what an arbitration agreement must contain to maximize chances of judicial enforcement.

Nine

Creating a Fair (and Enforceable) Arbitration Agreement

A S DISCUSSED IN CHAPTERS 3 THROUGH 5, COM-
pulsory arbitration is not yet a permanent feature of
the employment landscape. The Supreme Court has left
several significant issues unaddressed, giving it ample opportunity to restrict the applicability of compulsory arbitration. Moreover, Congress can
always amend any of several federal statutes to accomplish the same result.
Congress is unlikely to take such action if arbitration lives up to its potential as a fair and efficient method of resolving employment disputes. If,
however, employers abuse employment arbitration by imposing one-sided
agreements on employees, political pressure will mount on Congress to
protect employees from such abusive agreements, and the days of compulsory arbitration are likely to be numbered. If employers wish to retain the
opportunity to implement compulsory arbitration procedures, they must
diligently assure that these are fair to employees.

Employers also have a more short-term interest in drafting fair procedure. The cases discussed in chapter 4 establish that, under the current
state of the law, virtually every claim an employee might bring against an
employer is arbitrable. The fact that a claim is arbitrable, however, does
not ensure that a court always will enforce an agreement to arbitrate it;
courts are unlikely to enforce agreements that unfairly hinder an employee's ability to obtain redress for legitimate claims. The Supreme Court's
decision in *Gilmer v. Interstate/Johnson Lane Corp.*,[1] by approving the
particular arbitration agreement at issue in that case, establishes many of
the threshold standards that an agreement must meet to be enforced.
However, the *Gilmer* Court left many standards unaddressed, and discussed others only in passing, leaving uncertainty as to exactly what an
arbitration agreement must contain to guarantee its enforcement.

This chapter discusses several different ways in which employment
arbitration agreements have been or could be challenged on fairness

grounds. For each of these grounds, the chapter first examines existing case law to delineate the minimum requirements currently required for obtaining enforcement. It then sets forth recommendations, both to courts regarding what the minimum standards should be, and to employers regarding how their agreement should be drafted, to maximize the probability of enforcement.

A. Drafting and Implementing Compulsory Arbitration Agreements

1. Must the Agreement Be in Writing?

Some employers have implemented compulsory arbitration agreements simply by announcing the compulsory arbitration policy as a new term and condition of employment. For example, in *Kinnebrew v. Gulf Insurance Co.*[2] and in *Lang v. Burlington Northern Railroad Co.*,[3] the federal district courts for the Northern District of Texas and the District of Minnesota, respectively, compelled arbitration of wrongful termination claims under arbitration procedures that unilaterally were established by the employers' verbal announcement. Similarly, in *Hathaway v. General Mills, Inc.*,[4] the Texas Supreme Court held that an employer may modify the conditions of at-will employment (in this case, sales commission terms) simply by giving an employee adequate notice; an employee who continues working is deemed to have accepted the new terms.[5]

Notwithstanding the cases upholding oral arbitration agreements, the Federal Arbitration Act (FAA)[6] requires courts to stay judicial proceedings only for "any issue referable to arbitration *under an agreement in writing*, ..."[7] Courts considering this writing requirement have not interpreted it strictly. For instance, in *Nghiem v. NEC Electronic, Inc.*,[8] the arbitration provision was contained in an employment handbook, which the employee had received but apparently had not been required to sign. The Ninth Circuit held that this was sufficient to satisfy the writing requirement, because while the FAA "requires a writing, it does not require that the writing be signed by the parties."[9] Additionally, since the employee had initiated the arbitration proceedings, the court concluded that an agreement to arbitrate could be inferred from this conduct.[10]

Similarly, the underlying employment agreement need not be in writing to satisfy the "agreement in writing" provision.[11] In *Durkin v. Signa Property & Casualty Corp.*,[12] the plaintiff was an at-will employee with no written employment contract. The arbitration provision that the employer sought to enforce was contained in a written dispute resolution policy that the employer had distributed to its employees, including the plaintiff. The policy provided that it "is part of the employment relationship," that both the employer and the employee will be bound" by the outcome of arbitration, and that the arbitration decision "will be enforceable in court."[13] The employer apparently did not, however, require employees to sign the policy. Nonetheless, the Federal District Court for the District of Kansas enforced the arbitration provision. The Court held that at-will employment satisfies the "agreement" requirement of the FAA, and that the employer's announcement of the arbitration policy, both verbally in a meeting and in writing by distributing its dispute resolution policy, sufficed to put the plaintiff on notice that the arbitration clause was a condition of her employment.[14]

Most employers that have instituted compulsory arbitration programs have opted not to gamble on the enforceability of a verbally announced arbitration policy and have, instead, taken various steps to obtain individual written arbitration agreements from new or current employees.[15] An employer has a tremendous amount of flexibility in deciding how to draft an arbitration agreement, and to which employees the agreement will apply.[16] For example, an employer who anticipates difficulty getting current employees to sign arbitration agreements might decide to impose an arbitration requirement on new hires only. If the employer is implementing a comprehensive dispute resolution program, such as that of Brown & Root discussed in chapter 8, a "new hire" approach would create significant administrative difficulties because it would force the employer to administer simultaneously both arbitration and litigation policies. Employers implementing such a system, or employers which do not anticipate a negative reaction from current employees, will want to impose arbitration across-the-board. A third alternative is to draft the agreement only for highly-paid "professional" employees.

A sample arbitration agreement is attached as Appendix A to this chapter. The sample agreement, which is drafted as a stand-alone individual agreement, may be modified to fit any of these three approaches.

a. Drafting the Agreement for New Hires Only

Drafting the arbitration agreement for new hires only is the easiest way to implement compulsory arbitration because it does not require the employer to convince current employees to sign the agreement. The agreement should be in writing and should contain a line for the employee's signature. It should explain which disputes will be settled by arbitration and which, if any, will not. It should define arbitration and make it clear that, by agreeing to arbitration, the employee is waiving the right to proceed in court. The new hire should be given an opportunity to consider the agreement before signing it and be encouraged to seek the advice of counsel. The agreement should use nonlegal and easy-to-understand language; it should be sufficiently clear to avoid the possibility of an employee claiming later that she did not understand what she was signing.

In addition to creating a separate, independent or stand-alone agreement, the employer might also consider adding a clause such as the following to its employment application: "By signing this agreement, the applicant agrees to submit all legal disputes concerning this application for employment (including claims of discrimination) to binding arbitration, and waives the right to proceed in court. Moreover, the applicant understands that a term and condition of employment with the Company is that both the Company and the employee agree to submit all legal disputes that arise from their employment relationship to binding arbitration, and that the parties hereby waive their right to proceed in court." Such a clause would permit the employer to compel arbitration not only of claims brought by new hires, but also of claims brought by applicants before they are hired. It also may suffice, by itself, to bind the employee to arbitrate all future disputes arising out of the employment relationship.[17]

b. Drafting the Agreement for Current Employees

Although drafting employment agreements for new hires only is the easiest way to implement employment arbitration, an across-the-board implementation of arbitration is easier to administer because, as of the implementation date, all employees are covered by the same policy. There are two ways that employers might draft an across-the-board arbitration agreement. The first is to draft comprehensive stand-alone agreements, containing all terms of the arbitration agreement, or incorporating by reference the rules promulgated by a neutral entity, such as the American Arbitration Association (AAA), for each employee's signature. The disadvantage to this approach is that a comprehensive arbitration agreement might be several pages long, and this could be intimidating to employees. An alternative approach is to put the terms of the agreement in an employee handbook, and then incorporate those terms by reference in a separate stand-alone agreement signed by the employee.

(1) Comprehensive Stand-Alone Agreements

A stand-alone arbitration agreement for current employees should contain the same elements as the agreement described above for new hires. The sample agreement appended to this chapter is a stand-alone agreement. Rather than specifying all the procedures to be used when proceeding to arbitration, the sample agreement simply incorporates the AAA rules by reference.

Some commentators have argued that the employer must provide the employee with some independent consideration—such as an increase in salary or benefits—to make a stand-alone arbitration agreement valid.[18] This should not, however, be necessary, because both parties to the arbitration agreement give up the same procedural rights, such as the right to trial by jury, the right to extensive discovery, and a broad right to appeal.[19] Therefore, the employer's consideration for the employee's waiver of these procedural rights is the employer's waiver of identical rights. Similarly, an arbitration agreement will not fail for lack of mutuality so long as the employer, like the employee, is bound by the arbitration agreement.[20]

(2) Employee Handbooks

The employer might instead choose to implement the arbitration agreement by adding the policy to its employee handbook. The handbook should contain all the terms of the agreement in nonlegal, easy-to-understand language and, like agreements for new hires and individual employees, should clearly explain the consequences of signing an arbitration agreement.

The advantage to including an arbitration agreement in an employee handbook is that the agreement submitted for the employee's signature can be much simpler and easier to understand. The problem with this approach is that most employers go to great lengths to make certain that courts do *not* interpret the handbook as a binding contract. Employers do this because employees frequently cite handbooks in breach of contract cases to argue that the employer has abrogated an at-will employment relationship, or has contractually promised to follow the disciplinary procedures outlined in the handbook.[21] A court is unlikely to enforce an arbitration agreement contained in a handbook if the handbook states that it is not contractually binding.[22] For example, in *Heurtebise v. Reliable Business Computers, Inc.*,[23] the Michigan Supreme Court refused to enforce an arbitration agreement in an employment handbook because the handbook stated that its provisions did "not create any employment or personnel contract, express or implied."[24]

To avoid this problem, an employer wishing to implement an arbitration policy through its handbook should require employees to sign individual written acknowledgments that refer to the terms detailed and summarized in it.[25] For example, in *Topf v. Warnaco, Inc.*,[26] the arbitration provision which the defendant sought to enforce was contained in the employee handbook. On his first day of work, the plaintiff signed an "Acknowledgment of Receipt of the Warnaco Employee Handbook," which provided:

I [ ] understand that this Handbook is not and was not intended to serve as a contract between Warnaco and myself regarding the nature or duration of my employment with Warnaco, accept that this handbook is our entire agreement concerning each party's right to arbitrate employment disputes and to terminate the employment relationship with or without cause at any time, and that no one towards Warnaco is authorized to make an exception to this understanding, except an officer of Warnaco who does so in writing.[27]

The Federal District Court for the District of Connecticut enforced the arbitration agreement.

As the *Topf* case makes clear, requiring employees to sign written acknowledgments referring to arbitration provisions in their employee handbook effectively converts the handbook provision into a stand-alone arbitration agreement. Like the agreements for new hires and the stand-alone agreements discussed previously, the language in both the handbook and the written acknowledgments should be nonlegal and easy to understand. The acknowledgment should state clearly that it incorporates by reference the pertinent handbook provisions and that it constitutes a binding contract.

c. Drafting the Agreement for "Professional" Employees Only

A third alternative is to require employment arbitration agreements only for highly paid "professional" employees. Highly paid employees are, on average, more likely to hire a lawyer, more likely to bring suit, more likely to win in litigation,[28] and if they win, more likely to receive larger damage awards than lower-level employees.[29] Employers, therefore, may not object to lower-level employees' litigating their employment disputes, while they may insist on arbitrating suits brought by highly paid employees since the latter have a greater potential to bring financial disaster to the employer. Moreover, highly paid employees are far less likely than lower-paid employees to convince courts not to enforce their arbitration agreements, since they are presumed to have sufficient business acumen and bargaining power to have entered into the agreements knowingly and voluntarily.[30]

2. Is the Agreement Clearly Drafted?

The arbitration agreement must be drafted both broadly enough to encompass all possible employment claims, and specifically enough so that an employee cannot later claim that she did not realize, on signing the agreement, that the type of claim she is bringing must be arbitrated. To make the agreement sufficiently broad, the agreement should contain language such as: "The parties agree that any legal or equitable claims or disputes arising out of or in connection with the employment, the terms and conditions of employment, or the termination of employment, will be settled by binding arbitration."[31] The agreement also should specify that it applies not only to claims brought by the employee against the employer, but also to claims brought by the employee against other workers related to employment with the employer. For example, in *DeGaetano v. Smith Barney, Inc.*,[32] an employee sued both her employer and her supervisor in his individual capacity. The court held that the arbitration agreement signed by the employee was applicable not only to the claims asserted against the employer, but also to the claims asserted against the supervisor because the agreement made arbitrable "disagreements [that] may arise between an individual employee and [Smith Barney] or between employees in a context that involves his/her employer."[33] The court, therefore, granted a motion to compel arbitration on all of the employee's claims.[34]

The broad language mentioned in the previous paragraph should be followed by a list of the types of employment disputes that are arbitrable.[35] This will ensure that an employee who later brings suit cannot argue that her claim is not covered by the arbitration agreement. For example, in *Farrand v. Lutheran Brotherhood*,[36] the Seventh Circuit refused to compel arbitration of an age discrimination claim because it was unclear whether the arbitration agreement covered that type of claim. Similarly, in *Prudential Insurance Co. of America v. Lai*,[37] the Ninth Circuit refused to compel arbitration of a sexual harassment claim because the arbitration agreement did not explicitly state that it applied to such employment disputes.

An arbitration provision also should specify that it applies to claims arising under statutory or common law doctrines that did not exist at the time the arbitration agreement was signed. This is necessary because at least one court has refused to enforce an arbitration agreement where the statute under which the employee asserted his claim had not been enacted when the agreement was signed.[38] The arbitration provision also should specify that it applies only to "legal or equitable" claims in order to prevent employees from taking to arbitration every trivial disagreement that they have at the workplace. An example of language that is both sufficiently broad and sufficiently specific is found in the second paragraph of the sample agreement in the Appendix.

3. Is the Agreement Adhesive or Coercive?

Several commentators have argued that courts should deny enforcement of compulsory employment arbitration agreements because such agreements are adhesive,[39] that is, constitute adhesion contracts.[40] An adhesion contract is a "standardized contract, which, imposed and drafted by the party of superior bargaining strength, relegates to the subscribing party only the opportunity to adhere to the contract or reject it."[41] Generally, an adhesion contract is fully enforceable.[42] However, under state contract law principles, such a contract will not be enforced if it is not within the reasonable expectation of the weaker party, or if it contains terms which are unduly oppressive or unconscionable.[43]

An employment arbitration agreement, especially if presented to a large group of lower-level employees on a take-it-or-be-fired basis, is almost certainly an adhesion contract. State adhesion law principles, however, do not control cases brought under federal law. As a result, the argument that an arbitration agreement was allegedly the product of adhesion is not a defense to the enforcement of the arbitration clause under the FAA.[44]

Even if state contract law principles will not bar the enforcement of an adhesive employment arbitration agreement, federal law principles may operate to that effect. Although *Gilmer* rejected the suggestion that all employment arbitration agreements are unenforceable merely because they are imposed on a take-it-or-leave-it basis by an employer with greater bargaining power than its employees,[45] the Court also stated that "courts should remain attuned to well-supported claims that the agreement to arbitrate resulted from the sort of fraud or overwhelming economic power that would provide grounds 'for the revocation of any contract.' "[46]

The showing required to support revocation of an arbitration agreement on the basis of fraud or coercive inducement is extremely onerous. As discussed in chapter 4, it is not enough for an employee to claim that she has been coerced or defrauded into signing the entire employment agreement; this issue "is for the arbitrators and not for the courts."[47] Instead, the employee must prove that her agreement to the arbitration clause itself was the product of fraud or coercion.[48] This severability doctrine has been criticized for artificially isolating the arbitration agreement from the underlying agreement of which it is a part.[49] This doctrine is unlikely to affect stand-alone arbitration agreements because the arbitration and underlying agreements are one and the same. However, when an arbitration provision is inserted into a larger employment contract, to justify nonenforcement of the contract the employee will have to make the almost impossible showing that the arbitration clause, apart from the rest of the agreement, was the product of fraud or coercion.[50]

In some cases, employees have argued that their stand-alone arbitration agreements should not be enforced because of the conditions under which the agreements were signed. In *Maye v. Smith Barney Inc.,*[51] the plaintiffs claimed that their arbitration agreements should not be enforced because they each were told to sign their names approximately seventy-five times on a variety of documents (including an arbitration agreement) without anyone explaining the contents of the documents and without an adequate opportunity to read most of them.[52] They also complained that when they were told to sign these documents the atmosphere was "intimidating, hurried, and tense."[53] The United States District Court for the Southern District of New York nonetheless granted the employer's motion to compel arbitration, citing the rule that one "who signs or accepts a written contract, in the absence of fraud or other wrongful act on the part of another contracting party, is conclusively presumed to know its contents and to assent to them."[54] However, in *Berger v. Cantor Fitzgerald Securities,*[55] a different judge from the Southern District of New York refused to compel arbitration where the plaintiff advanced a similar argument. In *Berger,* the arbitration clause was contained in the plaintiff's U-4 form (the same form at issue in the Supreme Court's *Gilmer* case), which provided that disputes arising out of the plaintiff's employment must be submitted to mandatory arbitration according to NASD rules. Berger, the discharged employee, claimed (1) that he had been misled by the employer into believing the U-4 form did not contain an arbitration agreement, (2) that he was not given sufficient time to read the agreement before signing it, and (3) that he was never given a copy of the NASD manual referred to in the U-4 form. The Court denied the employer's motion to compel, and instead ordered the parties to engage in discovery concerning the circumstances surrounding Berger's signing of the U-4 form. The Court distinguished *Maye* by noting that, in that case, the one-page arbitration agreement contained a detailed explanation of the arbitration procedures and expressly defined the employment disputes covered by the agreement, whereas in *Berger,* the U-4 form merely made reference to the NASD rules with which Berger was not provided.[56]

The safest route for the employer simply is to ensure that the terms of its arbitration agreements are clearly spelled out and are not oppressive or unconscionable. These conditions will be met if the employer avoids the temptation to overreach by, for example, limiting employees' ability to obtain relief. For instance, in *Golinea v. Bob Baker Toyota,*[57] an employee attempted to persuade the court to deny enforcement of an arbitration agreement on the grounds that the agreement was adhesive. The court noted that the arbitration clause merely substituted the arbitral forum for the litigation forum, and that all provisions in the agreement applied equally to both parties.[58] The court held that, under these circumstances, the agreement was enforceable under both state and federal law.[59] By contrast, the court in *Pony Express Courier Corp. v. Morris,*[60] refused to compel arbitration pursuant to an agreement that, among other things, limited the damages the employee was entitled to seek and did not permit discovery. Adhering to the suggestions made in this chapter will maximize the probability that an agreement will be enforced.

4. Does the Agreement Convert At-Will Employment to Just-Cause Employment?

Most nonunion American workers are employed at-will, meaning that they can quit or be fired at any time, for any reason, unless that reason is otherwise made illegal by law (for example, the laws forbidding certain types of discrimination). By contrast, most unionized American workers are employed pursuant to collective bargaining agreements, which almost always provide that the employer can only fire an employee if it can show "good cause" to do so. Employers invariably prefer that the employment relationship be at-will rather than just cause, because at-will employment gives employers the maximum amount of flexibility in discharge or layoff decisions. An at-will employee can only challenge the employer's discharge decision if she can find a specific legal ground (such as discrimination) for doing so, and the burden is on her to prove that the employer's decision was illegal.[61] An employee employed under a just-cause provision can challenge the employer's discharge decision under any circumstances, and the burden is on the employer to prove that the discharge was justified.[62]

An important issue for at-will employers, then, is whether a compulsory arbitration agreement between an employer and an otherwise at-will employee can legally or practically convert at-will employment to just-cause employment. Some commentators have argued that it can.[63]

One way that arbitration might convert at-will employment into just-cause employment is if arbitrators imply from the arbitration agreement itself parties' intent to convert the relationship to just cause. Many labor arbitrators will imply a just-cause limitation in any collective bargaining agreement that is silent regarding discharge requirements, on the theory that to do otherwise would "reduce to a nullity the fundamental provision of a labor-management agreement—the security of a worker in his job."[64] Despite the dissimilarity between simple arbitration and collective bargaining agreements, it is nonetheless possible that arbitrators might imply a just-cause limitation from a simple arbitration agreement. Similarly, an arbitrator might perceive that it is her job to decide the case in accordance with what she considers fair and just, rather than strictly following the law.[65] These risks are enhanced if the arbitrator is an experienced union arbitrator familiar with just-cause employment but not with at-will employment.

A second way that an arbitration agreement might limit at-will employment is by introducing a contract into an otherwise contract-free employment relationship. The argument is that, by doing so, the employer raises the possibility that the arbitration agreement will give courts the opportunity to imply an obligation between the parties to deal with one another fairly and in good faith,[66] as the courts of many states do in all contractual relationships, within the context of the agreement to arbitrate.

The effect of the implied doctrine of good faith and fair dealing on at-will employment relationships covered by an arbitration agreement likely will be minimal, however, for two reasons. First, relatively few states recognize the doctrine.[67] Second, and more importantly, the implied duty to act in good faith would apply only to the scope of the contract—the arbitration agreement—and not to the employment relationship generally.[68] Thus, even in states that recognize the doctrine, though the employer would be under a duty to arbitrate in good faith, the employer would not be under such a duty when demoting or discharging an employee. For this reason, the doctrine of good faith and fair dealing is unlikely to extend just-cause protection to otherwise at-will employees merely through introducing an arbitration agreement.

Another way that arbitration might convert at-will employment into just-cause employment is if the employer attempts to oversell the arbitration agreement. Say, for instance, that an employer adopts a comprehensive dispute resolution system, such as the one created by Brown & Root and discussed in chapter 8. If the employer (or the employer's supervisors) tells employees that the agreement guarantees them "fairness" or "workplace justice" or "due process," these statements might be interpreted by courts or arbitrators as creating a contractual obligation on the employer only to discharge employees "fairly" or "justifiably" or "after due process": *i.e.,* only to discharge employees for cause.[69] Moreover, a disclaimer in the arbitration agreement purporting to preserve at-will employment may not override inconsistent representations and conduct.[70] Therefore, an employer who wishes to maintain an at-will employment relationship must not oversell an arbitration agreement.

Finally, arbitration might have the practical effect of turning at-will employment into just-cause employment merely because it is much easier to pursue a claim in arbitration than in litigation. The antidiscrimination laws permit anyone, regardless of their race or gender,[71] to challenge any adverse employment action taken against them by their employer. So long as the employee casts her claim in the mold of alleged discrimination, the employer must articulate, if not prove, a legitimate, nondiscriminatory reason for its action.[72] This, many have argued, has converted the United States from a system of at-will employment to a system of for-cause employment, at least with regard to the classes of persons (such as minorities and women) who easily can make a colorable allegation of discrimination.[73]

In the current litigative system, many people who feel that they have been treated unfairly by their employer are constrained from challenging the employer by the high costs of litigation and the difficulty of finding a lawyer to represent them.[74] Because arbitration is much simpler and less expensive than litigation, however, one would expect a larger number of employees to challenge employer conduct if they could do so through arbitration rather than litigation.[75] This is of significant concern to employers, and is a major reason why many employers have hesitated to adopt compulsory arbitration.

A simple arbitration agreement should not be interpreted to imply just-cause employment. As discussed in chapter 2, an arbitration agreement, by itself, does not change the parties' underlying substantive employment rights, but merely changes the forum in which those rights are resolved. Thus, the principles supporting the implication of a just-cause standard from a collective bargaining agreement do not apply to an arbitration agreement because the "fundamental provision" of an arbitration agreement is merely to agree to arbitration, not, as in collective bargaining, to trade job security for industrial peace.[76] However, since this distinction might be lost on a labor arbitrator, an employer wishing to preserve the at-will relationship should ensure that its arbitration agreement does not otherwise abrogate the at-will relationship, and should specify that an employee is only entitled to arbitrate claims involving allegations that the employer acted illegally (as opposed to arbitrarily or without cause).

B. Procedures for Selecting Arbitrators

One of the most pervasive criticisms of compulsory arbitration systems concerns the way arbitrators are selected. This criticism has centered on the securities industry's arbitration rules, which, as discussed in chapter 7, have resulted in a pool of arbitrators that (1) has strong ties to the employers against whom discrimination is alleged, (2) has little or no substantive knowledge of employment law, and (3) is demographically unrepresentative of the general population.

The Supreme Court's *Gilmer* decision, because it was based on a case arising out of the securities industry, often has been treated by courts as having approved that industry's procedures for selecting arbitrators. In *Gilmer*, the Court rejected the plaintiff's argument that arbitration of his age discrimination claim should not be compelled because of the possibility that his case ultimately would be decided by biased arbitrators. The Court noted that the securities industry arbitration rules under which Gilmer's case was to be arbitrated require that the parties be informed of the arbitrators' backgrounds, and allowed one peremptory challenge and unlimited challenges for cause, and require arbitrators to disclose "any circumstances which might preclude [them] from rendering an objective and impartial determination."[77] The Court held that these procedural safeguards were sufficient to protect Gilmer from the possibility of biased arbitrators.[78] Further, the Court indicated that the FAA, by providing that courts may overturn arbitration decisions "[w]here there was evident partiality or corruption in the arbitrators," also protects employees from biased arbitrators.[79]

A similar case is *Saari v. Smith Barney, Harris Upham & Co.*[80] In *Saari*, an employee in the securities industry sought to avoid enforcement of his employment arbitration agreement on the ground that, because the panel of arbitrators would be drawn from the securities industry, the arbitrators necessarily would be biased. The Ninth Circuit disagreed, stating that " '[m]istrust of the arbitral process' " was clearly rejected as a reason for avoiding arbitration by the Court in *Gilmer*."[81]

Gilmer and *Saari* could be interpreted as prohibiting any prearbitration attempts to avoid enforcement of arbitration agreements on the basis of potential bias. By this argument, an employee could not claim bias until after an arbitral award had been rendered. Only then could she appeal the award, and even then, the appeal would be brought under the extremely narrow judicial review standards discussed in part F of this chapter. However, in addition to rejecting Gilmer's prearbitration attempt to avoid enforcement on the basis of bias, the *Gilmer* Court also stated that "claimed procedural inadequacies [of arbitration] . . . [are] best left for resolution in specific cases."[82] This suggests that employees *can* mount a preaward challenge to the process of selecting arbitrators, but that the plaintiffs in the above-cited cases simply failed to develop an adequate factual record to support their challenge. Neither the plaintiff in *Gilmer* nor the plaintiff in *Saari,* for example, introduced evidence of the causes of bias listed above; instead, they simply issued, as the *Gilmer* Court characterized them, "generalized attacks" raising the mere *possibility* of bias. A showing that bias is inherently part of the securities industry's process for selecting arbitrators might (and should) persuade a court not to enforce an arbitration agreement.

Some commentators have argued that arbitral bias is an inherent part of *all* compulsory arbitration agreements because of the employer's unique status as a repeat player in arbitration.[83] In traditional labor arbitration between an employer and a union, both parties participate in arbitration with equal frequency. In employment arbitration, however, the employer alone is a repeat player, because the employee is unlikely to participate in arbitration more than once or twice in his or her lifetime. This gives employers two distinct advantages.

First, the employer is likely to have more and better information about proposed arbitrators, allowing the employer to choose an arbitrator who is more likely to render a decision favorable to the employer. Employers will track the records and reputations of arbitrators through networking and internal recordskeeping; nonunionized employees simply have neither the institutional capacity nor the resources to do the same. The problem might even become self-perpetuating since arbitrators, knowing that employers, but not employees, are likely to be aware of their award record, may consciously or subconsciously favor the employer.

Second, knowledge that the employer is far more likely than the employee to have an opportunity to hire an arbitrator for a successive case may, consciously or subconsciously, induce the arbitrator to favor the employer in a current case. This problem will be particularly acute in areas where a single employer employs a disproportionately large percentage of workers, where there is a limited pool of potential arbitrators, or where only a small number of employers have instituted compulsory arbitration agreements.

The twin problems of information asymmetry and institutional temptation may be ameliorated somewhat by the establishment of a "plaintiff bar" to share information about arbitrators in much the same way as it is made available to employers.[84] It is unlikely, however, that any such organization of employees or employees' advocates could ever match the organizational efficacy of employers. An alternative approach to combating these problems, discussed in Part E of this chapter, is to require that all arbitral decisions be published and easily accessible to everyone. This would give employees and employees' representatives access to the arbitral records over which employers currently enjoy a virtual monopoly, and provide arbitrators a strong incentive to be impartial.

This "institutional bias" approach to challenging employment arbitration agreements has not yet been tested in the courts. The language and tenor of *Gilmer* indicate that the Court is unlikely to be receptive to any argument that arbitrators are inherently biased. Absent a judicially- or congressionally-imposed requirement that arbitrators issue written opinions, and absent some mechanism for making these opinions publicly available, problems of inherent arbitral bias are likely to remain a concern for the foreseeable future.

A distinctive approach to challenging arbitral bias was taken by the plaintiff in *Olson v. American Arbitration Association, Inc.*[85] Olson filed suit alleging intentional infliction of emotional distress in connection with her employment. Her employer filed a motion to compel arbitration based on an arbitration clause in Olson's employment agreement. The trial court granted the motion. Before the arbitration hearing was held, Olson filed a second suit. This time, she claimed that the American Arbitration Association, a private, non-profit organization that provides arbitration services, had misrepresented to the public that it provided impartial arbitration services through neutral arbitrators, and that this violated the Texas Deceptive Trade Practices Act. Specifically, she argued that AAA's arbitration panels are biased in favor of employers because (1) the panels are unfairly stacked with lawyers who primarily represent employers in employment disputes, (2) a vast majority of the panelists are men, (3) a vast majority of the panelists are white, (4) a vast majority of the panelists are lawyers who do not represent a cross-section of society, and (5) AAA receives substantial contributions from employers.[86]

The employer filed a 12(b)(6) motion for failure to state a claim. The court granted the motion. Noting that Olson's contention that her panel of arbitrators would be biased was "speculat[ion] based on stereotypical characteristics," the court held that even if her allegations were true, they were insufficient by themselves to show bias.[87]

The *Olson* case is unique because Olson sued AAA directly for damages, rather than arguing in the suit against her employer that her arbitration agreement should not have been enforced due to arbitral bias. Because the dispute with her employer had not yet been arbitrated, AAA had not yet inflicted any damages on her for which she could obtain relief; by contrast, if she had raised the argument in the suit against her employer, the court would have had the option of refusing to enforce the arbitration agreement. Moreover, Olson's claim of bias was substantially less compelling than claims of bias that could be made against the securities industry, since Olson did not allege that her particular employer had any inappropriate ties to AAA or to the pool of potential arbitrators.

Notwithstanding *Gilmer, Saari,* and *Olson,* employers should be extremely careful to avoid even the appearance of bias in the selection of arbitrators. At a minimum, compulsory arbitration procedures should ensure that employees and their attorneys have an equal opportunity to participate in the selection of arbitrators. Ideally, they should be chosen by mutual agreement or, alternatively, by use of a neutral source of nominations of potential disinterested arbitrators. This is the method used successfully for many years in the collective bargaining agreement context.[88] In the nonunion context, the AAA and the Center for Public Resources (CPR) are available to nominate potential arbitrators. In *Williams v. Katten, Muchin & Zavis,*[89] the arbitration agreement at issue provided that if the parties were unable to agree upon an arbitrator within sixty days after a dispute arose, one would be chosen according to AAA rules. The court upheld this procedure against an employee's claim of bias.[90]

C. Representations by Attorneys

Most reported cases about compulsory employment arbitration involve employees, represented by attorneys, who attempt to avoid the effect of their arbitration agreement and instead litigate their case. As will be discussed in chapter 10, it is not surprising that employees who can find representation are likely to prefer litigation over arbitration; employees unable to find representation invariably will prefer arbitration to litigation, and hence will not challenge their arbitration agreement in court. Nonetheless, because virtually every employee who has been ordered to arbitration has been represented by an attorney, and since every arbitration agreement that has been challenged in court to date has permitted the employee to be represented by an attorney, an employer would be ill advised, in an arbitration agreement, to forbid the employee legal representation.

Frequently, employers will insert into their arbitration agreements a clause similar to the following: "The employee has the right to be represented by an attorney at all times. However, if the employee elects not to bring a lawyer to the arbitration hearing, the Company also will agree not to bring a lawyer to the hearing."[91] A mutual agreement not to use lawyers has the obvious advantage of saving both parties the high price of attorneys' fees. Moreover, recent studies suggest that this decision is unlikely to affect the outcome of the dispute.[92] Orley Ashenfelter and David Bloom, for example, have collected empirical evidence concerning the use and nonuse of attorneys in final-offer arbitration proceedings for New Jersey public safety employees (primarily police officers) in the arbitration of discharge grievances, in the arbitration of civil disputes in Pittsburgh, and in the arbitration of child custody disputes in California. After reviewing the data, the authors noted that the outcome of disputes is roughly the same if either both parties or neither party is represented by an attorney. Where only one party is represented by an attorney, however, that party's likelihood of prevailing increases substantially. Ashenfelter and Bloom therefore concluded that, where (as in arbitration) the method of dispute resolution allows the parties a realistic option of representing themselves, the decision to retain lawyers presents a prisoner's dilemma: Although it would be in both parties' best interest to represent themselves, both nonetheless will rationally hire lawyers to avoid the "sucker's payoff"[93] a party receives when her opponent hires a lawyer but she does not.[94]

A clause such as the one presented in the above paragraph avoids this dilemma by reducing the risk an employee would incur by deciding not to hire a lawyer. In one sense, however, it is misleading. If an employee agrees not to bring a lawyer to the arbitration hearing, it is unlikely that she will hire a lawyer to help her develop her case. The employer, however, being far more likely to deal with employment disputes on a recurrent basis, probably has on staff or easily available a lawyer who is familiar with the arbitration process and who can and will help prepare the employer's case and witnesses for the arbitration, even if that lawyer does not attend the hearing itself. Although it is unclear empirically how much of an advantage this might give the employer over the employee, it probably can be assumed that the employer would not bring in lawyers unless it perceived there was some advantage to doing so.

D. Discovery

Another criticism leveled at compulsory arbitration in *Gilmer* and elsewhere is that arbitral discovery is more limited than judicial discovery, and that this compromises an employee's ability to prove discrimination. Proving disparate treatment would be difficult without discovery because a plaintiff bringing such a case must prove that she was treated differently than other similarly-situated nonclass members.[95] Therefore, she must discover evidence of how those nonclass members were treated.[96] Proving disparate impact[97] would be impossible[98] without the opportunity to obtain from an employer statistical information about how the employment practice in question affects different demographic segments of the employee population.[99]

The NYSE rules approved by the Supreme Court in *Gilmer* permitted document production, information requests, depositions, and subpoenas.[100] The Court, after noting the availability of such discovery, observed that "by agreeing to arbitrate, a party 'trades the procedures and opportunity for review of the courtroom for the simplicity, informality, and expedition of arbitration.' "[101] In *Williams,* the arbitration agreement incorporated by reference AAA discovery rules.[102] The employee there argued that the AAA rules inadequately protected her statutory rights because the rules contained no provision specifically permitting or denying discovery. The court noted, however, that the AAA rules authorize an arbitrator to subpoena witnesses and documents either independently or upon the request of a party.[103] The court held that this was sufficient to protect the employee's right to obtain discovery.[104]

Because the rules at issue in *Gilmer* explicitly permitted a significant range of discovery, it is unclear whether courts will require explicit discovery rules as a condition precedent to enforcing employment arbitration agreements and if so, the nature and breadth of discovery rules that may be found sufficient. To ensure enforcement, arbitration procedures ideally should specifically permit at least the types of discovery to which the Supreme Court referred in *Gilmer.* Alternatively, agreements should incorporate by reference the AAA's Employment Dispute Resolution Rules.

Discovery is and should be less formal in arbitration than in litigation, because this informality is how arbitration derives its principal advantages.[105] However, the fact that an employment claim is being arbitrated rather than litigated does not diminish the need for complete discovery. Restrictions on discovery fall hardest on employees since the employer already possesses almost all relevant documents and data, such as personnel files and employee demographic information.[106] Employers' attempts to unduly restrict employees' access to adequate discovery should be closely scrutinized by the courts. Employees should not be bound by an arbitration agreement if the terms of that agreement deny them access to relevant documents and information, and, thus, make it impossible for them to prove their case.

E. Written Opinions

In *Gilmer*, the plaintiff argued that arbitration could not adequately protect employees' statutory rights because employment arbitrators are not required to issue written opinions.[107] This, Gilmer argued, would result in the public being unaware of employers' discrimination policies.[108] He also argued that it would hamper effective appellate review[109] and stifle development of the law.[110] The *Gilmer* Court held that these concerns did not justify denying enforcement of Gilmer's compulsory arbitration agreement. First, the Court stated that the securities industry arbitration rules require arbitrators to issue written, detailed opinions and to make those opinions publicly available.[111] However, as discussed in chapter 7, the Court was mistaken. The securities industry arbitration rules require the arbitrator to issue a written *award,* which does little more than state who shall receive what and when the individual shall receive it.[112] The arbitrator is not required to issue an *opinion* giving reasons for the award.[113]

The Court advanced two additional reasons for rejecting Gilmer's argument that his arbitration agreement should not be enforced because of the lack of written arbitral opinions. One was that courts would continue to issue judicial opinions because not all employers and employees are likely to sign binding arbitration agreements.[114] The other was that Gilmer's argument was not unique because settlement agreements, which are encouraged by the ADEA and other federal antidiscrimination statutes, similarly fail to produce written opinions.[115]

The Court's mistaken analysis of the securities industry arbitration rules, and its enforcement of Gilmer's arbitration based on that mistaken analysis, makes it unclear whether written arbitral opinions are a prerequisite to obtaining judicial enforcement of employment arbitration agreements. An employer drafting an employment arbitration agreement is subject to four possible interpretations of the law regarding written opinions. First, a written opinion might be required in every arbitration. Second, a written opinion might be required at the request of either party. Third, a written opinion might be required only upon the request of both parties. Finally, written opinions might be prohibited altogether.

The Supreme Court's enforcement of Gilmer's arbitration agreement based on the Court's mistaken assumption that the agreement required the issuance of written opinions should caution employers against adopting the latter two approaches. A prudent employer wishing to maximize the probability that its compulsory arbitration agreement will be enforced will require the arbitrator to issue a written opinion either in all cases or upon either party's request.

Apart from enforcement concerns, there are two additional reasons why written opinions are useful. The first is catharsis. A well-written opinion can convince the parties that the arbitrator heard and understood their positions and that the award is basically sound.[116] If this is the case, the award is less likely to be challenged in court.

The second purpose of opinion writing is to aid judicial review. A reviewing court cannot ascertain whether the arbitrator correctly followed the law unless the arbitrator states the law in writing and applies it to the facts of the case.[117] Written opinions are critical to any meaningful judicial review of the substantive matters at issue in a case.

One commentator has suggested that requiring written opinions can operate as a market substitute for judicial review. Speaking in the context of arbitration in the securities industry, which, as discussed in chapter 7, is plagued with arbitrators unschooled in employment law, Judith Vladeck has suggested that required opinion writing would expose incompetent arbitrators as "the damn fools that you thought they were," and that parties thereafter would refuse to select them as arbitrators in future cases.[118] Similarly, as discussed in Section B of this chapter, written opinions that are published and easily accessible can help diminish the informational advantage employers have in arbitrator selection procedures, and can help create a strong incentive for arbitrators to remain impartial.

Courts should refuse to enforce arbitration agreements that do not require arbitrators to issue written opinions either in all cases or at the request of either party. There are good reasons why the parties may choose to forego a written opinion; one is that the lack of an opinion virtually guarantees the finality of the arbitral award by making substantive review impossible. However, as discussed in the next section of this chapter, the public interest in ensuring the proper application of employment law underscores the importance of substantively correct arbitral decisions, which cannot be guaranteed absent the opportunity to obtain substantive judicial review. The decision to forego such review to obtain prompt resolution of the dispute should be a joint one, and should not unilaterally be imposed on the employee by the employer.

F. Judicial Review

Another basis on which compulsory arbitration has been challenged is limited opportunity for judicial review.[119] The FAA allows a reviewing court to vacate an arbitration award in limited circumstances, including "[w]here the award was procured by corruption, fraud or undue means"; "[w]here there [existed] evident partiality or corruption [by] the arbitrators"; where there existed specified misconduct by the arbitrators, or "[w]here the arbitrators exceeded their powers."[120] However, federal courts have tended to add a gloss to these provisions[121] and, in effect, to require that an arbitrator must grant the parties a fundamentally fair hearing.[122] The courts seem to agree that a fundamentally fair hearing requires notice, an opportunity to be heard and to present relevant and material evidence and argument before the arbitrators, and impartiality on the part of the arbitrators.[123]

When an arbitrator is called upon to interpret a clause contained in a commercial contract, or a term in a collective bargaining agreement, she is interpreting "private" law—law contractually created by the parties to govern those parties and no one else. Under these circumstances, it is appropriate to permit parties to agree in advance that the arbitrator's decision will not be appealable because the arbitrator misinterpreted the contract or misconstrued the underlying facts. It is assumed that the parties knew that they were agreeing to limited judicial review when they signed the arbitration agreement, and that, since any arbitral mistake affects only the parties themselves, they should be held to their bargain. Parties trading their right to appeal for a faster and less expensive method of dispute resolution should not be permitted to repudiate that bargain if the outcome of their case was not as they had hoped.

When statutory claims are involved, however, there is a public interest in the manner in which the statutory law is interpreted and applied.[124] Title VII, for example, was intended not only to give individual employees private redress for suffering discrimination, but also to "implement the public interest" in obliterating all traces of employment discrimination.[125] Thus, when an arbitration award is challenged based on the arbitrator's purported misapplication of statutory law, "there is a tension between the tradition of limited judicial review of arbitration awards and the presence of an independent public interest in ensuring that the law is correctly and consistently being applied."[126]

The Supreme Court considered this tension in *Mitsubishi Motors Corp. v. Soler Chrysler-Plymouth, Inc.*[127] In *Mitsubishi*, the Court distinguished prearbitration attempts to avoid enforcing an arbitration agreement from postarbitration attempts to vacate an award. Regarding the former, the Court held that the FAA requires a presumption that the arbitrator will decide the dispute in accordance with applicable law.[128] The mere possibility that an arbitrator will misapply the law, therefore, will not serve as a basis for refusing to enforce an arbitration agreement.[129]

On the other hand, the argument that an arbitral decision already rendered is based on a misapplication of the law may justify a court's vacation of the award. To this end, the Court stated that "the national courts of the United States will have the opportunity . . . to ensure that the legitimate interest in the enforcement of . . . [statutory] laws ha[ve] been addressed."[130] The Court stopped far short, however, of indicating that an arbitral award would be reviewable for factual or legal error in the same way as an adjudication by a trial court: "While the efficacy of the arbitral process requires that substantive review at the award enforcement stage remain minimal, it would not require intrusive inquiry to ascertain that the tribunal took cognizance of the [statutory] claims and actually decided them."[131] This language seems to imply that courts will examine arbitral awards only to ensure that statutory issues were considered and decided, which is markedly different from "ensur[ing] that the legitimate interest in the enforcement of [statutory] laws ha[ve] been addressed."

The lower courts, in reviewing arbitral decisions involving statutory claims, have refused to reverse such an award based on the "mere" fact that the arbitrator incorrectly interpreted or applied the law.[132] Instead, courts have stated that they only will reverse an arbitrator's award if the arbitrator acted in "manifest disregard of the law."[133] This standard—a judicially-created addition to the statutory grounds set forth in the FAA for vacating an award[134]—requires a showing that "the arbitrator 'understood and correctly stated the law but proceeded to ignore it.' "[135] Curiously, although dozens of cases discuss and define the "manifest disregard" standard, no arbitration award ever has been vacated on this ground.[136]

A more liberal standard of review has been proposed in the Model Employment Termination Act. META prohibits the discharge of covered employees except for "good cause,"[137] but limits damages[138] and recommends that all workplace disputes be resolved by binding arbitration.[139] It limits judicial review of arbitral awards to such grounds as fraud and corruption, an abuse of authority by the arbitrator, or a prejudicial error of law.[140] This "prejudicial error of law" standard is significantly broader than the "manifest disregard" standard that courts have used in the context of either collective bargaining or the FAA for vacating an arbitrator's award because the arbitrator misinterpreted or misapplied the law.[141] The META standard would permit a court to reverse any arbitration decision where the arbitrator's incorrect interpretation or application of the law adversely affects the rights of a party, making appellate review of arbitration awards significantly more common.

One commentator has asserted that imposing an appellate system on employment arbitration would, by obviating the finality of the award and guaranteeing a lengthy and expensive appellate process, defeat the primary purposes of arbitration. While this may be true, it is equally true that the current absence of arbitral opinions and the narrow review standard frustrate the public interest in ensuring the correct application of statutory employment laws. A different approach would better serve both the purpose of arbitration and the public interest. Arbitrators should be required to issue written opinions containing findings of fact and conclusions of law, and an accessible record of the proceedings should be available.[142] The opinions should be made publicly available and easily accessible. Courts should continue to apply the "manifest disregard of the law" standard, which will ensure that the most egregious errors of law are corrected while avoiding a postarbitration stampede to the courthouse.[143] The accessibility of arbitral opinions will ensure, as Vladeck suggests, that parties to future arbitrations are able to screen out potential arbitrators whose arbitral records demonstrate that they are incapable of correctly applying the law.

G. The Arbitrator's Ability to Award Relief

Employment arbitration agreements also have been criticized because of the limited authority of arbitrators to award relief. Prior to the decision in *Gilmer*, Professor Richard Shell wrote that the remedial powers of arbitrators in securities industry employment disputes "are limited to granting or denying relief requested by the particular parties before them and do not include monitoring long-term injunctive relief or making sweeping institutional reforms."[144] Shell, thus, concluded that securities arbitration procedures "simply would not be suited to implementing the systemic, institutional interests embodied in Title VII."[145]

The *Gilmer* court, while not directly addressing Professor Shell's concerns about institutional and long-term injunctive relief, nonetheless discussed generally the argument that the arbitrator's ability to award relief was too limited. The Court first noted that the securities industry's arbitration rules at issue in *Gilmer* granted arbitrators the authority to award equitable relief and to hear class actions.[146] The Court further opined that even if such authority were lacking, it would not justify a conclusion that arbitral procedures were inadequate to protect employees' statutory rights.[147]

Many federal employment antidiscrimination statutes, as well as most state common law torts, authorize punitive damage awards. As a counter-measure, some employers, when implementing employment arbitration systems, have inserted clauses that limit arbitrators' authority to award punitive and other types of damages.[148] It remains to be seen whether the courts will compel arbitration of discrimination claims under agreements containing such limitations.

It can be argued in such circumstances that the employee has waived, by contractual agreement, her right to seek the specified types of damages. As Judge Richard Posner pointed out in *Bararati v. Josephthal, Lyon & Ross, Inc.*:

> short of authorizing trial by battle or ordeal or, more doubtfully, by a panel of three monkeys, parties can stipulate to whatever procedures they want to govern the arbitration of their disputes; parties are as free to specify idiosyncratic terms of arbitration as they are to specify any other terms in their contract. For that matter, parties to adjudication have considerable power to vary the normal procedures, and surely can stipulate that punitive damages will not be awarded.[149]

Advocates of this approach square it with the FAA by interpreting the FAA as a mandate to courts requiring enforcement of all arbitration agreements "according to the terms of the parties' agreement,"[150] regardless of what those terms might be.

But what if an arbitration agreement stipulates that an employee "agrees to submit all employment disputes, including discrimination claims, to binding arbitration provided, however, that the arbitrator may award no relief for any claim based on sex discrimination"? Has the employee waived her opportunity to pursue a sex discrimination claim? Clearly not. Because Title VII vests in employees certain rights that are nonwaivable,[151] a prospective waiver of substantive Title VII rights is un-enforceable under well-established Title VII case law.[152] So what of a prospective waiver of the right to seek certain types of damages? Although *Gilmer* makes it clear that parties to an employment agreement prospec-tively may waive or alter certain statutory procedures for enforcing sub-stantive Title VII rights (such as the right to sue in court), it is less clear whether *Gilmer* authorizes the parties prospectively to waive their Title VII right to seek statutorily authorized categories of damages.

A clue may lie in the Court's statement in *Gilmer* that "[b]y agreeing to arbitrate a statutory claim, a party does not forgo the substantive rights afforded by the statute; it only submits to their resolution in an arbitral, rather than a judicial forum."[153] Although the Court here is referring to arbitration under the FAA, this interpretation of the FAA coincides nicely with the Title VII distinction between substantive rights, which are not prospectively waiveable, and procedural rights, which are. This substantive/procedural distinction gives the Court an easy way to reconcile its interpretation of the FAA in *Gilmer* with its prior interpretations of Title VII.

So is the statutory right to seek punitive damages a nonwaiveable substantive right or a waiveable procedural one? In the 1995 decision of *Mastrobuono v. Shearson Lehman Hutton, Inc.*,[154] the Court held that such a right is a substantive right.[155] Nonetheless, the decision itself could be interpreted as inconsistent with the proposition that the right to seek punitive damages is inherently nonwaiveable. In that case, the Mastrobuonos sued Shearson under various securities laws, claiming that Shearson had churned their account. After the trial court ordered the parties to arbitrate the dispute in accordance with an arbitration agreement they had signed, the case was arbitrated. The arbitrator issued a decision in favor of the Mastrobuonos, awarding them both compensatory and punitive damages. Shearson then moved to vacate the punitive damages portion of the award on the ground that the arbitration agreement contained a choice of law provision designating that the agreement would be construed in accordance with the law of New York, and on the ground that New York law prohibited arbitrators from awarding punitive damages. The Supreme Court held that the arbitration agreement was ambiguous as to whether the arbitrator would be permitted to award punitive damages, and that this ambiguity should be resolved in favor of the Mastrobuonos.[156] The Court, therefore, held that the arbitrator retained the authority to award punitive damages, and reinstated the punitive damages part of the award.[157]

Because the decision was based on ambiguity in a particular arbitration agreement, it is extremely narrow, applicable only to that specific contract and to no other.[158] Moreover, the Court specifically distinguished the situation in *Mastrobuono* from the one that most often arises in the context of employer arbitration agreements: a clause drafted by the employer that explicitly forbids the arbitrator from awarding punitive damages. The Court noted that "[a]s a practical matter, it seems unlikely that petitioners . . . had any idea that by signing a standard-form agreement to arbitrate disputes[,] they might be giving up an important substantive right," such as the right to seek punitive damages.[159]

Instead of basing its decision on the narrow ground of ambiguity in the contract, the Court instead could have held that the right to seek punitive damages is inherently nonwaiveable. It is possible, therefore, that the Court might enforce a clear waiver of punitive damages. This proposition, however, is speculative. The underlying claim in *Mastrobuono* was based on securities law, not Title VII. The strong Title VII case precedent establishing the nonwaiveability of substantive rights might easily convince the Court to interpret the FAA consistently with Title VII. Therefore, by calling the right to seek punitive damages a substantive right, the Court may have paved the way for a later decision to equate "substantive" with "non-waiveable."

Assuming that statutorily permitted categories of damages are non-waiveable, the issue turns to whether such damages, when purportedly (though ineffectively) "waived" by agreement, may be awarded by the arbitrator, or whether they may (or must) be awarded by a court. In *Mastrobuono*, that decision was easy because the purported waiver of punitive damages operated through a choice of law provision rather than an explicit waiver. If, however, a waiver were to state, "The Arbitrator shall have no authority to award punitive damages," a court could not simply strike the waiver and order the punitive damages issue to be submitted to arbitration. This is because any award of punitive damages by the arbitrator would exceed the scope of the arbitrator's contractual authority, and this is a statutory ground for vacating an arbitral award. In such a situation, courts have two options.

The majority of courts that have addressed the issue to date have held that a party with a statutory right to seek punitive damages may do so notwithstanding an arbitral agreement to limit damages. This issue has arisen several times in New York, where state law forbids an arbitrator to award punitive damages.[160] The first option is to sever the punitive damage claim from the rest of the case, require the parties to submit the nonpunitive damages part of the case to arbitration, and stay the punitive damages part for resolution by the court after an arbitration award has been made. This approach has been adopted by several New York courts confronted with this issue.[161]

An example of a court adopting this approach is *Kinnebrew v. Gulf Insurance Co.*[162] In *Kinnebrew*, the United States District Court for the Northern District of Texas ordered to arbitration plaintiff's claims under the federal Equal Pay Act[163] and the Texas Commission on Human Rights Act[164] even though the arbitration agreement did not provide for the award of punitive damages, attorneys' fees, or equitable relief.[165] The court reasoned that an employee's right to such relief was not a "substantive" right and, therefore, was waiveable.[166] (This reasoning probably will not survive *Mastrobuono*.) However, by retaining jurisdiction in the case "to consider any statutory remedies to which [a] plaintiff is entitled after arbitration is completed,"[167] the court left open the possibility that it would allow the employee to recover these types of relief in a subsequent judicial action.

The second option for courts faced by an arbitration agreement with a "no authority to award punitive damages" clause is to strike the arbitration clause altogether and allow the entire claim to be litigated. The Ninth Circuit adopted this option in *Graham Oil Co. v. Arco Products Co.*,[168] which involved a suit by a gasoline retailer alleging that its supplier unlawfully raised its prices in violation of the federal Petroleum Marketing Practices Act (PMPA).[169] The supplier sought to compel arbitration on the basis of an arbitration agreement. The Ninth Circuit agreed with the supplier that generally this dispute would be arbitrable, since an agreement to submit statutory claims to arbitration "constitutes nothing more than an agreement to substitute one legitimate dispute resolution forum for another and involves no surrender of statutory protections or benefits."[170] In this case, however, the court held that the arbitration agreement expressly forfeited the retailer's statutory right to recover punitive damages and attorneys' fees and altered the statute of limitations.[171] Noting that the purpose of the PMPA was to protect retailers from the "dominant economic power" exercised by suppliers,[172] the court declined to sever the offending provisions and, instead, refused to enforce the arbitration agreement, permitting the retailer to seek redress for all its claims in court.[173]

The Ninth Circuit did not indicate in *Graham* whether its treatment of the arbitration clause necessarily would be the same in cases not involving the PMPA, such as employment cases. At least one court has indicated, however, that an arbitration agreement could be struck in its entirety because the agreement does not permit statutorily authorized damages. In *Johnson v. Hubbard Broadcasting, Inc.*,[174] Johnson, a former employee claiming sexual harassment under Title VII, urged the court to invalidate the agreement on the ground that its remedy provisions were inconsistent with her Title VII rights. The arbitration agreement at issue apparently limited Johnson's award to out-of-pocket damages (as interpreted by the employer, the agreement permitted economic damages such as back pay and lost benefits but excluded punitive damages and damages for pain and suffering) and forbade any award of attorneys' fees.[175] The Federal District

Court for the District of Minnesota compelled arbitration of the claim pending the arbitrator's determining the meaning of the damage limitations. In doing so, however, the court stated that "should the arbitrator find that the terms of the arbitration agreement deny Johnson the opportunity to recover the full array of statutory remedies available under state and federal law, the agreement would contravene federally and state established remedial measures, possibly rendering the agreement unenforceable as unconscionable."[176]

The New York approach is more consistent than the Ninth Circuit's method with current law favoring enforcement of arbitration agreements. The New York approach preserves the employees' statutory right to enumerated damages while enforcing an agreement to arbitrate the merits of the underlying dispute. It also discourages employers from insisting on arbitral provisions restricting employees' abilities to seek the relief to which they are statutorily entitled. Two cases (one in arbitration and one in litigation) exist where previously there was only one; if the employee prevails in arbitration on the issue of liability, the punitive damage claim will be tried in court, probably to a jury. This inefficient process will obviate most, if not all, of the advantages of proceeding through arbitration.[177] As a result, it likely will take only a few rulings in this direction to convince employers not to attempt to limit arbitral relief.

Although compulsory employment arbitration is finding increasing favor in the courts, an agreement requiring arbitration of statutory discrimination claims must be scrupulously fair to ensure judicial enforcement.[178] The agreement should be in writing, should specify the types of employment disputes that are covered by the agreement, and should specify the persons or parties to whom the agreement applies. It should permit both parties to participate equally in the selection of arbitrators either by mutual choice or from a pool of disinterested neutrals. It should permit ample discovery, including document production, information requests, depositions, and subpoenas. The arbitration agreement should require the arbitrator to issue a written opinion. It should not attempt to limit the arbitrator's ability to award relief by, for example, forbidding an award of punitive damages or attorneys' fees. In short, the arbitral process that is substituted for litigation should be, in appearance as well as substance, scrupulously fair to the employee.

Even under the current state of the law, which is highly deferential to employment arbitration agreements, agreements that do not meet the standards listed above generally will not be enforced by courts. Courts cannot, however, police every employer's arbitration agreement. If courts are overwhelmed with petitions from employees claiming, justifiably, that they have been forced to sign one-sided agreements, courts are unlikely to continue looking upon compulsory arbitration with favor. As discussed in chapters 3 and 4, both the courts and Congress can easily bring a short end to the future of compulsory arbitration if the alternative is permitting employers to trample on employees' legal employment rights. If employers wish to continue to enjoy the benefits of arbitrating their employment claims, they must ensure that their employees benefit also.

Appendix A. Employment Agreement

The parties agree that employment is at-will, and that either party may terminate the employment relationship at any time for any or no reason. Any agreement abrogating the at-will relationship must be in writing and signed by both employee and employer.

The parties further agree that any legal or equitable claims or disputes arising out of or in connection with the employment, the terms and conditions of employment, or the termination of employment will be settled by binding arbitration. This agreement applies to the following allegations, disputes, and claims for relief, but is not limited to those listed: wrongful discharge under statutory law and common law; employment discrimination based on federal, state or local statute, ordinance, or governmental regulations; retaliatory discharge or other action; compensation disputes; tortious conduct; contractual violations (although no contractual relationship, other than at-will employment and this agreement to arbitrate, is hereby created); ERISA violations; and other statutory and common law claims and disputes, regardless of whether the statute was enacted or whether the common law doctrine was recognized at the time this Agreement was signed.

The arbitration proceedings shall be conducted in [city, state] in accordance with the National Rules for the Resolution of Employment Disputes (National Rules) of the American Arbitration Association (AAA) in effect at the time a demand for arbitration is made. The employee is entitled to representation by an attorney throughout the proceedings at his or her own expense; however, the employer agrees not to use an attorney in the arbitration hearing if the employee agrees to the same.

One arbitrator shall be used and shall be chosen by mutual agreement of the parties. If, within thirty days after the employee notifies the employer of an arbitrable dispute, no arbitrator has been chosen, an arbitrator shall be chosen by AAA pursuant to its National Rules. The arbitrator shall coordinate and limit as appropriate all prearbitral discovery, which shall include document production, information requests, and depositions. The arbitrator shall issue a written decision and award, stating the reasons therefor. The decision and award shall be exclusive, final, and binding on both parties, their heirs, executors, administrators, successors, and assigns. The costs and expenses of the arbitration shall be borne evenly by the parties.

The parties understand that by signing this agreement, they are agreeing to substitute one legitimate dispute resolution forum (arbitration) for another (litigation), and thereby are waiving their right to have their disputes resolved in court. This substitution involves no surrender, by either party, of any substantive statutory or common law benefit, protection, or defense.

The parties agree that this is not intended to add to, create, or imply any contractual or other right of employment. The parties' employment relationship is at-will, and no other inference is to be drawn from this Agreement.

Employee	(Date)	Employer (Date)

Ten

The Policy Implications of Compulsory Employment Arbitration

EVEN IF WE ASSUME THAT ALL EMPLOYERS ADOPT-
ing compulsory employment arbitration procedures do
so in a way that is scrupulously fair to employees, this
does not answer the broader question of whether compulsory arbitration
is an acceptable way to resolve employment disputes involving issues of
public law. Parties to an arbitration agreement effectively waive several
critical procedural rights available to them in litigation, among them the
right to trial by jury, the right to obtain full discovery of their case, the
right to have their case litigated and tried under the Federal Rules of Civil
Procedure and Evidence, and (except under very narrow circumstances)
the right to appeal the arbitrator's incorrect application of the law.[1] Although both employer and employee waive these rights, the disadvantages
of such a waiver often fall heaviest on the employee. Because most employment laws were created to protect employees, an enforcement mechanism
that overwhelmingly benefits employers will defeat the purpose for which
the laws were enacted.

The current litigative method of employment dispute resolution, while
preserving these procedural rights, imposes heavy costs (economic and
otherwise) on the parties—costs that often fall heaviest on employees and
greatly restrict their opportunities to vindicate their legal rights. Arbitration can ease these costs significantly, giving more employees a better
opportunity to pursue their claims. Arbitration, therefore, may be an appropriate method for resolving legal employment disputes if, on balance,
the benefits of arbitration for employees, such as better access to adjudication, outweigh the disadvantages occasioned by the loss of procedural
rights. The benefits commonly associated with arbitration include the
speed with which claims are resolved, the finality of an arbitral award,

145

the relatively low cost of arbitration, the expertise of the adjudicator, the informality of the proceedings, and the less confrontational atmosphere of arbitral proceedings.

Arbitration, if implemented fairly and properly, can be of great benefit to both employers and employees. However, because it is a private dispute resolution mechanism, drafted by employers, and often imposed on employees on a sign-it-or-be-fired basis, it can be abused by employers who draft unfair, one-sided agreements that effectively eviscerate employees' substantive employment rights. Although courts can, to some extent, police arbitration agreements by refusing to enforce egregiously unfair ones, courts have neither the resources nor the desire to review every employer's arbitration agreement.

The current experiment with compulsory arbitration is an apt response to these competing concerns. Where an employee challenges in court a particular compulsory arbitration agreement imposed by an employer, courts should only enforce the agreement if it is fundamentally fair to employees. At a broader level, we as a society should only permit employers to adopt compulsory arbitration systems if the courts are able, through the adjudication of particular cases, to ensure that compulsory arbitration is not used to weaken employment rights that have been erected over the past fifty years. If too many employers draft one-sided agreements, and courts are unable to keep up with their attempts to abuse employment arbitration, then either Congress or the Supreme Court should end the experiment with compulsory arbitration. Employers should recognize that this is a significant possibility, and should, as a matter of self-interest if nothing else, bend over backward to draft fair agreements. If the overwhelming number of employers implementing compulsory arbitration do so through agreements that are fair to employees, then courts should confirm compulsory arbitration as a legitimate method of employment dispute resolution while simultaneously continuing the current refusal to enforce agreements that are unfair to employees.

This chapter will begin by describing the procedural rights that parties waive by agreeing to arbitration, and the benefits that arbitration offers over litigation. Each of these rights and benefits will be assessed as to its relative effect on both employers and employees. Next, this chapter will consider several broader concerns about compulsory arbitration, such as the prospect of employers unilaterally imposing arbitration agreements on unwilling employees, the effect of compulsory arbitration on the enforcement of important public policies such as nondiscrimination, and the possibility that employers will abuse employment arbitration by using it to vitiate employees' substantive employment rights. Finally, the chapter will conclude with some final remarks concerning the future of compulsory employment arbitration.

A. Lost Procedural Rights

The American system of litigation represents an extremely formal, highly complex, and often technical method of resolving disputes. Formality is not necessarily a bad thing. It can help ensure that like cases are treated uniformly, that cases progress in an orderly and predictable way from inception to trial to appeal, and that the parties are given equal access to factual information about the dispute. Procedural formalities often are designed to help protect a party with a meritorious case from being overwhelmed by a party with a significant advantage in political influence, financial resources, or access to information.[2] In the employment context, these procedures may offer more to the employee than they to the employer.

1. Trial by Jury

Most employment disputes involve an attempt to answer three basic questions: (1) What did the employer do to the employee? (the factual issue); (2) was the employer's conduct illegal under the law? (the legal issue); and (3) if the answer to question two is yes, how much money would it take to compensate the employee for her damages? (the damage issue). Under traditional tort law, issues one and three generally are decided by a jury,[3] and question two by a judge. Until 1991, all three questions were decided by the judge under Title VII and other federal antidiscrimination statutes. The Civil Rights Act of 1991 changed this structure by giving questions one and three to the jury.[4]

Arbitration vests full authority for all three questions in the arbitrator, regardless of whether the dispute arises under federal or state, statutory or common law. The transfer of the authority to decide factual issues and damages from the jury to an arbitrator generally is viewed as more favorable to employers than employees, because, for three reasons, employers generally distrust juries.

First, employers often perceive juries as less predictable than judges or arbitrators.[5] Employers may believe that a jury's decision on issues of liability and damages is less likely than one made by a judge or arbitrator to correspond to the facts of the case. To some extent this may be true. The presentment of "facts" in the courtroom is hardly a model for effective communication, and may easily result in jury confusion or an inadequate grasp of what is relevant or important. Moreover, a person is likely to serve on a jury in an employment case only once in a lifetime; therefore, compared to judges and arbitrators who see such cases regularly, she is at a distinct disadvantage in evaluating the merits of a particular case or assessing damages.[6] However, this perception of jury unpredictability may equally be due to employers' tendency to view their cases from their own perspective (most likely a formal, legal perspective) rather than from the less formal and more pragmatic perspective of an employee or juror.

Second, employers often feel that jurors are the "peers" of employees, not employers, and that jurors are likely to award substantial damages to a sympathetic plaintiff regardless of the legal merits of the case. Many employers believe that jurors do this because they feel that even if the employer is not responsible for the plaintiff's woes, the employer can more easily compensate for those woes than can the unfortunate employee. Again, there probably is some truth to this. Jurors are far more likely to be employees than employers, and as such they may be predisposed to view employment disputes through an employee's eyes. However, the small amount of empirical data available concerning the outcome of employment cases demonstrates that juries render findings of liability in less than half of all employment cases that go to a jury.[7] Moreover, Brown & Root's experience with arbitration, discussed in chapter 6,[8] indicates that arbitrators may be more likely than juries to render a verdict in favor of employees.

Third, many employers believe that jurors are far more likely than judges or arbitrators to award "jackpot" jury awards, which are damage awards far out of proportion to what the employer perceives to be fair compensation for the harm allegedly inflicted. This is certainly true, at least to some extent. Informal experience with employment arbitration indicates that arbitrators are extremely unlikely to render the multimillion dollar amounts becoming increasingly common in jury awards, and, if longstanding practice in the arbitration of traditional labor disputes is any guide, punitive damages in employment cases are not likely to be awarded with great frequency in the future.[9] However, Brown & Root's experience with employment arbitration demonstrates that smaller arbitral awards are likely to be offset by the greater frequency with which findings of liability are entered. This may indicate the purported tendency of arbitrators to "split the baby" in hard cases—to give the employee some relief, but less than she would be entitled to if the employer clearly were wholly at fault.

In theory, a large employer might be unaffected by the tradeoff between lower average awards and higher rates of liability if these are balanced evenly. In practice, however, employers are extremely fearful of large damage awards, for several reasons. A single seven-digit award may cause a small-to-medium-sized company to go out of business. Even if the company is large, and can absorb the cost of a large award, such an award may jeopardize the prestige of in-house counsel responsible for overseeing the litigation. A large award also may generate news headlines and other adverse publicity that the company would find embarrassing.

This fear of large damage awards magnifies the amount that employers are willing to spend to settle a given case, and increases the bargaining power of employees in settlement negotiations. By eliminating jury trials (and therefore the possibility of windfall damage awards), arbitration decreases the likelihood that an employee will receive a large prearbitration settlement. This in turn may have residual effects on the employee's ability to attract competent counsel to pursue her case. Thus, although employers' distrust of juries is not entirely justified, the transfer from the jury to an arbitrator to decide issues of liability and damages nonetheless represents a significant net gain for employers.

2. Full Discovery

Discovery is the process by which parties to a lawsuit obtain knowledge of facts relevant to the suit that are known by the opposing parties and witnesses.[10] The philosophy underlying the federal and state rules of civil procedure considers thorough discovery necessary to avoid prejudicial surprise at trial;[11] to disclose fully the nature and scope of the controversy;[12] to narrow, simplify, and frame the relevant issues;[13] and to enable a party to obtain the information needed to prepare for trial.[14] Trial is seen as a search for truth,[15] rather than a game in which the result depends on the fortuitous availability of evidence or the skill and strategy of attorneys.[16]

The Federal Rules of Civil Procedure, as well as parallel state rules, evince a strong policy favoring thorough discovery.[17] These rules explicitly permit the parties to discover relevant facts by, among other means, taking depositions, sending interrogatories, sending requests for admissions, and obtaining documents.[18] The parties need not obtain approval from the court before seeking such discovery. Additionally, the federal rules and some state rules require the parties to disclose certain relevant facts as a matter of course shortly after a lawsuit is filed.[19]

As discussed in chapter 7, a generous allotment of discovery is absolutely crucial to the employee in most employment cases, because the employer possesses most of the information (such as demographic profiles of the workforce, records of personnel decisions, personnel files, and disciplinary notices) without which the employee would be unable to prove her case.[20] This is particularly true when, as in many cases, the employee's employment is terminated. Without discovery, she may have no way of learning if she was replaced by someone of a different race, sex, or other protected classification. Adequate discovery is essential to the employee regardless of whether the case is tried in a judicial or arbitral forum because without it, the employee may have no case.

Discovery is important to employers also, although for a different reason. Employers use discovery to get admissions from the employee, which the employer will use in an attempt to get the case dismissed prior to adjudication. Presumably, the same evidence—despite when obtained during the trial process—used to justify the pretrial dismissal of a case will result in the posttrial dismissal of that case, or, at the very least, in a finding by the trier of fact of no liability. Discovery thus usually is less crucial in developing the employer's case than developing that of the employee. For the employer, discovery represents a cost-and risk-cutting trial avoidance strategy, whereas for the employee, it often is her only hope for developing a case.

Discovery generally is less available in arbitration than in litigation because, as the Supreme Court recognized in *Gilmer*, parties to an arbitration agreement trade the formalities and comprehensive discovery provisions of judicial procedure for the less formal and more expedited discovery procedures of arbitration.[21] Arbitration is faster and less expensive than litigation in large part because discovery is less extensive and, ideally, less adversarial. Instead of scheduling depositions and sending interrogatories and requests for production of documents as a matter of course, most arbitral procedures require that the parties coordinate all discovery through the arbitrator. For example, the American Arbitration Association's rules authorize such discovery "as the arbitrator considers necessary to a full and fair exploration of the issues in dispute,"[22] thereby giving the arbitrator discretion over whether, and under what circumstances, discovery will be permitted.

As discussed in chapter 7, arbitration agreements that unduly restrict an employee's access to adequate discovery should not be enforced. This does not mean, however, that arbitral discovery should be as extensive as litigative discovery. Arbitral discovery should be limited to whatever will allow the parties to discover facts necessary to proving their cases. Some restrictions on discovery—and certainly a closer monitoring of discovery by arbitrators than judges currently perform—is essential to preserving the advantages arbitration offers over litigation. However, because an employee is uniquely dependent on discovery to develop a case, any restrictions on discovery are likely to benefit the employer at the employee's expense.

3. Rules of Civil Procedure and Evidence

Parties to an arbitration agreement forego certain formalities in exchange for the informality and expedition of arbitration, one of which is strict compliance with rules of civil procedure and evidence.[23] Where both employer and employee are represented by able counsel, the absence of formal rules may favor the employer because, as with discovery, procedural rules help level the playing field. In many cases, however, employees are unable to retain competent counsel to represent them on employment matters. This problem is discussed later in this chapter.

Where an employee is not represented by counsel, the absence of formal rules is of great benefit to the employee. It is extremely difficult for a nonlawyer to navigate the complex and often unwritten rules governing pretrial and trial procedures, even when judges, as they usually do, bend over backward to accommodate the novice.[24] Most law students spend at least three semesters studying the rules of civil procedure and evidence. Even then, they must undergo a substantial amount of practical training and/or mentoring before they can litigate a case competently on their own. Under these circumstances, the absence of formal rules may help to prevent an employee's case from being dismissed, or her evidence from being stricken, merely because she failed to follow some obscure procedural rule that she did not understand.

4. Appeal

As discussed in chapter 7, an arbitrant's right to appeal is extremely limited. She may not appeal an arbitrator's finding of fact, may only appeal the arbitrator's application of the law if the arbitrator knowingly used the wrong legal standard, and may only appeal procedural issues if the arbitrator was obviously biased or did not afford her an opportunity to present her case. The effect of these onerous restrictions on the right to appeal is that arbitration decisions are, for all practical purposes, the final and virtually unreviewable determination of the parties' dispute. This significantly reduces the time and expense it takes to resolve the dispute, because even an unsuccessful appeal of litigation can take years and tens of thousands of dollars in legal fees.

In any case, whether litigated or adjudicated, the beneficiary of a liberal right to appeal is the party who lost the case at trial or on summary disposition by the adjudication. This is so even if the appeal is likely to be unsuccessful, because the prospect of a protracted and expensive appeals process might persuade a nonappellant to settle a case, even one provisionally won on its merits. As discussed earlier in this chapter, employers win more than half of all jury trials; they win an even greater percentage of trials decided by judges.[25] Employees, therefore, have the most to lose by giving up the right to appeal because they cannot use the appeals process as a bargaining tool to compel settlement.

If the rights waived by parties to an arbitration agreement are tallied up as on a scorecard, the employer wins three to one. The one area of advantage to employees—waiver of the necessity for strict compliance with the rules of procedure and evidence—only benefits employees unrepresented by counsel; otherwise, like the other three waived rights, it works to the advantage of employers. Although restrictions on liberal appellate rights offer employers a slight advantage, restrictions on discovery and the waiver of the right to trial by jury give employers great tactical advantages by making it more difficult for employees to prove their cases and by minimizing the bargaining power they can exert in settlement negotiations. Thus, it is generally agreed that, on balance, the waiver of procedural rights occasioned by the signing of a compulsory arbitration agreement disproportionately favors employers.[26] It should come as no surprise, therefore, that in virtually every reported employment case in which one party is seeking to compel arbitration, it is the employer who favors arbitration and the employee who would prefer to remain in court.

B. Perceived Advantages of Arbitration

Both employers and employees give up important procedural rights by agreeing to arbitrate their disputes, and the burden of these foregone rights is borne most heavily by employees. Arbitration, however, represents a tradeoff between strict adherence to procedural formality and efficiency. Its relative informality allows the procedures to be tailored to the dispute, rather than the other way around, resulting in certain benefits, such as the faster and less expensive resolution of the dispute. Like the burdens of foregone procedural rights, many of these benefits redound primarily to employees. This section discusses those benefits and, as in the prior section, compares their relative effects on employers and employees.

1. *Speed*

Federal court caseloads are burgeoning, and state court dockets are not far behind.[27] Judges are swamped by criminal cases that force them to curtail time spent on civil cases.[28] At the same time, civil cases are proliferating, led by federal employment litigation that increased 2,166 percent between fiscal years 1970 and 1989.[29]

Overloaded judicial dockets mean that litigated employment claims generally take, at a minimum, several years to get to trial from the date that suit is filed.[30] The review process conducted by federal and state equal employment opportunity agencies (discussed in chapter 6) can add another year if the employee or her attorney truncates the agency's investigation by requesting an early right-to-sue letter; the process can add an additional two to four years if the employee allows the agency to conduct a full investigation and to attempt conciliation.[31] An employee fortunate enough to make it to trial and receive a favorable judgment must wait for years to recover damages as the case is kept alive in the appellate courts.[32] Employment cases that are not settled or concluded by summary disposition commonly take three to five years from inception to final disposition. In fact, cases lasting a decade or more are not unheard of.[33]

By streamlining the discovery and appellate processes and utilizing an adjudicator with the time to take a hands-on approach to the case, arbitration can resolve in months a dispute that would take years in court.[34] The longest it has ever taken Brown & Root to resolve a dispute under its Dispute Resolution Program is a little over two years. Sixty-five percent of its disputes (nonlegal as well as legal) were resolved within four weeks; only twenty-one out of 1,529 total disputes took more than a year to resolve.[35] Thus arbitration can significantly decrease the amount of time that an employment dispute is outstanding.

Both employers and employees benefit from a faster resolution time. The employee can put the dispute behind her, and, if the employment relationship has been severed, can focus on new employment. The employer can eliminate the opportunity costs resulting from employees spending time on litigation rather than engaging in productive activity. Shorter resolution time is one of many factors making arbitration significantly less expensive than litigation, and, again, benefiting both parties.

Although both parties clearly are helped by an expedited dispute resolution process, employees have the most to gain. This is because employers invariably have greater financial resources than employees,[36] and thus are better situated to engage in litigation by attrition. Most employees simply cannot afford to pay the attorneys' fees and costs that it takes to litigate a case for several years. Even when an employee is able to engage an attorney on a contingency fee basis, which means that the attorney collects no compensation unless and until the plaintiff receives a settlement check or damage award, the employee nonetheless often must pay for litigation expenses, and put working and personal life on hold until the litigation is complete.

Moreover, the liberal discovery rules afforded by the rules of civil procedure provide employers with ample opportunity to delay trial indefinitely.[37] It is always possible to claim that more documents, records, and depositions are needed before discovery is "complete," and an overworked trial judge is unlikely to complain too loudly about motions to postpone the trial date. An employer believing that an employee has a valid claim has ample motive to delay trial indefinitely, because doing so will both pressure the employee to accept a smaller settlement as her resources dwindle,[38] and extend into the distant future the date that settlement or judgment must be paid out. Delay also may deter future suits by other employees by fostering the employer's reputation for vigorously defending and delaying all of its employment cases.[39] Current procedural rules, therefore, give employers both the means and the incentive to abuse discovery by using it to pressure employees to settle their cases for less than they are worth. By reducing the time between the inception of an employment dispute and the award, arbitration disproportionately benefits employees by minimizing employers' opportunity to "bleed" employees through protracted litigation.

2. Cost

Litigating an employment dispute is expensive. An informal survey of plaintiff lawyers conducted in 1992 revealed that it costs between $10,000 and $60,000 in attorney's fees and expenses to take a plaintiff's employment case through trial.[40] Similarly, a 1988 study of California employment cases found that pretrial legal fees for defending these cases averaged $25,000 and that the total legal bill for defending cases going to trial averaged approximately $80,000.[41] Because these figures are several years old and because legal fees have not held steady during that time, these figures probably understate significantly the cost of litigating an employment case today.[42]

The high cost of litigation imposes significant burdens on both employers and employees. The employer, when faced with a suit by an employee or a former employee, may either make an early settlement regardless of the merits of the claim, or face the immediate prospect of high legal costs.[43] An employer's decision to adopt a strategy of delay will have only a small effect on immediate legal costs, and over the life of a case will drive these costs up substantially. Although settling a given case early often is less expensive for the employer than litigating it, early settlement encourages other employees to file suit, even if they have questionable claims, in the hope that the employer will settle to avoid litigation costs.[44] The high cost of litigation is one of the main reasons many employers currently are considering implementing compulsory arbitration agreements.[45]

As troublesome as high litigation costs are for employers, they are even more disastrous for employees. Few employees have between $10,000 and $60,000 readily available to fund an employment lawsuit, particularly if, as often is the case, the lawsuit arises from termination of employment.[46] Employees, therefore, depend on contingency fee arrangements with plaintiff attorneys if they are to find counsel to prosecute their case. Plaintiff lawyers, however, are aware that employment cases are expensive to litigate. Even when success in litigation is certain, the potential recovery must be above $60,000 to make the attorney's contingent share of the recovery cover the anticipated costs of litigation.[47] When success is uncertain, a lawyer will be unlikely to take the case on a contingency basis unless there are excellent prospects for early settlement or there is a realistic chance of recovering an extremely large damage award.

Few employees, even those with valid allegations of discrimination or wrongful discharge, can convince an attorney, before a lawsuit is filed, that they are relatively certain to receive a large damage award. For one thing, employment cases are extremely difficult for a plaintiff attorney to evaluate in an initial assessment interview. Rarely does the employee possess a "smoking gun" document proving that she was the victim of discrimination; seldom does the employee possess any supporting documentation at all. Most employees walk into the attorney's office with nothing but a story to tell—a story that the attorney knows may be colored by conscious or subconscious exaggeration or misunderstanding. From the perspective of the attorney, the story is unverifiable at this stage, because most, if not all, of the witnesses remain employed by the employer, and the attorney's rules of ethics forbid her from contacting these employees.[48] This makes it virtually impossible for a plaintiff attorney to assess the likely outcome of the case without first hearing the employer's version of what happened, and this seldom occurs until after the case has been filed and discovery has begun.

Even if the attorney is convinced of the merits of the case, provable damages may not be high enough to cover litigation costs. A significant component of the damages awarded in most successful employment cases is lost wages. Lost wages will be minimal, however, for employees who are still employed by the employer, who were terminated but quickly found other employment, or who did not receive a high annual salary. If suit can be grounded in tort, lost earnings can be embellished by emotional distress and punitive damages, but courts and juries are wary of permitting recovery on tort grounds except in the most egregious employment cases.[49] The 1991 Civil Rights Act gives employees the right to recover certain compensatory damages (with statutorily-capped limits on recovery),[50] but this may not be enough to convince a plaintiff attorney that the case is worth taking.

Provisions in statutes such as Title VII that allow successful plaintiffs to recover their reasonable attorneys' fees[51] will encourage some plaintiff attorneys to accept cases in which an employee might otherwise go unrepresented.[52] Such provisions do not, however, assure employees whose rights have been violated that they will find an attorney to vindicate those rights, for four reasons.[53] First, attorney's fees are awarded only if the employee prevails, and the amount will not be adjusted to compensate for the possibility that the case would have been lost.[54] This significantly decreases the incentive for plaintiff attorneys to take cases that are not sure winners. Furthermore, as discussed above, very few employment cases look like sure winners when they are first presented to an experienced plaintiff attorney.

Second, several courts have held that when an employee prevails on some, but not all, of her claims, attorneys' fees can only be recovered for the time spent pursuing the successful claims.[55] An attorney who takes the case is obligated professionally to pursue all possible claims, including questionable claims, despite a substantial risk that she will not be compensated for all of her work. This creates a significant incentive for her to decline representation.

Third, the attorney risks the possibility of a feeless settlement. If an employer makes a settlement offer that does not provide for attorneys' fees, the lawyer is obligated to communicate the offer to the employee,[56] and the employee has the right to accept it.[57] Once burned by such a settlement, an attorney is likely to think twice about taking another employment case with the expectation of collecting a statutory fee award.

Finally, it is possible that neither the employee nor her lawyer can finance the entire litigation, even if they believe they are relatively certain to receive a large payout at the conclusion of the suit. The attorney must invest hundreds of hours in the litigation; the employee typically must front thousands of dollars in filing fees, expert fees, deposition fees, and other expenses. Unemployed workers, as well as the solo practitioners and small firms that comprise the majority of plaintiffs' civil rights lawyers, often lack the reserves to commence (or conclude) a case lasting ten years or more.

The high cost of employment litigation has made it impossible for the majority of Americans to pursue even obviously valid employment claims.[58] The reported cases demonstrate that relatively few plaintiffs are hourly wage or clerical workers; most are professionals, executives, or middle-to-upper-management employees.[59] Lower-income employees cannot afford to hire a lawyer, and this leaves them with virtually no chance of obtaining representation in employment cases.[60] A recent survey of attorneys who regularly represent employees in employment cases revealed that approximately 5 percent of the employees requesting representation[61] had their cases accepted. Even assuming that a substantial proportion of employees were denied representation because of the apparent lack of meritorious claims, the survey indicates that many employees with valid claims cannot obtain representation. Because employees seldom can finance employment litigation on their own, they are left with no way to vindicate their legal rights. To these employees, the laws designed to protect them are chimerical.

Arbitration is significantly less expensive than litigation.[62] Although no formal studies or surveys have been conducted to ascertain the cost to an employee of bringing an employment claim to arbitration, the Bureau of National Affairs reports that "[o]n average, companies find that they can arbitrate between fifteen and twenty cases for the cost of one wrongful discharge lawsuit."[63] As discussed in chapter 6, Brown & Root cut its outside legal expenses in half after adopting its dispute resolution program, even after accounting for the company reimbursing employees for *their* legal expenses in pursuing legal claims. The substantially reduced costs of adjudication, coupled with a much shorter time frame for receiving an award, makes it possible for employees to attract competent counsel far more often than currently is possible in litigation.[64] Moreover, the reduced costs of arbitration may enable a greater number of employees to afford to pay their attorneys hourly rather than contingency fees, allowing them to keep everything recovered in their arbitral award rather than paying 30–40 percent to their attorneys under the contingency fee arrangement.

3. Informality

Another much-touted advantage of arbitration is its relative informality as compared to litigation. This informality can be manifested in two ways, each of which disproportionately benefits employees.

First, the employment arbitration agreement may eliminate some of the statutory roadblocks to adjudication. As discussed in chapter 6, Title VII and parallel state statutes establish an elaborate set of procedures, such as filing a timely charge of discrimination with the Equal Employment Opportunity Commission (EEOC) or a similar state administrative agency, with which employees must comply before they can file a lawsuit. Because these procedures already are confusing to experienced employment lawyers,[65] they pose an even more difficult obstacle for an unrepresented employee trying to navigate the prejudicial process.

Some employment arbitration agreements may dispense with the requirement that employees jump through these procedural hoops before proceeding to arbitration. For example, an agreement that permits or requires an employee to request arbitration immediately after an incident has arisen or within a short specified time frame[66] may be interpreted as waiving the employer's opportunity to contest the claim on the ground that the employee has failed to satisfy procedural prerequisites. On the other hand, an agreement specifying that an arbitral award may only be made in accordance with applicable law, requiring employees to satisfy procedural prerequisites to filing suit as a precondition for arbitration, or preserving all applicable legal defenses, may preserve the employer's right to require the employee to comply with the legal procedural requirements. Even under an agreement with these provisions, however, an employer may be willing to waive the procedural prerequisites in individual cases, whether to encourage the prompt resolution of the dispute or in the hope that the employee will not avail herself of her right to inform state and federal equal employment opportunity agencies about allegedly discriminatory practices.

The second way that arbitration is less formal than litigation is in how the adjudication itself is conducted. A trial is an extremely formal proceeding, governed by hundreds of written and unwritten rules that take years to master. Although it is possible for a nonlawyer to take a case to trial on her own behalf, it is not easy. Most employees are so intimidated by the legal process that they may not pursue their case at all if they cannot find a lawyer to take it.

Arbitration is much simpler than litigation. Instead of being governed by the federal and state rules of civil procedure and evidence, which (with explanatory commentary) can fill as many as forty-four volumes,[67] most arbitration is controlled by rules that fill no more than a few pages. The rules promulgated by the American Arbitration Association (AAA), for example, are contained on twenty-one pamphlet pages, and provide for everything from how arbitration is initiated to choosing the arbitrator to the hearing itself. They are straightforward and easy for a nonlawyer to understand.

The simplicity of arbitral rules reflects the simplicity of the arbitral hearing itself. Generally, the arbitrator begins by explaining how the hearing will be conducted and by administering an oath to the witnesses. The arbitrator then invites each of the parties to give a short summation of what they expect the evidence will show. Next, each side has the opportunity to tell its story and to present witnesses and evidence. Parties may cross-examine one another's witnesses, and occasionally the arbitrator may question a witness. After presenting evidence, each party gives a closing statement summarizing the evidence and explaining why the arbitrator should find in its favor. The arbitrator generally concludes the hearing by telling the parties when and how they will be notified of the decision and award.

One of the major advantages of arbitration is that its simplicity makes lawyers superfluous. An employee can pursue a claim in arbitration with little difficulty even if she cannot find a lawyer to represent her. To be sure, she will be at a disadvantage if the employer brings a lawyer to the arbitration hearing, but the difference between having and not having a lawyer in arbitration is minor compared with litigation. Moreover, most employers are willing to agree not to bring a lawyer to the hearing if the employee agrees to the same, because this will substantially reduce the employer's legal fees.[68]

Arbitration thus provides access to a forum for adjudicating employment disputes for employees whom the litigation system has failed.[69] Procedural rights, such as the right to trial by jury, extensive (and often excessive) discovery, and formal rules of procedure and evidence, mean little to employees who cannot find an attorney to take their case, and who, therefore, feel that the doors to justice are closed to them. Arbitration gives these employees a ready opportunity to have their claims heard.

4. Ecumenism

Litigation is nothing if not adversarial. As discussed above, it can take years to bring an employment dispute to trial. By that time, what may have started out as a misunderstanding or mistake that could have been remedied by reinstatement and a few thousand dollars in lost wages has turned into a battle of epic proportions. Perceptions of the parties and witnesses have been irreversibly colored and polarized by years of conflict.[70] Emotional and economic damages that were minimal or did not exist at the time the dispute arose have accumulated, compounded, and assumed an importance far out of proportion to the nature of the dispute.[71] Inexpensive and simple remedies, such as reinstatement and an apology, have become impossible.[72]

These are not inevitable features of any employment dispute. They are, however, the pervasive result of our adversarial system of litigation.[73] Although a discharged employee may be shocked and depressed, these feelings are unlikely to become either devastating or permanent unless the employee litigates her discharge. Litigation forces the employee to invest scores of hours and thousands of dollars in an entrenched legal position. With alienation from former coworkers, the employee loses an important part of her professional network. She becomes strongly focused on past wrongs at the expense of her present and future career. Litigation also can be emotionally traumatic. The years spent building mistrust and suspicion may affect permanently an employee's personality, making it difficult for her to maintain meaningful relationships or find and hold subsequent jobs. The time and emotional commitment required to pursue litigation forces the employee to place her personal and professional life on hold for years.[74]

Arbitration offers a way to avoid intractable confrontation. Because arbitration can be completed in months rather than years, the conflict can be resolved before the parties have drawn lines in the sand, and while relatively inexpensive remedies are still an option.[75] The informal nature of the process avoids forcing parties to stake out polar positions that later become difficult or impossible to retract. A comprehensive dispute resolution program, such as the one designed by Brown & Root and discussed in chapter 6, can result in the vast majority of employment disputes being settled by mutual agreement, avoiding direct confrontation entirely. The benefits to both employers and employees of resolving employment disputes in this way are as obvious as they are enormous.

C. Public Concerns

Thus far, this chapter has examined compulsory arbitration by comparing its relative effects on employers and employees. In addition to this calculus of the parties' private gains and losses, there is the broader issue of whether the public at large is well served by sanctioning compulsory arbitration as a method of resolving employment disputes. This section examines several aspects of that issue.

1. Employers' Imposition of Arbitration Agreements on Unwilling Employees

Compulsory employment arbitration agreements typically are drafted by employers, who then require their employees to sign the agreements as a condition of employment. The employees, often employed at-will, can reject the agreement by seeking employment elsewhere. However, the costs of doing so can be enormous for an employee with a significant amount of tenure invested in her current employer, or for an employee who, for any number of possible reasons, may have difficulty finding comparable employment. One might, therefore, legitimately ask companies such as Brown & Root what, if their dispute resolution program is as good as they claim, and if employees benefit from it and like it, would the company lose by making the arbitration agreement voluntary?

The argument that employee participation in employment arbitration programs should be voluntary can be made in two ways. First, one might argue that before a dispute arises employees should be given the choice of whether or not to sign an agreement to arbitrate future employment claims. Second, one might argue that an employer should not be permitted to ask an employee to sign an arbitration agreement until *after* a dispute has arisen.

a. Voluntary Predispute Arbitration Agreements

Permitting predispute arbitration agreements, but forbidding employers from demanding that employees sign them as a condition of employment, would not necessarily sound the death knell for compulsory arbitration. This approach still would allow employers to implement their arbitration programs all at once; the only difference from the way this usually is done now is that employees would be able to choose to sign the agreement rather than being confronted with a take-it-or-be-fired (or not hired) demand. The effect of this form of implementation, insofar as employees who elect to sign agreements are concerned, would be identical to that of an across-the-board mandatory approach: all employees who sign the agreement would be required to arbitrate, rather than litigate, any future employment claims. The crucial difference, from an employer's perspective, is that not all employees would be covered by the program, because they could choose not to participate.

Few employers have approached employment arbitration programs in this way. One possible reason for this relates to the up-front costs of designing a compulsory arbitration program. Employers might feel that if few employees voluntarily sign arbitration agreements, the employer savings in litigation costs will not offset the start-up costs of the program, and therefore will not be worth the employer's while to establish such a program. However, the costs of establishing a simple employment arbitration program—one that simply exchanges arbitration for litigation—is minimal, and involves little more than an attorney spending a few hours drafting an agreement, and a personnel manager or other management representative coordinating the employees' signing of individual agreements. While start-up costs for more extensive dispute resolution programs, such as the one designed by Brown & Root discussed in chapter 6, will be far higher, the benefit to employees of such a program is much greater. If the program is truly fair, the employer should expect a high level of voluntary employee participation.

Another possible reason why employers are unlikely to favor voluntary predispute arbitration agreements is the administrative convenience of instantly bringing all employees within the new program. A two-track dispute resolution system, one (involving arbitration) for employees willing to sign arbitration agreements and another (using the current litigative model) for other employees, could be difficult to administer, especially for employers using a multi-level comprehensive dispute resolution process such as that of Brown & Root. This argument is far less persuasive, however, when made by employers who seek simply to exchange the litigation forum for arbitration.

A third reason why employers might not favor voluntary predispute agreements is that employees may resent the perceived inequity when one worker signs an arbitration agreement while another, similarly situated, does not. Say, for instance, that two women, Rosita and Sally, work side-by-side on an assembly line, and that Rosita has elected to sign an arbitration agreement but Sally has not. Both were given undeservedly poor rankings on their last performance evaluation by their sexist male supervisor, and these low rankings caused them to be denied pay raises which they deserved. Rosita, in accordance with her arbitration agreement, takes her dispute to arbitration and, six weeks later, the arbitrator awards her a retroactive raise. Sally, however, is unable to find a lawyer to represent her because her damages are too small to justify the costs of a lawsuit. She is likely to resent Rosita's award and to expect, with some moral force, the company to give her a raise commensurate with Rosita's despite her having no contractual right to the benefits of arbitration. In other words, she wants the benefits of arbitration without having given up—as Rosita did —the right to sue.

Of course, this could go the other way as well. Say the supervisor asks both Rosita and Sally to have sex with him, then fires them when they refuse. Rosita arbitrates and gets reinstated (under a different supervisor) with back pay and $20,000 damages for emotional pain and suffering. Sally has little difficulty finding a lawyer for this case, files suit, and receives, on top of her back pay, a $1.2 million punitive damage award. Rosita—and every other employee of the company who elected to sign an arbitration agreement—will justifiably question whether they made the right decision.

A final reason why employers might disfavor voluntary implementation of predispute arbitration agreements is that the approach compromises arbitration's risk-management advantage to the employer. From an employer's perspective, one of the principal advantages of across-the-board employment arbitration is that it permits the employer to eliminate the risk of jackpot jury verdicts. Many, if not most, employers would prefer being exposed to more frequent arbitration awards that the company easily can afford to facing the possibility of even one catastrophically large jury award that could put the company out of business or on the front page of the *Wall Street Journal*. An across-the-board implementation of compulsory arbitration allows the company to all but guarantee that an employment lawsuit will not result in an award having this effect. Voluntary implementation of predispute arbitration reduces the risk of a catastrophic award only in proportion to the number of employees who voluntarily sign arbitration agreements, if in fact it reduces the risk even that much.[76]

For these reasons, very few employers that have adopted predispute employment arbitration programs have given employees the choice of whether to opt into the program. Even when employers do so, however, it questionable just how "voluntary" most programs are. It is not difficult to imagine an employer giving a new employee a stack of ten or fifteen employment documents to sign and only a few minutes to sign them.[77] Nor is it reasonable to assume that, even under the best of circumstances, more than a small percentage of employees will read and understand agreements they sign committing them to binding arbitration.[78] Instead, an employee usually signs the agreement with little or no thought of future employment law violations[79] or of what effect the agreement will have on obtaining redress for such a violation.

One possible solution is to require employers to explain fully to employees the consequences of signing a compulsory arbitration agreement. As discussed in chapter 7, the prudent employer will explain the agreement in writing, will recommend that the employee consult an attorney before signing the agreement, and will give the employee several days to consider the agreement before signing it—all to avoid the possibility that the employee later will claim that she did not understand what she was signing or did not understand that the agreement would cover a particular type of dispute she would prefer to litigate. At best, however, this is only a partial solution because most employees do not anticipate future employment disputes at the time they are hired.[80] They are unlikely to place as high a value on the rights they are waiving as they would if the agreement were presented to them after a dispute had arisen.[81] Compulsory arbitration may, therefore, be seen as "encouraging" employees to undervalue the rights that Congress or the courts considered sufficiently important to provide for judicial enforcement, even if the signing of the arbitration agreement is both informed and voluntary. This has led some commentators to suggest that employers should not be permitted to present employees with arbitration agreements until after a dispute has arisen.[82]

b. Voluntary Postdispute Arbitration Agreements

An obvious advantage to permitting only postdispute arbitration agreements is that doing so allows the parties to decide whether to arbitrate only after they fully appreciate the impact that decision will have on a concrete dispute. This advantage, however, also makes it very unlikely that the parties will agree to arbitrate their dispute. When a predispute agreement is signed, neither party knows whether, *ex ante,* they will prefer arbitration or litigation. If the future claim involves a large potential damage award and legal liability is relatively certain, it likely will be the employee who will favor litigation and the employer who will favor arbitration. Conversely, if the future claim involves a small potential damage award and legal liability is questionable, the employee probably will have an extremely difficult time finding legal counsel to represent her, at least on a contingency basis, and therefore probably will favor arbitration over litigation. If employees sign a predispute arbitration agreement with full knowledge of the consequences of doing so, it is because the benefits of arbitration plus the benefits of getting a job with, or remaining employed by, a particular employer exceed those of retaining the right to litigate a future employment dispute.

Assume, for example, that Rosita and Sally, on their first day of work for Megacorp, each were given a copy of Megacorp's employment arbitration agreement and were told that they had a week to sign and return it. Each took it to an attorney, who explained to them the consequences of signing the agreement. Each decided that the benefits of arbitration plus the benefits of employment with Megacorp outweighed any they might have by retaining their risk to sue, and decided to sign the agreement.

A year later, Rosita is fired for not having sex with her supervisor and Sally is discriminatorily denied a pay raise. Other things being equal, Sally probably will be happy to go to arbitration, while Rosita probably would much rather litigate her claim. However, because both Rosita and Sally have signed arbitration agreements, both must take their claims to arbitration.

Change the facts, however, and assume that neither Rosita nor Sally signed predispute arbitration agreements, and that the law only permits Megacorp to present employees with an arbitration agreement after a dispute has arisen. Megacorp almost certainly will never offer Sally an arbitration agreement because the company knows that Sally will have a difficult time finding a lawyer to pursue her claim. Megacorp, therefore, would prefer to confine Sally's options to litigation, knowing that she probably will be unable to pursue her claim in the courts. Similarly, if Megacorp offers Rosita an arbitration agreement, she rationally will refuse to sign it, knowing that the nature of her claim makes it likely that she will do better in litigation than arbitration. This demonstrates that, even if predispute arbitration agreements are rational for both parties, postdispute arbitration agreements likely will be irrational for at least one party, and therefore probably will not be signed. Once the cards are on the table and it is clear who will win and who will lose by going to arbitration, agreement becomes extremely unlikely.

This phenomenon also explains why such a large proportion of compulsory employment arbitration cases involve employer attempts to enforce arbitration agreements against employees who clearly would prefer to stay in court. An employer that, after a dispute has arisen, discovers that an arbitration agreement will benefit an employee in that particular dispute, cannot easily challenge the arbitration agreement in court. Since the employer almost certainly drafted the agreement, and is the party with the greater bargaining power, a court is not likely to permit the employer to avoid the effects of its own agreement. More importantly, the employer wants to be able to enforce the arbitration agreement in the next case, when arbitration might have the effect of benefitting the company. Because the employer is a repeat player in the arbitration game, and by virtue of its having adopted a compulsory arbitration program after calculating that over time it benefits more from arbitration than litigation, the employer does not want to do anything that might jeopardize future enforceability of its arbitration agreements. A judicial decision that an arbitration agreement is unenforceable in one case makes it more likely that the agreement will not be enforced in the next case.

An employee, however, is unlikely to be a repeat player in the arbitration game, and has little stake in whether the employee's arbitration agreement is enforced over time. If, after a dispute has arisen, she discovers that it benefits her to take her claim to arbitration, she will arbitrate her case quietly and happily without challenging the arbitration agreement in court. If, however, she discovers after the dispute has arisen that her prospects are better in litigation than arbitration, she has an incentive to challenge the arbitration agreement. Thus it is not accurate to infer, from the mere fact that most reported arbitration cases are brought by employees seeking to avoid arbitration, that arbitration inherently favors employers over employees. Rather, this effect stems from the fact that employers, but not employees, have a strong disincentive to avoid the effects of the arbitration agreement when it is to their advantage to do so in one particular case.

A rational employee will challenge an arbitration agreement in court whenever the advantage to be gained by litigating, multiplied by the probability of successfully avoiding arbitration, exceeds the costs of attempting to avoid arbitration. For example, if it costs $2,000 to file a lawsuit and oppose an employer's motion to compel arbitration, and the probability that the employee will convince the judge to deny the employer's motion and let the employee litigate her case is twenty percent, then a rational employee will challenge an arbitration agreement in court any time she believes that the advantage to be gained by arbitrating instead of litigating exceeds $10,000.

This may help explain why judges are so reluctant to allow arbitration agreements to be successfully challenged in court. The costs of judicially challenging on employment arbitration agreement are likely to be relatively uniform and relatively low—a few hundred dollars in filing fees to file the lawsuit, a few thousand dollars in attorneys' fees (at most) to draft a complaint, and a few thousand dollars (at most) to respond to the employer's motion to compel. The advantage to be gained by litigating rather than arbitrating may be huge in certain cases, particularly if the facts create the significant possibility of a punitive damage award. Under these circumstances, judicial challenges to arbitration agreements will be fairly common unless the probability of those challenges succeeding is extremely low.

Frequent judicial refusals to enforce arbitration agreements would have two effects. First, by increasing the number of judicial challenges, it would destroy or significantly diminish the advantages arbitration offers even in cases where the arbitration agreement ultimately is enforced. A dispute cannot be resolved within weeks if the parties first must wait six months to a year for a judge to rule on a motion to compel. Second, it would tend to give employees the benefit of the arbitration agreement without requiring them to assume the risks. An employee who easily and successfully can challenge arbitration agreements on the basis of, for example, unequal bargaining power, is for all practical purposes given the opportunity to "cherry pick" her forum—to go to arbitration when it benefits her, and otherwise to go to court. It would not be fair to allow employees to void an arbitration agreement simply because they discovered *ex post* that it did not operate to their benefit. A gamble is not unfair merely because the gambler loses. In any event, employers are not likely to agree to arbitration under these circumstances.

This is not to say, however, that courts should hesitate to strike employment arbitration agreements that are unfair to employees. Employers should be put on notice that courts will not enforce such agreements, and that employers adopt them at their own peril. On the other hand, if the advantages of arbitration are to be realized to their fullest potential, it must be equally clear that fair agreements universally will be enforced.

2. Proper Enforcement of Civil Rights Laws

As discussed in chapter 7, many employment rights, particularly those conferred by statute, were designed not only to benefit employees privately, but also to achieve public ends, such as the elimination of employment discrimination. Many commentators have argued that this "public interest" aspect of statutory rights interpretation and application provides a strong argument for returning the enforcement of those rights to public tribunals.[83] By itself, however, this is not much of an argument against compulsory arbitration. If arbitration results in the proper enforcement of statutory employment rights, then the public interest has been vindicated, regardless of whether the forum is public or private. In fact, by giving low-income employees access to an adjudicatory forum that currently is unavailable to them, arbitration may serve the public interest in a way that litigation cannot.

The public interest involves more than merely ensuring that violators are punished and victims are made whole. The broader public interest consists of insuring, at the least possible cost, that employment laws are not violated. Employers are discouraged from engaging in unlawful employment practices not only by the possibility that they will be ordered (by judge, jury, or arbitrator) to pay large damage awards, but also by the stigma that attaches to an employer who is publicly branded a discriminator. Whereas judicial decisions are available to the public and may even be reported in the popular press when the conduct is particularly egregious or widespread, or the damage award is particularly large, arbitration is confidential, and few people other than the parties involved likely will know the outcome of a given case.[84]

Publicity from employment cases has several effects, all of which tend to increase the effectiveness of the employment laws. First, it discourages publicity-conscious employers from engaging in unlawful behavior. Second, it educates both employers and employees about what is, and what is not, legal behavior in the workplace. Finally, it serves as a constant reminder that we, as a society, do not tolerate conduct such as invidious discrimination in the workplace. Every case reported in the popular media reminds employees that they have certain rights that society considers important, that employers are required to respect, and for which the law provides a remedy if those rights are not respected.

3. Prospects for Abuse by Employers

As discussed earlier in this chapter, the right to a legal remedy may be chimerical if the employee's only option is litigation and the employee is unable to find a lawyer to pursue her claim. While arbitration can minimize this problem, it also presents a different problem which can result in the nonenforcement of employment rights. Because arbitration is a private dispute resolution system designed by employers, these same employers are able to abuse the system by requiring employees to sign away their substantive employment rights. The case law abounds with examples of employers taking this approach, such as the example of Pony Express Courier Corp. in chapter 1. Fortunately, most of those cases end with the courts' refusing to enforce the agreement or issuing an injunction requiring the employer to withdraw the agreement. Courts are not equipped, however, to scrutinize arbitration agreements drafted by every employer in this country.

Employers should take their cues from these cases and make certain that arbitration agreements are scrupulously fair to employees. Employers should avoid all temptations to overreach by making certain they do not unduly restrict employee access to discovery, skew the process of selecting arbitrators, or limit the arbitrator's ability to award relief. Adhering to the suggestions made in chapter 9 will help ensure that employees are treated fairly and that the agreement is enforced.[85]

Compulsory employment arbitration offers tremendous benefits to both employers and employees. It can reduce significantly the costs and time involved in resolving disputes. It also provides a forum for adjudicating grievances to employees currently shut out of the litigation system. Finally, it presents an opportunity for parties to resolve their differences in a way that promotes, rather than discourages, maintaining the employment relationship.

With this opportunity, however, comes the risk that employers will abuse arbitration by using it to eviscerate employees' statutory employment rights. Some employers already have tried to do this by, for example, conditioning their employees' continued employment on signing an agreement that not only provides for dispute resolution by arbitration, but also purports to waive employees' rights to discovery or the recovery of certain types of damages. In judicial challenges to such lopsided agreements, courts appropriately have refused to enforce them. Courts have, however, enforced agreements which, though less lopsided, nonetheless disproportionately favor employers, such as in the securities industry where an employer organization controls the selection of arbitrators. Such enforcement exemplifies a strong judicial policy favoring arbitration, and is one indication that compulsory employment arbitration probably is here to stay.

Employment arbitration is not, however, a panacea for disputes arising within the nonunionized workplace. The dangers of employer abuse require courts to be vigilant in ensuring that arbitration agreements do not become a vehicle for eliminating employees' legal protections. Nonetheless, given the litigation system's current inability to provide any meaningful forum to so many employees who feel that they have suffered legal wrongs in the workplace, compulsory arbitration, properly implemented, can be a significant improvement over litigation.

Notes

Chapter One. An Introduction to Employment Arbitration

1. *Take This Job and . . . Promise Not to Sue*, SACRAMENTO BEE, July 7, 1996, at E1; *Securities Regulators Keep Sex Bias Cases under Wraps*, TAMPA TRIBUNE, June 23, 1996, at 1; Tom Lowry, *Can Wall Street Police Itself? Harassment Case Points Up Secrecy*, USA TODAY, May 23, 1996, at 5B; Jill Hodges, *EEOC Argues against Hubbard Policy; Race Discrimination Suit Questions KSTP-TV's Employment Agreement*, STAR TRIBUNE, May 18, 1996, at 1D; Ted Wendling, *Judge Says Employer Can Require Arbitration*, CLEVELAND PLAIN DEALER, March 15, 1996, at 3B; Maria Scao, *The New Face of Justice: Arbitration, Mediation, and Other Forms of Private Legal Resolution Are Now a Mainstream Alternative to the Public Justice System*, THE BOSTON GLOBE, Feb. 18, 1996, at 87.

2. Marshall W. Grate, *Binding Arbitration of Statutory Employment Discrimination Claims*, 70 U. DET.-MERCY L. REV. 698, 719 (1993).

3. Richard A. Bales and Reagan Burch, *The Future of Employment Arbitration in the Non-Union Sector*, 45 LAB. L.J. 627, 635 (1994).

4. Ronald Turner, *Compulsory Arbitration of Employment Discrimination Claims with Special Reference to the 3 A's—Access, Adjudication and Acceptability*, 31 WAKE FOREST L. REV. 231, 294 (1996).

5. Pub. L. No. 102–66, 105 Stat. 1071, 1081 (codified in scattered sections of 42 U.S.C.).

6. 42 U.S.C. § 118.

7. See chapter 4.

8. *See, e.g.,* DeGaetano v. Smith Barney, Inc., 70 Fair Employ. Prac. Cas. (BNA) 401 (S.D.N.Y. 1996).

9. 500 U.S. 20 (1991).

10. William M. Howard, *Arbitrating Employment Discrimination Claims: Do You Really Have To? Do You Really Want To?*, 43 DRAKE L. REV. 255, 255 (1994); Stephen J. Ware, *Employment Arbitration and Voluntary Consent*, 25 HOFSTRA L. REV. 84, 100 (noting that since *Gilmer*, "more employers have begun to insist upon arbitration agreements as a condition of employment.").

11. *Big Companies Use ADR for Worker Cases: Factfinding Most Popular, GAO Study Finds*, 13 ALTERNATIVES TO HIGH COST LITIG. 127, 128 (1995).

12. E. Patrick McDermott, *Survey of 92 Key Companies: Using ADR to Settle Employment Disputes*, 50 DISP. RESOL. J. 8 (1995).

13. *Take This Job, supra* note 1, at E1.

14. Dun & Bradstreet Information Services, *Dun's Million Dollar Disc Plus* (3d Q. 1996).

15. Pony Express Courier Corp. v. Morris, 921 S.W.2d 817, 819 (Tex. App.—San Antonio 1986, n.w.h.). On December 6, 1996, the author telephoned Richard Taylor, Pony Express's human resources manager, to enquire about the company's employment arbitration policy. Mr. Taylor stated that each of the company's employees has the policy "in

fine print somewhere, but it [the policy] is never enforced. I really can't tell you any more about it than that." Mr. Taylor refused to answer any further questions. His averment that the policy is never enforced is belied by the case cited above, in which the company attempted to enforce the arbitration agreement against a warehouse worker in San Antonio, Texas, who alleged she had been discriminated against on the basis of sex and sexually harassed.

16. *Model Termination Act Would Improve Remedies Available to Fired Employees,* St. Antoine Says, DAILY LAB. REP. (BNA) No. 94, at A-2 (May 14, 1992); Randall Samborn, *At-will Doctrine under Fire,* NAT'L L.J., Oct. 14, 1991, at 40. For general discussions of the META, see Theodore J. St. Antoine, *The Making of the Model Employment Termination Act,* 69 WASH. L. REV. 361 (1994); Theodore J. St. Antoine, *Employment-at-will—Is the Model Act the Answer?* 23 STETSON L. REV. 179 (1993).

17. Model Employment Termination Act § 3(a)-(b)(1991), 7A U.L.A. 71 (Supp. 1995).

18. *Id.*

19. Andrew Leigh, *States May Change Rules for Fired Workers' Rights,* INVESTOR'S BUS. DAILY, Jan. 3, 1992, at 8.

20. *See, e.g.,* law review articles cited in Richard A. Bales, *Compulsory Arbitration of Employment Claims: A Practical Guide to Designing and Implementing Enforceable Agreements,* 47 BAYLOR L. REV. 591, 593–94 n. 14 (1995)(hereinafter *"Compulsory Arbitration"*); *see also* Margaret A. Jacobs, *Riding Crop and Slurs: How Wall Street Dealt with a Sex-Bias Case,* WALL ST. J., June 9, 1994, at A-1; John W. Zinsser, *Employment Dispute Resolution Systems: Experience Grows but Some Questions Persist,* 12 NEGOTIATION J. 151, 158 (1996).

21. Chappell, *Arbitrate . . . and Avoid Stomach Ulcers,* 2 ARB. MAG., Nos. 11–12, 6, 7 (1944); *see also* Gates v. Arizona Brewing Co., 95 P.2d 49, 50 (Ariz. 1939); Stockwell v. Equitable F. & M. Ins. Co., 134 Cal. App. 534, 25 P.2d 873 (3d Dist. 1933). One court has stated that a true arbitration agreement contains the following five elements: (1) a third-party decisionmaker, (2) a mechanism for ensuring neutrality with respect to the rendering of the decision, (3) a decisionmaker chosen by the parties, (4) an opportunity for both parties to be heard, and (5) a binding decision. Cheng-Canindin v. Renaissance Hotel Associates, 50 Cal. App. 4th 676, 684, 57 Cal. Rptr.2d 867, 872 (Cal. App. 1 Dist. 1996).

22. Originally, "compulsory arbitration" referred to arbitration that was imposed on the parties by operation of law. *See, e.g.,* Herbert Roof Northrup, COMPULSORY ARBITRATION AND GOVERNMENT INTERVENTION IN LABOR DISPUTES: AN ANALYSIS OF EXPERIENCE, 9–50 (Labor Policy Association ed., 1966); Jere S. Williams, *The Compulsory Settlement of Contract Negotiation Labor Disputes,* 27 TEX. L. REV. 587 (1949); *Should the Federal Government Require Arbitration of Labor Disputes in All Basic American Industries?,* 26 CONG. DIG. 193, 195 (1947). Recently, however, the phrase has been used, as it is in this book, to refer to prospective arbitration agreements between employers and employees. *See Compulsory Arbitration, supra* note 20, at 594.

23. Mitsubishi Motors Corp. v. Soler Chrysler-Plymouth, Inc., 473 U.S. 614, 628 (1985)(stating that by agreeing to arbitrate, a party "does not forego the substantive rights," but "only submits to their resolution in an arbitral, rather than a judicial form.").

24. For discussions of the at-will rule, see Jay M. Feinman, *The Development of the Employment at-Will Rule,* 20 AM.. & J. LEGAL HIST. 118 (1976); Mayer G. Freed and Daniel Polsby, *The Doubtful Providence of "Wood's Rule" Revisited,* 22 ARIZ. ST. L.J. 551

(1990); Jay M. Feinman, *The Development of the Employment-at-Will Revisited,* 23 ARIZ. ST. L.J. 733 (1991).

25. *But see* Jean R. Sternlight, *Panacea or Corporate Tool?: Debunking the Supreme Court's Preference for Binding Arbitration,* 74 WASH. U. L. Q., 637 (1996)(arguing that arbitration profoundly affects substantive rights).

26. 42 U.S.C. § 2000e-2 (a)(1994).

27. 42 U.S.C. § 1981A (b)(1994).

28. *See, e.g.,* Perry A. Zirkel and J. Gary Lutz, *Characteristics and Functions of Mediators: A Pilot Study,* 36 ARB. J. 15 (1981); Lon L. Fuller, *Mediation—Its Forms and Functions,* 44 S.CAL. L. REV. 305 (1971); William E. Simkin, MEDIATION AND THE DYNAMICS OF COLLECTIVE BARGAINING (1971).

29. These circumstances are discussed in chapter 9.

30. 1 Kings, 3:16–28 (King James).

31. Robin Lane Fox, THE SEARCH FOR ALEXANDER, 113–14 (1980).

32. AAA, ARBITRATION NEWS, 2 (1963).

33. See chapter 2, part A.

34. William M. Howard, *The Evolution of Contractually Mandated Arbitration,* 48 ARB. J. 27, 28 (1993); Daniel E. Murray, *Arbitration in the Anglo-Saxon and Early Norman Periods,* 16 ARB. J. 193 (1961).

35. Frances Kellor, ARBITRATION AND THE LEGAL PROFESSION: A REPORT PREPARED FOR THE SURVEY OF THE LEGAL PROFESSION (1952).

36. John P. McMahon, *Implementation of the U.N. Convention on Foreign Arbitral Awards in the U.S.,* 26 ARB. J. 65 (1971); *see also* Scherk v. Alberto-Culver Co., 94 S. Ct. 2449 (1974).

37. Lolita Browning, *Olympics '96: Is There an Arbitrator in the House?* TEXAS LAWYER, July 22, 1996, at 6.

38. For the historical development of labor arbitration in the United States, see Dennis R. Nolan and Roger I. Abrams, *American Labor Arbitration: The Early Years,* 35 U. FLA. L. REV. 373 (1983); Robben Wright Fleming, THE LABOR ARBITRATION PROCESS, 1–30 (1965); Edwin Emil Witte, HISTORICAL SURVEY OF LABOR ARBITRATION (1952); E. L. Oliver, *The Arbitration of Labor Disputes,* 83 U. PA. L. REV. 206 (1934).

39. Richard A. Bales, *A New Direction for American Labor Law: Individual Autonomy and the Compulsory Arbitration of Individual Employment Rights,* 30 HOU. L. REV. 1864, 1875–78 (1994).

40. Jesse Freidin and Francis S. Ulman, *Arbitration and the War Labor Board,* 58 HARV. L. REV. 309 (1945).

41. The President's National Labor-Management Conference, Nov. 5–30, 1945 (U.S. Dept. of Labor, Div. of Labor Standards, Bull. No. 77, 1946), 42–43.

42. United Steelworkers of Am. v. American Mfg. Co., 363 U.S. 564 (1960)(holding that arbitrators, not courts, should decide the arbitrability of grievances); United Steelworkers of Am. v. Warrior & Gulf Navigation Co., 363 U.S. 574 (1960)(holding that courts should refuse to order a grievance to arbitration only if the collective bargaining agreement's arbitration clause cannot be interpreted to cover the dispute); United Steelworkers of Am. v. Enterprise Wheel & Car Corp., 363 U.S. 593 (1960)(holding that courts should not review the merits of an arbitrator's award so long as the award "draws its essence" from the collective bargaining agreement).

43. See chapter 2, part D.

44. *See, e.g.,* Katherine Van Wezel Stone, *The Legacy of Industrial Pluralism: The Ten-*

sion between Individual Employment Rights and the New Deal Collective Bargaining System, 59 U. CHI. L. REV. 575, 578–84 (1992).

45. Michael Goldfield, THE DECLINE OF ORGANIZED LABOR IN THE UNITED STATES, 10 (1987).

46. *Data for 1994 Shows Membership Held Steady at 16.7 Million,* DAILY LAB. REP. (BNA) No. 27, at D-1 (Feb. 9, 1995).

47. *Id.*

48. *See Union Coverage of U.S. Private Workforce Predicted to Fall Below 5 Percent By 2000,* DAILY LAB. REP. (BNA) No. 241 (Dec. 18, 1989), at A-1.

49. *See* Stone, *supra* note 44, at 588–93.

50. 1 Arthur Larson, WORKMEN'S COMPENSATION LAW, § 5.30 (1994).

51. *Id.* at § 4.50.

52. *See* 29 U.S.C. §§ 201–19 (1994).

53. *See* J. Joseph Huthmacher, SENATOR ROBERT F. WAGNER AND THE RISE OF URBAN LIBERALISM, 203–04 (1968)(noting that, according to Senator Wagner, the fixing of minimum wages and maximum hours was merely a foundation for future efforts of labor and industry to work out their conflicts and problems among themselves); *see also* Clyde W. Summers, *Labor Law as the Century Turns: A Changing of the Guard,* 67 NEB. L. REV. 7, 9 (1989)(noting that the FLSA was intended to support collective bargaining).

54. *See* 29 U.S.C. § 206(d)(1994).

55. 42 U.S.C. § 2000e-2 (1994).

56. 29 U.S.C. §§ 621–34 (1994)(prohibiting workplace discrimination on the basis of age).

57. *Id.* §§ 651–78 (setting guidelines for workplace safety).

58. *Id.* §§701–961 (providing equal opportunities to individuals with disabilities).

59. *Id.* §§ 1001–1461 (protecting employee pension benefits).

60. 42 U.S.C. § 2000e(k)(1994)(prohibiting workplace discrimination on the basis of pregnancy, childbirth, and related medical conditions).

61. 5 U.S.C. §§ 1101–8913 (1994).

62. 29 U.S.C. §§ 2001–09 (1994)(prohibiting the use of lie detectors and polygraphs in the workplace except under narrowly specified conditions).

63. *Id.* §§ 2101–09 (requiring notice to employees before plant closings and mass layoffs).

64. 42 U.S.C. §§ 12101–213 (1994)(prohibiting discrimination in employment on the basis of disability).

65. *Id.* § 1981a (providing for damages in cases of intentional discrimination in employment).

66. 29 U.S.C. § 2601 (1994)(allowing employees to take leave for family and medical emergencies).

67. *See* Charles C. Heckscher, THE NEW UNIONISM: EMPLOYEE INVOLVEMENT IN THE CHANGING CORPORATION, 160 (1988)(noting that state laws in some jurisdictions protect employees from discrimination based on sexual orientation, political involvement, marital status, medical condition, and criminal records).

68. For general discussions of whistle-blowers, see Stewart J. Schwab, *Wrongful Discharge Law and the Search for Third-Party Effects,* 74 TEX. L. REV. 1943, 1966–72 (1996).

69. Stone, *supra* note 44, at 592 (citing *Individual Employment Rights Manual,* 9A LAB. REL. REP. (BNA) 540–92 (1991)).

70. *See, e.g.,* Scott G. Cairns and Carolyn V. Grady, *Drug Testing in the Workplace:*

A Reasoned Approach for Private Employers, 12 GEO. MASON U. L. REV. 491, 520–30 (1990)(recognizing private employers' use of drug testing and discussing statutory limits such as requirements of probable cause, confidentiality, and notice); Judith M. Janssen, *Substance Abuse Testing and the Workplace: A Private Employer's Perspective,* 12 GEO. MASON U. L. REV. 611, 636–39 (1990)(citing examples of state laws limiting drug and alcohol testing by private employers).

71. *See* Joleane Dutzman, Comment, *State Criminal Prosecutions: Putting Teeth in the Occupational Safety and Health Act,* 12 GEO. MASON U. L. REV. 737, 738–39 (1990)(noting the recent use of criminal penalties to supplement OSHA and enforce health and safety mandates); S. Douglas Jones, Comment, *State Prosecutions for Safety-Related Crimes in the Workplace: Can D.A.'s Succeed Where OSHA Failed?,* 79 KY. L.J. 139, 14–47 (1990–91)(discussing the increasing use of state criminal prosecutions to enforce workplace safety requirements).

72. *See, e.g.,* Katherine Van Wezel Stone, *Employees as Stakeholders under State Non-shareholder Constituency Statutes,* 21 STETSON L. REV. 45, 45–47 (1991)(discussing non-shareholder constituency statutes, which create fiduciary duties on the part of corporate directors toward those other than shareholders). For examples of such statutes, see *Appendix,* 21 STETSON L. REV. 279, 279–93 (1991).

73. MONT. CODE ANN. §§ 39-2-901 to -915 (1993)(prohibiting discharge of an employee in retaliation for the employee's refusal to violate public policy, for reporting a violation of public policy, in violation of express provisions of employer's personnel manual, or without good cause after completion of employee's probationary period).

74. P.R. LAWS ANN. tit. 29, § 185a (1985 & Supp. 1990)(providing indemnity for workers dismissed without good cause).

75. V.I. CODE ANN. tit. 24, § 65 (1993)(protecting employees from wrongful discharge).

76. Summers, *supra* note 53, at 13.

77. *Id.* at 13–14; *see, e.g.,* Toussaint v. Blue Cross & Blue Shield, 292 N.W.2d 880, 892 (Mich. 1980)(holding that employer statements of policy, such as personnel manuals, can give rise to contractual rights in employees).

78. Summers, *supra* note 53, at 13; *see, e.g.,* Foley v. Interactive Data Corp., 765 P.2d 373, 398 (Cal. 1988); Fortune v. National Cash Register Co., 364 N.E.2d 1251, 1256–57 (Mass. 1977).

79. *See, e.g.,* Ohanian v. Avis Rent A Car Sys., Inc., 779 F.2d 101, 103–04 (2d Cir. 1985).

80. Pugh v. See's Candies, Inc., 171 Cal. Rptr. 917, 925–27 (Cal. Ct. App. 1981).

81. Summers, *supra* note 53, at 13; *see also* Schwab, *supra* note 68.

82. *See, e.g.,* Wagenseller v. Scottsdale Memorial Hosp., 710 P.2d 1025, 1035 (Ariz. 1985); Phipps v. Clark Oil & Ref. Corp., 396 N.W.2d 588, 592–94 (Minn. Ct. App. 1986), *aff'd,* 408 N.W.2d 569 (Minn. 1987).

83. *See, e.g.,* Frampton v. Central Ind. Gas Co., 297 N.E.2d 425, 428 (Ind. 1973).

84. *See, e.g.,* Palmateer v. International Harvester Co., 421 N.E.2d 876, 879–81 (Ill. 1981); Nees v. Hocks, 536 P.2d 512, 516 (Or. 1975).

85. *See, e.g.,* Wilson v. Monarch Paper Co., 939 F.2d 1138, 1139–41 (5th Cir. 1991).

86. For general discussions concerning individual rights, see *New Direction, supra,* note 32, at 1874–81; Dennis P. Duffy, *Intentional Infliction of Emotional Distress and Employment at Will: The Case against "Tortification" of Labor and Employment Law,* 74 B.U. L. REV. 387, 421–27 (1994); Robert J. Rabin, *The Role of Unions in the Rights-Based*

Workplace, 25 U.S.F. L. Rev. 169, 174–87 (1991); Stone, *supra* note 44, at 584–93; Summers, *supra* note 53, at 11–14 (1988).

87. The EEOC currently has a backlog of almost 88,000 claims, 99.5 percent of which it will not litigate on behalf of the claimant. U.S. GAO Report, EEOC's Expanding Workload: Increases in Age Discrimination and Other Changes Call for a New Approach, GAO/HEHS-94-32, at 13 (February 9, 1994).

88. *New Direction, supra* note 32, at 1879–80.

89. Clark Kerr, *More Peace—More Conflict,* Proceedings of the 28th Annual Meeting of NA 8, 14 (1976).

90. *See* Sarah Rudolph Cole, *Incentives and Arbitration: The Case Against Enforcement of Executory Arbitration Agreements between Employers and Employees,* 64 U.M.K.C. L. Rev. 449, 449 (1996).

91. *See* Bales and Burch, *supra* note 3, at 627, 633.

92. *See* chapter 8.

93. *See* Duffy, *supra* note 86, at 423; William B. Gould, IV, *Stemming the Wrongful Discharge Tide: A Case for Arbitration,* 13 Employee Rel. L.J. 404, 413–14 (1988); Eric Schnapper, *Advocates Deterred by Fee Issues,* Nat'l L.J. , Mar. 28, 1994, at C1.

94. See chapter 6.

95. *See* Margaret A. Jacobs, *Rulings Show Judges Are Growing Skeptical of Mandatory Arbitration,* Wall St. J., Dec. 22, 1994, at B2.

96. 9 U.S.C. §§ 1–16 (1994).

Chapter Two. The Emergence of Compulsory Arbitration

1. Vynior's Case, 8 Coke 81 b; Kill v. Hollister, 95 Eng. Rep. 532 (K.B. 1746); Oregon & W. Mortgage Sav. Bank v. American Mortg. Co., 35 F. 2, 23 (C.C.D. Or. 1888); Allen v. Watson, 16 Johns 205; Jones v. Harris, 59 Miss. 214.

2. *Oregon & W. Mortgage,* 35 F. at 23; Waters v. Taylor, 15 Ves. Jr. 10; Harcourt v. Ramsbottom, 1 Jac. & Walk 505; *see also* Atlantic Fruit Co. v. Red Cross Line, 276 F. 319, 321 (S.D.N.Y. 1921).

3. Scott v. Avery, 4 H. L. Cas. 811; *see also* Kulukundis Shipping Co. v. Amtor Trading Corp., 126 F.2d 978 (2d Cir. 1942)(concluding that judicial suspicion of arbitration originated as a means of protecting judges' incomes).

4. 52, 53 Vict. Ch. 49.

5. Austrian Lloyd Co. v. Gresham Society, 1 K. B. 249 (1903); Manchester Ship Canal Co. v. Pierson & Son, 2 Q. B. 606 (1900).

6. *See, e.g.,* Insurance Co. v. Morse, 87 U.S. 445, 453 (1874); Doyle v. Continental Ins. Co., 94 U.S. 535, 538 (1876); Perkins v. United States Elec. Light Co., 16 F. 513 (C.C., S.D.N.Y., undated). Some courts held that while an agreement to arbitrate liability was invalid and unenforceable, an agreement to arbitrate damages, even when made a precondition to civil suit, was valid and enforceable. *See, e.g.,* Hamilton v. Home Ins. Co., 137 U.S. 370, 383–87 (1890); Hamilton v. Liverpool & London & Globe Ins. Co., 136 U.S. 242, 255–57 (1890).

7. 222 F. 1006 (S.D.N.Y. 1915).

8. *Id.* at 1011 (noting the absence of a statute validating arbitration agreements that would "modernize" the ideas of judges).

9. *Id.* at 1007 (stating that "a more unworthy genesis [of the rule permitting unilateral revocation of arbitration agreements] cannot be imagined"), 1012 (implying that the Court could not find convincing reasons for application of the rule), 1009 ("Yet it is surely a

singular view of judicial sanctity which reasons that, because the Legislature has made a court, therefore everybody must go to the court.").

10. *Id.* at 1010–11.

11. *Proceedings of the American Bar Association,* 45 A.B.A. Rep. 19, 75 (1920).

12. *See* Note, Erie, Bernhardt, *and Section 2 of the United States Arbitration Act: A Farrago of Rights, Remedies, and a Right to a Remedy,* 69 YALE L.J. 847, 854 n.41 (1960).

13. Gilmer v. Interstate/Johnson Lane Corp., 500 U.S. 20, 24 (1991).

14. 43 Stat. 883 (1925).

15. 9 U.S.C. §§ 1–16 (1994).

16. *Id.*

17. Moses H. Cone Memorial Hosp. v. Mercury Constr. Corp., 460 U.S. 1, 25 n.32 (1983); Robert Lawrence Co. v. Devonshire Fabrics, Inc., 271 F.2d 402, 408 (2d Cir. 1959).

18. *Moses H. Cone,* 460 U.S. at 24; Southland Corp. v. Keating, 465 U.S. 1, 10 (1984).

19. This issue is discussed in chapter 4.

20. 346 U.S. 427 (1953).

21. 15 U.S.C. § 77 (1994).

22. *Wilko,* 346 U.S. at 430–35.

23. 15 U.S.C. § 77N (1994).

24. *Wilko,* 346 U.S. at 435.

25. *See, e.g.,* American Safety Equip. Corp. v. J.P. Maguire & Co., 391 F.2d 821, 827 (2d Cir. 1968); Hunt v. Mobil Oil Corp., 444 F. Supp. 68, 70–71 (S.D.N.Y. 1977).

26. United Steelworkers of Am. v. Warrior & Gulf Navigation Co., 363 U.S. 574, 582 (1960); United Steelworkers of Am. v. Enterprise Wheel & Car Corp., 363 U.S. 593, 597 (1960); United Steelworkers of Am. v. American Mfg. Co., 363 U.S. 564 (1960).

27. Textile Workers Union v. Lincoln Mills, 353 U.S. 448 (1957)(discussed in chapter 3).

28. 29 U.S.C. § 185 (1994).

29. *American Mfg. Co.,* 363 U.S. at 567–68.

30. *Warrior & Gulf Navigation,* 363 U.S. at 582–83.

31. *Enterprise Wheel,* 363 U.S. at 597.

32. *See* R. Bales, *A New Direction for American Labor Law: Individual Autonomy and the Compulsory Arbitration of Individual Employment Rights,* 30 Hous. L. Rev. 1863, 1867–71 (1994); Note, *Arbitration After Communications Workers: A Diminished Role?,* 100 Harv. L. Rev. 1307, 1309 (1987).

33. *See* 29 U.S.C. §§ 151–66 (1994).

34. *See* Mark Barenberg, *The Political Economy of the Wagner Act: Power, Symbol, and Workplace Cooperation,* 106 Harv. L. Rev. 1379, 1423 (1993)(stating that "while the diminished bargaining power of individual workers vitiated the normative force of their voluntary choice to submit to the authority of the large-scale enterprise, collective bargaining would empower workers sufficiently to cleanse that choice of duress"); Harry Shulman, *Reason, Contract, and Law in Labor Relations,* 68 Harv. L. Rev. 999, 1000 (1995)(explaining that the NLRA established a "bare legal framework that is hardly an encroachment on the premise that wages and other conditions of employment be left to autonomous determination by employers and labor"); *see also* 29 U.S.C. § 151 (1988)(citing the "inequality of bargaining power" between centralized employers and employees "who do not possess full freedom of association or actual liberty of contract" as a reason that the NLRA was needed); 78 Cong. Rec. 3678 (1934)(statement of Sen. Wagner), reprinted in 1

LEGISLATIVE HISTORY OF THE NATIONAL LABOR RELATIONS ACT 1935, at 20 (1949)(arguing that there must be equality of bargaining power that is accomplished through the employees' right to participate in collective bargaining).

35. John R. Commons and John B. Andrews, PRINCIPLES OF LABOR LEGISLATION 43 (4th rev. ed. 1936)(stating that employees are empowered by collective bargaining and minimum wage laws that create equal bargaining power between employees and their employer).

36. David E. Feller, *A General Theory of the Collective Bargaining Agreement*, 61 CAL. L. REV. 663, 742 (1973)(noting that "the enforcement mechanism . . . is the essence of the industrial collective bargaining agreement" assuming that both labor and management comply with the jointly agreed rules).

37. *See Warrior & Gulf Navigation*, 363 U.S. at 580 (noting that "[a] collective bargaining agreement is an effort to erect a system of industrial self-government").

38. *See* Clinton S. Golden and Harold J. Ruttenberg, THE DYNAMICS OF INDUSTRIAL DEMOCRACY 37 (1942)(noting that in the early 1940s the role of the NLRB shifted from an enforcer of collective bargaining agreements to a supervisor of elections, and that this event marked the end of an era during which unions and management looked to government for the solution of their problems); William M. Leiserson, *Constitutional Government in American Industries*, 12 AM. ECON. REV. 75 (1922)(noting the shift in sovereignty from the hands of owners and managers into a democratic system).

39. *See Enterprise Wheel & Car*, 363 U.S. at 594–96 (noting that a collective bargaining agreement will often provide for the use of arbitration to settle disputes); *Warrior & Gulf Navigation*, 363 U.S. at 582 (noting that an arbitrator brings experience and competence in the subject matter to the grievance process that a judge might not possess); *American Mfg. Co.*, 363 U.S. at 568–69 (noting that arbitration will be used for all grievances involving interpretation of the collective bargaining agreement).

40. *See Warrior & Gulf Navigation*, 363 U.S. at 581 (stating that arbitration of collective bargaining agreement provisions creates a "system of private law"); Leiserson, *supra* note 38, at 75 (stating that trade agreements result in a predictable, constitutional-like form of business government); Katherine Van Wezel Stone, *The Legacy of Industrial Pluralism: The Tension Between Individual Employment Rights and the New Deal Collective Bargaining System*, 59 U. CHI. L. REV. 575, 623 (1992)(stating that workplace legislation is enacted and contained in the collective bargaining agreement).

41. George W. Taylor, *Preface,* to Freidin, LABOR ARBITRATION AND THE COURTS (1952)("In a very real sense, the parties who establish their own labor arbitration machinery create a judicial procedure where none has existed."); Leiserson, *supra* note 38, at 63 (noting how arbitration can be used to settle grievances, much like a court's judicial power); Stone, *supra* note 40, at 623 (stating that arbitration is supposed to supply a neutral vantage point for enforcing workplace rules).

42. *See* Alexander v. Gardner-Denver Co., 415 U.S. 36, 52 (1974)(noting that the integral role of arbitration in the industrial pluralist system helps establish "industrial self-government"); *Warrior & Gulf Navigation*, 363 U.S. at 581 (recognizing that "the grievance machinery under a collective bargaining agreement is at the very heart of industrial self-government" and that "[a]rbitration is the means of solving the unforeseeable by molding a system of private law for all the problems which may arise").

43. *See Enterprise Wheel & Car*, 363 U.S. at 597 (upholding an arbitral award "so long as it draws its essence from the collective bargaining agreement[,]" and stating that an arbitration award that relies on external law instead of the collective bargaining agreement fails this test); *Warrior & Gulf Navigation*, 363 U.S. at 582 (noting that the arbitrator's

authority is limited only by the collective bargaining agreement's terms); Harry T. Edwards, *Labor Arbitration at the Crossroads: The 'Common Law of the Shop' v. External Law,* 32 ARB. J. 65, 90–91 (1977)(stating that arbitrators should be reluctant to decide public law issues because they may be wrong and, if followed by a court out of deference to the arbitrator, they may distort the development of precedent); Theodore J. St. Antoine, *Judicial Review of Labor Arbitration Awards: A Second Look at* Enterprise Wheel *and its Progeny;* Bernard D. Meltzer, *Ruminations About Ideology, Law, and Labor Arbitration,* 34 U. CHI. L. REV. 545, 557–59 (1967)(stating that "parties typically call on an arbitrator to construe and not to destroy their agreement"); 75 MICH. L. REV. 1137, 1140–43 (1977)(stating that an award must "draw its essence" from the collective bargaining agreement in order to be valid and enforceable)(quoting *Enterprise Wheel & Car,* 363 U.S. at 597). The late Dean Shulman stated that "[a] proper conception of the arbitrator's function is basic. He is not a public tribunal imposed upon the parties by superior authority which the parties are obliged to accept. He has no general charter to administer justice for a community which transcends the parties. He is rather a part of a system of self-government created by and confined to the parties. He serves their pleasure only, to administer the rule of law established by their collective agreement." Shulman, *supra* note 34, at 1016.

44. *See* Katherine Van Wezel Stone, *The Post-War Paradigm in American Labor Law,* 90 YALE L. J. 1509, 1515 (1981).

45. *Warrior & Gulf,* 363 U.S. at 578.

46. Samuel Estreicher, *Arbitration of Employment Disputes Without Unions,* 66 CHI-KENT L. REV. 753, 758 (1990).

47. *See* G. Richard Shell, *The Role of Public Law in Private Dispute Resolution: Reflections on* Shearson/American Express, Inc. v. McMahon, 26 AM. BUS. L.J. 397, 404; (1988). *See, e.g.,* Romyn v. Shearson Lehman Bros., 648 F. Supp. 626, 632 (D.C. Utah 1986)(RICO); Breyer v. First National Monetary Corp., 548 F. Supp. 955, 959 (D.C.N.J. 1982)(Commodities Exchange Act); Aimcee Wholesale Corp. v. Tomar Prods., Inc., 237 N.E.2d 223, 225 (1968)(Sherman Antitrust Act).

48. 415 U.S. 36 (1974).

49. *Id.* at 42.

50. *Id.* at 43.

51. *Id.* at 49.

52. *Id.* at 57.

53. *Id.* at 53.

54. *Id.* at 57–58.

55. *Id.* at 56.

56. 450 U.S. 728 (1981).

57. *Id.* at 742.

58. *Id.* at 743.

59. 466 U.S. 284 (1984).

60. *See, e.g.,* Utley v. Goldman Sachs & Co., 883 F.2d 184 (1st Cir. 1989)(Title VII); Swenson v. Management Recruiters Int'l, Inc., 858 F.2d 1304 (8th Cir. 1988)(Title VII); Nicholson v. CPC Int'l, Inc., 877 F.2d 221 (3d Cir. 1989)(ADEA); *see also* Jones v. Baskin Flaherty, Elliot and Mannino, P.C., 661 F. Supp. 597, 604 (W.D. Pa. 1987)(ADEA); Steck v. Smith Barney, Harris Upham & Co., 661 F. Supp. 543, 544–47 (D.N.J. 1987)(ADEA); Horne v. New England Patriots Football Club, Inc., 489 F. Supp. 465, 467–70 (D. Mass. 1980)(ADEA). *Cf.* Pihl v. Thompson McKinnon Sec., 48 FAIR EMPL. PRAC. Cas. 922, 924–26 (E.D. Pa. 1988)(holding that ADEA claims are subject to compulsory arbitration).

61. Mitsubishi Motors Corp. v. Soler Chrysler-Plymouth, Inc., 473 U.S. 614

(1985)(compelling enforcement of a private contract to arbitrate claims arising under the Sherman Antitrust Act).

62. Rodriguez de Quijas v. Shearson/American Express, Inc., 490 U.S. 477 (1989)(compelling enforcement of a private contract to arbitrate claims arising under section 12(2) of the Securities Act of 1933).

63. Shearson/American Express, Inc. v. McMahon, 482 U.S. 220 (1987)(compelling enforcement of a private contract to arbitrate claims arising under both RICO and section 10(b) of the Securities Act of 1934).

64. *Mitsubishi*, 473 U.S. at 628 (citation omitted).

65. *McMahon*, 482 U.S. at 227.

66. *See., e.g.*, Michael Lieberman, *Overcoming the Presumption of Arbitrability of ADEA Claims: The Triumph of Substantive Over Procedural Values in* Nicholson v. CPC International, Inc., 138 U. Pa. L. Rev. 1817, 1826 (1990). The FAA presumption of arbitrability articulated in the *Mitsubishi* trilogy is analogous to the Section 301 presumption of arbitrability enunciated by the Court in the *Steelworkers* trilogy. *See* United Steelworkers v. Enterprise Wheel & Car Corp., 363 U.S. 593, 596 (1960); United Steelworkers v. Warrior & Gulf Navigation Co., 363 U.S. 574, 582 (1960); United Steelworkers v. American Mfg. Co., 363 U.S. 564, 569 (1960).

67. *See, e.g., McMahon*, 482 U.S. at 232 ("the streamlined procedures of arbitration do not entail any consequential restriction on substantive rights."); *Mitsubishi*, 473 U.S. at 628 ("By agreeing to arbitrate a statutory claim, a party does not forgo the substantive rights afforded by the statute; it only submits their resolution to an arbitral, rather than a judicial, forum.").

68. 473 U.S. 614 (1985).

69. 15 U.S.C. §§ 1–7 (1994).

70. *Mitsubishi*, 473 U.S. at 615.

71. *Id*. at 626.

72. *Id*. at 628 (citation omitted).

73. *Id*.

74. In dissent, Justice Stevens noted the Court's traditional distinction between arbitrable contractual (collectively bargained for) rights and nonarbitrable statutory rights, and cited *Gardner-Denver, Barentine, McDonald,* and *Wilko,* for the proposition that arbitration is not an appropriate vehicle for the final resolution of statutory rights. *Id*. at 647–50 (Stevens, J., dissenting).

75. *Id*.

76. *Id*. at 626–27.

77. 482 U.S. 220 (1987).

78. 18 U.S.C. §§ 1961–68 (1994).

79. 15 U.S.C. § 78j(b).

80. *McMahon*, 482 U.S. at 234.

81. *Id*. at 232 (citations omitted).

82. 490 U.S. 477 (1989).

83. 15 U.S.C. §§ 77a-77aa.

84. *Id*. §§ 77b-77e, 77j, 77k, 77m, 77o, 77s, 78a-78o, 78o-3, 78p-78hh.

85. *Rodriquez*, 490 U.S. at 481.

86. *Id*. at 483.

87. *Id*. at 486–87 (Stevens, J., dissenting).

88. 500 U.S. 20.

89. 29 U.S.C. §§ 621–34 (1988 & Supp. IV 1992).

90. *Gilmer,* 500 U.S. at 24 (quoting Gilmer v. Interstate/Johnson Corp., 895 F.2d 195, 197 (4th Cir. 1990)).

91. *Id.* at 30–35.

92. *Id.* at 33–35.

93. Courts holding that FAA arbitrability is triggered by the arbitration clause in a collective bargaining agreement include Austin v. Owens-Brockway Glass Container, Inc., 78 F.3d 875, 881 (4th Cir.), *cert. denied,*—U.S.—(1996); Bright v. Norshipco & Norfold Shipbuilding & Drydock Corp., 1997 WL 35519 (E.D. Va. 1997); Almonte v. Coca-Cola Bottling Co. of N.Y., Inc.,—F. Supp.—, 1997 WL 149328 at *5 (D. Conn. 1997); Brummett v. Copaz Packing Corp., 954 F. Supp. 160 (S.D. Ohio 1996); Jessie v. Carter Health Care Ctr., 930 F. Supp. 1174, 1176–77 (E.D. Ky. 1996); Knox v. Wheeling-Pittsburgh Steel Corp., 899, F. Supp. 1529, 1536–40 (N.D. W. Va. 1995)(requiring plaintiff to exhaust her collective bargaining agreement's arbitration procedure before litigating her Title VII claim in court). *See also* Katherine Van Wezel Stone, *Mandatory Arbitration of Individual Employment Rights: The Yellow Dog Contract of the 1990s,* 73 DENVER L. REV. 1017, 1036 (1996)(predicting that courts increasingly will apply the FAA unionized employees' federal statutory claims).

Courts holding that FAA arbitrability is not triggered by the arbitration clause in a collective bargaining agreement include Pryner v. Tractor Supply Co., 1997 WL 125936 at *12 (7th Cir. 1997); Varner v. National Super Markets, Inc., 94 F.3d 1209, 1213 (8th Cir. 1996); DiPuccio v. United Parcel Serv., 890 F. Supp. 688, 692–93 (N.D. Ohio 1995); Randolph v. Cooper Indus, 879 F. Supp. 518, 520–23 (W.D. Pa. 1994); Griffin v. Keystone Steel & Wire Co., 858 F. Supp. 802, 804 (C.D. III. 1994); Block v. Art Iron, Inc., 866 F. Supp. 380, 386–87 (N.D. Ind. 1994); Claps v. Moliterno Stone Sales, Inc., 819 F. Supp. 141, 147 (D. Conn. 1993). *See also* Darby v. North Mississippi Rural Legal Services, Inc., 1997 WL 88241 (N.D. Miss. 1997)(holding that a plaintiff need not exhaust grievance procedures contained in a collective bargaining agreement before filing suit alleging violation of statutory rights under the Americans with Disabilities Act).

See also Richard A. Bales, *The Discord between Collective Bargaining and Individual Employment Rights,* 77 BOSTON U.L. REV.—(1997); Amanda G. Dealy, Note, *Compulsory Arbitration in the Unionized Workplace: Reconciling Gilmer, Gardner-Denver, and the Americans with Disabilities Act,* 37 B.C. L. REV. 479 (1996); Martin H. Malin, *Arbitrating Statutory Employment Claims in the Aftermath of* Gilmer, 40 ST. LOUIS U.L.J. 77, 84–88 (1996).

94. *See, e.g.,* St. John v. Employment Dev. Dep't, 642 F.2d 273, 275 (9th Cir. 1981)(noting that the preferred method for promoting Title VII's goal of nondiscrimination is voluntary compliance and that this is the very reason the EEOC exists). The EEOC's statutory role as intermediator is discussed further in chapter 4.

95. *Gilmer,* 500 U.S. at 28 (stating that inability to file a private judicial action would not prevent one from filing a charge with the EEOC).

96. *Id.*

97. *Gilmer,* 500 U.S. at 29 (noting that Congress did not preclude arbitration in its recent ADEA amendments).

98. *Id.* (quoting 29 U.S.C. § 626(b)(1988)).

99. *Id.; cf.* 29 U.S.C. § 626(c)(1)(1994)(allowing plaintiffs to file ADEA suits in any competent jurisdiction).

100. *Gilmer,* 500 U.S. at 32–33; *see also Bills Relating to Sales and Contracts to Sell in*

Interstate Commerce; and a Bill to Make Valid and Enforceable Written Provisions or Agreements for Arbitration of Disputes Arising out of Contracts, Maritime Transactions, or Commerce Among the States or Territories or with Foreign Nations: Hearings on S. 4213 and S. 4214 Before the Subcomm. of the Senate Comm. on the Judiciary, 67th Cong., 4th Sess. 9 (1931)(statement of Senator Walsh)(using employment arbitration agreements as an example of adhesion contracts). This issue is discussed further in chapter 9.

101. *Gilmer,* 500 U.S. at 33.

102. *Id.* (quoting *Mitsubishi,* 473 U.S. at 627).

103. *Id.*

104. *Gilmer,* 500 U.S. at 30 (quoting *Rodriquez,* 490 U.S. at 481).

105. *Id.* (noting that the NYSE arbitration rules provide ample protection).

106. *Id.* at 30–31 (citing 9 U.S.C. § 10(b)(1988)).

107. *Id.* at 31 (quoting *Mitsubishi,* 473 U.S. at 628).

108. *Id.* at 31–32; *see also* United Steelworkers v. Enterprise Wheel & Car Corp., 363 U.S. 593, 598 (1960)(noting that arbitrators "have no obligation to the court to give their reasons for an award").

109. *Gilmer,* 500 U.S. at 31–33.

110. *Gilmer,* 500 U.S. at 32 n.4 (quoting *McMahon,* 482 U.S. at 232).

111. *Id.* at 32.

112. 9 U.S.C. § 1 (1994).

113. *Gilmer,* 500 U.S. at 25 n.2.

114. Christine Godsil Cooper, *Where Are We Going With Gilmer?—Some Ruminations on the Arbitration of Discrimination Claims,* 11 St. Louis Pub. L. Rev. 203, 226, 234 (1992).

115. *Id.* at 226–29; Michael G. Holcomb, Note, *The Demise of the FAA's "Contract of Employment" Exception?,* 1992 J. Dispute Resol. 213, 220–21 (1992); Jenifer A. Magyar, *Statutory Civil Rights Claims in Arbitration: Analysis of* Gilmer v. Interstate/Johnson Lane Corp., 72 B.U.L. Rev. 641, 653 (1992).

116. Slawsky v. True Form Founds. Corp. No. 91–1882, 1991 WL 98906 at 1 (E.D. Pa. 1991)(distinguishing *Gilmer* because the plaintiff's compulsory arbitration clause was located in a " 'contract of employment' that is exempt from the FAA"). Most post-*Gilmer* federal cases have avoided this issue the same way the Court in *Gilmer* did—by arguing that because the arbitration agreements at issue were contained in the plaintiffs' registration applications with the NYSE, the agreements were not part of a "contract of employment." *See, e.g.,* Bierdeman v. Shearson Lehman Hutton, Inc., 963 F.2d 378 (9th Cir.)(text on Westlaw), *cert. denied,* 506 U.S. 917 (1992); Willis v. Dean Witter Reynolds, Inc., 948 F.2d 305 (6th Cir. 1991); Alford v. Dean Witter Reynolds, Inc., 939 F.2d 229 (5th Cir. 1991), *reversing* 905 F.2d 104 (5th Cir. 1990).

117. *See, e.g.,* Weston v. ITT-CFC, 8 IER Cas. 503 (N.D. Tex. 1992); American Postal Workers Union, AFL-CIO v. United States Postal Serv., 823 F.2d 466, 473 (11th Cir. 1987); Stokes v. Merrill Lynch, Pierce, Fenner & Smith, Inc., 523 F.2d 433, 436 (6th Cir. 1975); Dickstein v. duPont, 443 F.2d 783, 785 (1st Cir. 1971); Signal-Stat Corp. v. Local 475, United Elec., Radio & Mach. Workers of Am., 235 F.2d 298, 303 (2d Cir. 1956), *cert. denied,* 354 U.S. 911, *reh'g denied,* 355 U.S. 852 (1957); Tenney Eng'g, Inc. v. United Elec. Radio & Mach. Workers of Am., Local 437, 207 F.2d 450, 452 (3d Cir. 1953); Malison v. Prudential-Bache Sec., Inc., 654 F. Supp. 101, 104 (W.D.N.C. 1987); *see also* Southland Corp. v. Keating, 465 U.S. 1, 11 (1984)(stating that the FAA withdrew from the states the power to require resolution in a judicial forum for a claim that the parties had

agreed to arbitrate, excepting arbitration agreements which are "part of a written maritime contract or a contract 'evidencing a transaction involving commerce.' ").

Chapter Three. The FAA "Contracts of Employment" Exclusion

1. *See, e.g.,* 1996 DAILY LAB. REP. No. 129 (BNA)(July 5, 1996).

2. Chapter 2, part B.

3. 9 U.S.C. § 1 (1996).

4. S. 4214 67th Cong., 4th Sess. (1922).

5. H.R. 13522, 67th Cong., 4th Sess. (1922).

6. Matthew W. Finkin, *"Workers' Contracts" Under the United States Arbitration Act: An Essay in Historical Clarification,* 17 BERKELEY J. EMPLOY. & LAB. L. 282, 283 (1996).

7. 45 ABA REP. At 295 (1992).

8. Hyman Weintraub, ANDREW FURUSETH: EMANCIPATOR OF THE SEAMEN (1959).

9. *See* Herbert Burstein, *The United States Arbitration Act—A Reevaluation,* 3 VILL. L. REV. 125, 130 (1958).

10. Proceedings of the 26th Annual Convention of the International Seamen's Union of America, 203 (1923) [hereinafter 26th Seamen's Union Convention]; Proceedings of the 45th Annual Convention of the American Federation of Labor 52 (1925) [hereinafter 45th AFL Convention].

11. *Sales & Contracts to Sell in Interstate and Foreign Commerce and Federal Arbitration; Hearings Before the Subcomm. of the Comm. on the Judiciary,* 67th Cong., 4th Sess. 9 (1923) [hereinafter *"Sales & Contracts"*]; 26th Seamen's Union Convention, *supra* note 10, at 203.

12. 26th Seamen's Union Convention, *supra* note 10, at 203, 205; Finkin, *supra* note 6, at 287–88, 292.

13. 38 Stat. 1164, as amended by 41 Stat. 1006.

14. 46 U.S.C. § 688.

15. 26th Seamen's Union Convention, *supra* note 10, at 205.

16. Finkin, *supra* note 6, at 282, 288.

17. 17 STAT. 267 (1872), 46 U.S.C.A. § 651 *et seq.* (1946)(seamen); 38 STAT. 103 *et seq.* (1913), 41 STAT. 469 *et seq.* (1920), 44 STAT. 577 (1926), 45 U.S.C.A. §151 *et seq.* (1946)(railroad employees); *see also* Tenney Eng'g, Inc. v. United Elec. Radio & Mach. Workers of Am., Local 437, 207 F.2d 450, 452 n. 7 (3d Cir. 1953); Amalgamated Ass'n of Street, Elec. Ry. & Motor Coach Employees of Am., Local Div. 1210 v. Pennsylvania Greyhound Lines, 192 F.2d 310, 313 (3d Cir. 1951).

18. Finkin, *supra* note 6, at 286–89.

19. Finkin, *supra* note 6, at 288–89.

20. 26th Seamen's Union Convention, *supra* note 10, at 205.

21. *Id.* at 204.

22. *Id.* (emphasis added).

23. Proceedings of the 27th Annual Convention of the International Seamen's Union of America 100 (1924).

24. *Sales & Contracts, supra* note 11, at 9.

25. *Id.*

26. *Id.*

27. *Id.* at 9–10.

28. *See* Finkin, *supra* note 6, at 297, 297 n.67.

29. Letter from Herbert Hoover, Secretary of the Department of Commerce, to Senator Thomas Sterling (Jan. 31, 1923), in *Sales & Contracts, supra* note 11, at 14 (emphasis added).

30. 48 A.B.A. REP. 287 (1923); *see Tenney Eng'g,* 207 F.2d at 452.

31. *Joint Hearings Before the Subcommittee of the Committees on the Judiciary, on S. 1005 and H.R. 647,* 68th Cong., 1st Sess. 2 (1924).

32. Burstein, *supra* note 9, at 130; Finkin, *supra* note 6, at 286, 297.

33. 45th AFL Convention, *supra* note 10, at 52.

34. *Report of the Standing Comm. on Commerce, Trade, and Commercial Law,* 51 A.B.A. REP. 385, 394 (1926).

35. 19 Am. Fed. of Lab. Weekly News Services No. 5 (April 13, 1929).

36. *Report of the Standing Comm. on Commerce, Trade, and Commercial Law,* 55 A.B.A. REP. 328, 328 (1930).

37. 353 U.S. 448, 458 (1957).

38. 29 U.S.C. § 185 (1996). The pertinent provision of Section 301 is as follows: "Suits for violation of contracts between an employer and a labor organization representing employees in an industry affecting commerce as defined in this Chapter, or between any such labor organizations, may be brought in any district court of the United States having jurisdiction of the parties, without respect to the amount in controversy or without regard to the citizenship of the parties."

39. Nathan P. Feinsinger, *Enforcement of Labor Agreements—A New Era in Collective Bargaining,* 43 VA. L. REV. 1261, 1265 (1957).

40. *See, e.g., Ex Parte* Birmingham Fire Ins. Co., 172 So. 99, 101 (Ala. 1937); Key v. Norrod, 136 S.W. 991 (1911).

41. Archibald Cox, *Grievance Arbitration and the Federal Courts,* 67 HARV. L. REV. 591, 591 (1954).

42. *See Textile Workers,* 353 U.S. at 446 (Frankfurter, J., dissenting)(interpreting the majority opinion in *Lincoln Mills* as rejecting "the availability of the Federal Arbitration Act to enforce arbitration clauses in collective bargaining agreements").

43. Cox, *supra* note 41, at 593.

44. *See* Gatliff Coal Co. v. Cox, 142 F.2d 876, 882 (6th Cir. 1944).

45. *See* Newberry v. United States, 256 U.S. 232, 257 (1921): "It is settled . . . that the power to regulate interstate and foreign commerce does not reach whatever is essential thereto. Without agriculture, manufacturing, mining, etc., commerce could not exist, but this fact does not suffice to subject them to the control of Congress." *See also* New York Central R.R. Co. v. White, 243 U.S. 188 (1917)(equating interstate commerce with interstate transportation); United States v. Lopez, 115 S. Ct. 1624 (1995)(discussing the history of the Supreme Court's definition of "commerce").

46. Lewittes & Sons v. United Furniture Workers of Am., 95 F. Supp. 851, 855 (S.D.N.Y. 1951); Wilson & Company v. Fremont Cake & Meal Co., 77 F. Supp. 364 (D. Neb. 1948); *but see Amalgamated Ass'n,* 192 F.2d at 313 (holding that the words "nothing herein contained" mean "nothing contained in Title 9"); Pennsylvania Greyhound Lines v. Amalgamated Ass'n, Div. 1063 193 F.2d 327, 328 (3d Cir. 1952)(holding that the arbitration act gave district court no authority to compel arbitration of collective bargaining contract of workers engaged in interstate commerce).

47. *But see* Asplundh Tree Expert Co. v. Bates, 71 F.3d 592, 601 (6th Cir. 1995)("The exclusionary clause [§1] does not employ the same broad language of § 2. If Congress had intended the exclusion to be as broad as the coverage, it would have used the same language in the exclusion clause.").

48. *See* Donahue v. Susquehanna Collieries Co., 138 F.2d 3, 6–7 (3d Cir. 1943); Watkins v. Hudson Coal Co., 151 F.2d 311, 320–21 (3d Cir. 1945); *cert. denied*, 327 U.S. 777 (1946) Donahue v. Susquehanna Collieries Co., 160 F.2d 661, 664 (3d Cir. 1947); *see also* Evans v. Hudson Coal Co., 178 F.2d 663, 663 (3d Cir. 1950).

49. 192 F.2d 310 (3rd Cir. 1951); *accord, Pennsylvania Greyhound*, 193 F.3d at 328.

50. *Amalgamated Ass'n*, 192 F.2d 310.

51. *See* H.R. REP. No. 255, 80th Cong., 1st Sess. I (1947).

52. Cox, *supra* note 41, at 595 n.12.

53. *See, e.g.*, International Union United Furniture Workers v. Colonial Hardwood Flooring Co., 168 F.2d 33, 35–36 (4th Cir. 1948); *Gatliff*, 142 F.2d at 879–80.

54. 350 U.S. 198, 201 (1956). This decision is discussed in greater detail in the second half of this chapter.

55. For a general discussion of whether collective bargaining agreements fall within the contracts of employment exclusion, see Douglas E. Ray, *Court Review of Labor Arbitration Awards under the Federal Arbitration Act*, 32 VILL. L. REV. 57 (1987).

56. 321 U.S. 332, 334–35 (1944).

57. *Lewittes*, 95 F. Supp. at 851; United Office & Professional Workers v. Monumental Life Ins. Co., 88 F. Supp. 602, 606 (E.D. Pa. 1950).

58. *See Amalgamated Ass'n*, 192 F.2d at 313; *Pennsylvania Greyhound*, 193 F.2d at 328; Mercury Oil Ref. Co. v. Oil Workers Int'l Union, 187 F.2d 980, 983 (10th Cir. 1951); Ludlow Mfg. & Sales Corp. v. Textile Workers Union, 108 F. Supp. 45, 49–50 (D. Del. 1952); Boston & Maine Transp. Co. v. Amalgamated Ass'n, 106 F. Supp. 334, 335 (D. Mass. 1952).

59. *See* Signal Stat Corp. v. Local 475, United Elec., Radio & Mach. Workers of Am., 235 F.2d 298, 302 (2d Cir. 1956), *cert. denied*, 354 U.S. 911 (1957).

60. *See, e.g., Amalgamated Ass'n*, 192 F.2d at 313; *Donahue*, 160 F.2d at 662; *see also* S. REP. No. 105, 80th Cong., 1st Sess. 15 (1947)(references to collective bargaining agreements as "employment contracts" permeated the debates on the LMRA); NLRB v. Rockaway News Supply Co., 345 U.S. 71, 76–77 (1953)(referring, in another context, to collective bargaining agreements as "employment contracts"); NLRB v. Sands Mfg. Co., 306 U.S. 332, 342 (1939)(same).

61. United Steelworkers of Am., C.I.O. v. Galland-Henning Mfg. Co., 241 F.2d 323, 327 (7th Cir.), *aff'd*, 354 U.S. 906 (1957).

62. *See* American Postal Workers Union v. United States Postal Serv., 823 F.2d 466, 473 (11th Cir. 1987)(recognizing that the position that collective bargaining agreements are not "contracts of employment" is the minority view with only two courts so holding).

Before the Supreme Court's *Lincoln Mills* decision, the circuit courts were split, with several of them holding that the FAA applied to collective bargaining agreements because they were not "contracts of employment." *See, e.g.*, Local 19, Warehouse, Processing & Distributive Workers Union v. Buckeye Cotton Oil Co., 236 F.2d 776, 781 (6th Cir. 1956), *cert. denied*, 354 U.S. 910 (1957); Local 205, United Elec. Radio & Mach. Workers v. General Elec. Co., 233 F.2d 85, 98 (1st Cir. 1956)(holding that the term "contract of employment" refers to an individual transaction rather than to a union-negotiated collective agreement), *aff'd on other grounds*, 353 U.S. 547 (1957); Hoover Motor Express Co. v. Teamsters, Local Union No. 327, 217 F.2d 49, 53 (6th Cir. 1954)(arguing that the FAA exception was not intended to apply to collective bargaining agreements).

Since *Lincoln Mills*, however, the circuits universally have held that collective bargaining agreements are "contracts of employment," and that they are outside the scope of the FAA. *See, e.g.*, United Food & Commercial Workers Local Union No. 7R v. Safeway Stores, Inc.,

889 F.2d 940, 944 (10th Cir. 1989); Bacashihua v. United States Postal Serv., 859 F.2d 402, 404–05 (6th Cir. 1988); Occidental Chem. Corp. v. Int'l Chem. Workers Union, 853 F.2d 1310, 1315 (6th Cir. 1988); American Postal Workers Union v. United States Postal Serv., 823 F.2d 466, 473 (11th Cir. 1987).

63. 207 F.2d 450 (3d Cir. 1953). *Tenney* itself illustrates the judicial confusion regarding interpretation of the FAA. Originally, the Third Circuit read Section 3 as distinct from Section 1, although the court did not consider whether a collective bargaining agreement was a contract of employment. *See Susquehanna*, 138 F.2d at 5; *Watkin*, 151 F.2d 311, 320 (3d Cir. 1945) *cert. denied*, 327 U.S. 777 (1946). Then, in *Amalgamated Ass'n*, 192 F.2d at 313, the court reversed its *Donahue* holding, but concluded that a collective bargaining agreement was a contract of employment and that the Arbitration Act did not apply. Finally, in *Tenney*, 207 F.2d at 453–54, the court modified its views to extend the stay provisions of the FAA to collective bargaining agreements involving employees not directly employed in interstate commerce.

64. *Id*. at 454.

65. *Id*. at 451.

66. *Id*. at 452–53 (citation omitted).

67. *Id*. at 454.

68. Cox, *supra* note 41, at 597.

69. *See Tenney*, 207 F.2d at 453.

70. Cox, *supra note* 41, at 597–98.

71. *See id*. at 598.

72. Finkin, *supra* note 6, at 298 (reviewing the legislative history of the FAA and concluding that the exclusion should apply to all employment contracts); Michael R. Holden, Note, *Arbitration of State-Law Claims by Employees: An Argument for Containing Federal Arbitration Law*, 80 CORNELL L. REV. 1695, 1714–25 (1995)(arguing that the FAA was intended to apply only to commercial contracts); Robert J. Lewton, Comment, *Are Mandatory Binding Arbitration Requirements a Viable Solution for Employers Seeking to Avoid Litigating Statutory Employment Discrimination Claims?* 59 ALBANY L. REV. 991, 1019 (1996)(suggesting that the exclusion should apply to all employment contracts "because no valid reason exists for varying the rule under which arbitration of statutory employment discrimination claims may be compelled, depending on the industry in which the plaintiff is employed"); Christine G. Cooper, *Where Are We Going with Gilmer?—Some Ruminations on the Arbitration of Employment Discrimination Claims*, 11 ST. LOUIS PUB. L. REV. 203, 231–34 (1992)(asserting that "[t]he purpose of expressly excluding contracts of seamen and railroad employees seems to have been to make sure they were excluded, not to limit the exclusion of others" and criticizing *Tenney's* use of ejusdem generis); Michael G. Holcomb, *The Demise of the FAA's "Contract of Employment" Exception?*, 1992 J. DISP. RESOL. 213, 220–21 (asserting that the Act was not meant to apply to disputes between employer and employee); Jennifer A. Magyer, *Statutory Civil Rights Claims in Arbitration: Analysis of* Gilmer v. Interstate/Johnson Lane Corp., 52 B.U.L. REV. 641, 652–53 (1992)(noting that the courts should be constrained because it was clear that Congress did not intend for the FAA to apply to contracts of employment).

73. In the First Circuit, see Dickstein v. duPont, 443 F.2d 783, 785 (1st Cir. 1971)(holding the FAA exclusion inapplicable because an account executive employed by a brokerage firm was not "engaged in foreign or interstate commerce"); Scott v. Farm Family Life Ins. Co., 827 F. Supp. 76, 77–78 (D. Mass. 1993)(applying a narrow construction of the FAA's exclusion of contracts of employment for workers engaged in foreign or interstate

commerce)(citing *Tenney*, 207 F.2d at 452). In the Second Circuit, see Signal-Stat Corp. v. Local 475, United Elec. Workers, 235 F.2d 298, 303 (2d Cir. 1956)(holding the FAA exclusion inapplicable because plaintiffs, who merely manufactured goods for sale in interstate commerce, were not themselves actually engaged in interstate commerce), *cert. denied,* 354 U.S. 911 (1957); Erving v. Virginia Squires Basketball Club, 468 F.2d 1064, 1069 (2d Cir. 1972)(holding the FAA exclusion inapplicable to a basketball player because he was not "actually in the transportation industry"); DiCrisci v. Lyndon Guar. Bank, 807 F. Supp. 947, 953 (W.D.N.Y. 1992)(noting that "the reference to seamen, railroad employees, or any other class of workers engaged in foreign or interstate commerce, suggests that Congress intended to refer to workers engaged in commerce *in the same way* that seamen and railroad workers are"); Powers v. Fox Television Stations, Inc., 923 F. Supp. 21, 23–24 (S.D.N.Y. 1996)(holding the FAA exclusion inapplicable to a television reporter because he was not employed "in the transportation industry"). In the Third Circuit, see Great Western Mortgage Corp. v. Peacock, 110 F.3d 222 (3d Cir. 1997); *Tenney,* 207 F.2d at 452 (holding that the FAA excludes only those workers who are "actually engaged in the movement of interstate or foreign commerce or in work so closely related thereto as to be in practical effect part of it"); Dancu v. Coopers & Lybrand, 778 F. Supp. 832, 834 (E.D. Pa. 1991)(holding that a consultant for state and local governments was not "actively involved in interstate transportation," and therefore was not excluded by the FAA), *aff'd mem.*, 972 F.2d 1330 (3d Cir. 1992). In the Fourth Circuit, see Rudolph v. Alamo Rent A Car, Inc., 952 F. Supp. 311 (E.D. Va. 1997); Malison v. Prudential-Bache Sec., Inc., 654 F. Supp. 101, 104 (W.D.N.C. 1987)(holding that although the work of a stockbroker involved interstate commerce, the FAA exception was inapplicable because it was "aimed at employees in transportation industries"). In the Fifth Circuit, see Rojas v. TK Communications, Inc., 87 F.3d 745, 747–798 (5th Cir. 1996)(construing the exclusion narrowly); Weston v. ITT-CFC, 8 Individual Empl. Rights Cas. (BNA) 503, 505 (N.D. Tex. 1992)(finding that the "weight of persuasive authority favors a narrow interpretation" of the FAA exclusion for workers engaged in interstate commerce); ITT Consumer Fin. Corp. v. Wilson, 8 Individual Emp. Rights Cas. (BNA) 802, 806 (S.D. Miss. 1991)(compelling arbitration, in part because the defendants were not "involved in the transportation industry"). In the Sixth Circuit, see Asplundh Tree Expert Co. v. Bates, 71 F.3d 592, 596–602 (6th Cir. 1995)(holding that the exclusionary clause should be construed narrowly to effectuate the FAA's policy favoring arbitration); Stokes v. Merrill Lynch, Pierce, Fenner & Smith, Inc., 523 F.2d 433, 436 (6th Cir. 1975)(recognizing that the parties had stipulated that their claims arose directly from their employment with Merrill Lynch in interstate commerce and did not seriously contend that as account executives, they fell within the exception from coverage in the FAA); Management Recruiters Int'l, Inc. v. Nebel, 765 F. Supp. 419, 422 (N.D. Ohio 1991)(holding the FAA exclusion inapplicable to an account executive because she was not engaged in interstate commerce or transportation). In the Seventh Circuit, see Miller Brewing Co. v. Brewery Workers Local Union No. 9, 739 F.2d 1159, 1162 (7th Cir. 1984)(holding that the FAA exclusion applies only to persons employed in transportation industries), *cert. denied,* 469 U.S. 1160 (1985); Pietro Scalzitti Co. v. International Union of Operating Eng'rs, 351 F.2d 576, 580 (7th Cir. 1965)(holding the FAA exclusion applicable only to "workers engaged in the movement of interstate or foreign commerce"). In the Eleventh Circuit, see American Postal Workers Union v. United States Postal Serv., 823 F.2d 466, 473 (11th Cir. 1987)(holding that postal workers are "engaged in interstate or foreign commerce within the meaning of the statutory exclusion"); Hydrick v. Management Recruiters Int'l, Inc., 738 F. Supp. 1434, 1435 (N.D. Ga. 1990)(holding the FAA exclusion applicable only to "workers actually engaged in interstate commerce")(quoting *American Postal Workers*, 823 F.2d at 473). In the D.C. Circuit, see Cole v. Burns Int'l Security Servs., 105 F.3d 1465, 1467, 1470–72 (D.C. Cir. 1997).

74. 468 F.2d 1064 (2d Cir. 1972).

75. *Id.* at 1069.

76. 807 F. Supp. 947, 950 (W.D.N.Y. 1992).

77. *Id.* at 953.

78. 215 F.2d 221, 224 (4th Cir. 1954).

79. *Id.* at 224.

80. *Id.* (citations omitted).

81. 859 F. Supp. 952 (D. Md. 1994).

82. *Id.* at 958.

83. 948 F.2d 305 (6th Cir. 1991).

84. *Id.*

85. *Id.* at 310; *see Miller Metal*, 215 F.2d at 224 (declining to adopt a narrow construction of Section 1 because the inclusionary language in Section 2 was intended to exercise the full extent of Congress' Commerce Clause power and reading the exclusionary clause narrowly would be inconsistent); Finkin, *supra* note 6, at 298 (advancing the same argument).

86. Willis, 948 F.2d at 310–11; *see also* Holden, *supra*, note 72, at 1714–25 (exhaustively reviewing the exclusion's legislative history and concluding that it was intended to remove *all* employment contracts from the purview of the FAA).

87. 71 F.3d 592, 600–01 (6th Cir. 1995).

88. *Id.* at 601.

89. *See, e.g.,* Holden, *supra* note 72, at 1751–54; R. Bales, *A New Direction for American Labor Law: Individual Autonomy and the Compulsory Arbitration of Individual Employment Rights,* 30 HOUSTON L. REV. 1863, 1904 (1994).

90. 218 F.2d 948 (2d Cir. 1955), *rev'd on other grounds,* 350 U.S. 198 (1956).

91. *Id.* at 951–52 (citations omitted).

92. *See Gilmer,* 500 U.S. at 33 (noting that there was "no indication in this case . . . that Gilmer, an experienced businessman, was coerced or defrauded into agreeing to the arbitration clause").

93. 415 U.S. 36 (1974).

94. John A. Gray, *Have the Foxes Become the Guardians of the Chickens? The Post-Gilmer Legal Status of Predispute Mandatory Arbitration as a Condition of Employment,* 37 VILL. L. REV. 113, 132–33 (1992); Charles A. Sullivan et al., EMPLOYMENT DISCRIMINATION: SPECIAL RELEASE ON THE CIVIL RIGHTS ACT OF 1991, at 93 (2d ed. 1992)("The more natural reading of [the FAA exclusion] is that it concerns collective bargaining agreements —contracts with 'classes of workers' ").

95. *See Asplundh Tree Expert Co.,* 71 F.3d at 601 ("The comment of the Chairman of the American Bar Association committee responsible for drafting the bill to the effect that the bill 'is not intended [to] be an act referring to labor disputes, at all' would tend to support the contention that the Act was not intended to apply to collective bargaining agreements, but sheds no further light on the issue of individual employment contracts."); *Miller Metal,* 215 F.2d at 224 (discussing the legislative history of the FAA exclusion and concluding that while "[n]o one would have serious objection to submitting to arbitration the matters covered by the individual contracts of hiring," the FAA could not be construed to permit compulsory arbitration of collective bargaining agreements); Richard E. Speidel,

Arbitration of Statutory Rights Under the Federal Arbitration Act: The Case for Reform, 4 OHIO ST. J. ON DISP. RESOL. 157, 168 n.43 (1989)("Congress probably intended to exclude collective bargaining agreements from the scope of the FAA."); Burstein, *supra* note 9, at 133 (arguing that the language "contract evidencing a transaction involving commerce" was inserted as in the exclusionary clause as a substitute for the earlier "transaction involving commerce" in order to preclude any construction that the bill applied to labor contracts as well as to commercial transactions).

96. *See* Samuel Estreicher, *Arbitration of Employment Disputes Without Unions,* 66 CHI-KENT L. REV. 753, 762 n.30 (1990)("There are . . . only two plausible readings [of the exclusionary clause]. One is to give the exclusionary clause its most natural reading, as a linguistic matter, and exempt all employment contracts involving employees in interstate commerce. The other is to read the clause in light of the opposition that led to its inclusion in the FAA and exempt only collective-bargaining agreement."); *Miller Metal,* 215 F.2d at 224 (discussing the legislative history of the FAA exclusion and concluding that while "[n]o one would have serious objection to submitting to arbitration the matters covered by the individual contracts of hiring," the FAA could not be construed to permit compulsory arbitration of collective bargaining agreements).

97. *See supra* notes 60–61 and accompanying text.

98. 26th Seamen's Union Convention, *supra* note 10, at 203–04, *cited at Textile Workers,* 353 U.S. at 466 n.2 (Frankfurter, J., dissenting).

99. Burstein, *supra* note 9, at 132–33.

100. *Id.* ("One thing is clear: organized labor had encouraged and relied upon collective bargaining agreements and it seems doubtful that the opposition of the American Federation of Labor [to the USAA] would have been limited to individual contracts."); Finkin, *supra* note 6, at 290.

101. *See generally* Wallace v. Christensen, 802 F.2d 1539, 1559 (9th Cir. 1986)(Kozinski, J., concurring)(noting that a court can cite legislative history to support practically any proposition).

Chapter Four. Applicability of the FAA to Other Employment Laws

1. *Gilmer,* 500 U.S. at 25–26.

2. *Id.* at 26.

3. *Id.* at 27–29.

4. *See* Austin v. Owens-Brockway Glass Container, Inc., 78 F.3d 875, 881–82 (4th Cir. 1996); *cert. denied,* 65 U.S.L.W. 3181 (Nov. 12, 1996); Almonte v. Coca-Cola Bottling Co. of N.Y., Inc., 959 F. Supp. 569, 1997 WL 149328 (D. Conn. March 13, 1997); Reese v. Commercial Credit Corp., 955 F. Supp. 567 (D.S.C. 1997); Brummett v. Copaz, 954 F. Supp. 160 (S.D. Ohio 1996); Golenia v. Bob Baker Toyota, 915 F. Supp. 201, 204–05 (S.D.Cal. 1996); Satarino v. A. G. Edwards & Sons, Inc., 941 F. Supp. 609 (N.D. Tex. 1996); Topf v. Warnace, Inc., 942 F. Supp. 762 (D. Conn. 1996); Pilanski v. Metropolitan Life Ins. Co., 1996 WL 622024 (S.D.N.Y. Oct. 28, 1996); Durkin v. Cigna Property & Casualty Corp., 942 F. Supp. 481 (D. Kan. 1996); Solomon v. Duke Univ., 850 F. Supp. 372, 373 (M.D.N.C. 1993).

5. *See* Kuehner v. Dickinson & Co., 84 F.3d 316, 318–20 (9th Cir. 1996); Hampton v. ITT Corp., 829 F. Supp. 202, 204 (S.D. Tex. 1993).

6. *Topf,* 1996 WL 607343.

7. *See* Saari v. Smith Barney, Harris Upham & Co., 968 F.2d 877, 881–82 (9th Cir.), *cert. denied,* 506 U.S. 986 (1992).

8. *See* Pritzker v. Merrill Lynch, Pierce, Fenner & Smith, Inc., 7 F.3d 1110, 1112 (3d Cir. 1993).

9. *See* Kinnebrew v. Gulf Ins. Co., 67 Fair Empl. Prac. Cas. (BNA) 189 (N.D. Tex. 1994).

10. *See Reese,* 955 F. Supp. 567; *Satarino,* 941 F. Supp. 609; *Pilanski,* 1996 WL 622024.

11. *See* McNulty v. Prudential-Bache Sec., Inc., 871 F. Supp. 567, 571 (E.D.N.Y. 1994).

12. *See* William v. Katten, Muchin & Zavis, 837 F. Supp. 1430, 1437 (N.D. Ill. 1993).

13. *See Austin,* 78 F.3d at 880–82.

14. *See* Rojas v. TK Communications, Inc., 87 F.3d 745, 747 (5th Cir. 1996); Alford v. Dean Witter Reynolds, Inc., 939 F.2d 229, 230 (5th Cir. 1991)(following *Gilmer* in comparing the similarities of Title VII and the ADEA and concluding that because of similar goals, they should both be subject to arbitration); *see also* Hirras v. National R.R. Passenger Corp., 10 F.3d 1142, 1146 (5th Cir.), *vacated,* 114 S. Ct. 2732 (1994)(remanding case for further consideration in light of Hawaiian Airlines, Inc. v. Norris, 512 U.S. 246 (1994)); *rev'd on other grounds,* 44 F.3d at 278 (1995)(holding that Title VII claims are subject to the compulsory arbitration provisions of the Railway Labor Act).

15. *See* Willis v. Dean Witter Reynolds, Inc., 948 F.2d 305, 307 (6th Cir. 1991)(holding that, in light of *Gilmer,* a Title VII sex discrimination claim was subject to arbitration).

16. *See* Nghiem v. NEC Electronic, Inc., 25 F.3d 1437, 1441 (9th Cir.), *cert. denied,* 115 S. Ct. 638 (1994); Bierdeman v. Shearson Lehman Hutton, Inc., 963 F.2d 378 (9th Cir.); (citing *Mago* and holding a sex discrimination claim pursuant to Title VII arbitrable), *cert. denied,* 506 U.S. 917 (1992); Mago v. Shearson Lehman Hutton, Inc., 956 F.2d 932, 935 (9th Cir. 1992)(holding that because the ADEA and Title VII "are similar in their aims and substantive provisions," the latter could be held to compulsory arbitration); *see also* Saari v. Smith Barney, Harris Upham & Co., 968 F.2d 877, 882 (9th Cir.)(holding that an employer may compel arbitration of a claim brought under the Employee Polygraph Protection Act), *cert. denied,* 506 U.S. 986 (1992).

17. *See* Bender v. A.G. Edwards & Sons, Inc., 971 F.2d 698, 700–01 (11th Cir. 1992)(holding Title VII claims arbitrable after finding "no reason to distinguish between ADEA claims and Title VII claims").

18. Several district courts have reached the same conclusion. *See, e.g.,* Sheller v. Frank's Nursery & Crafts, Inc., 957 F. Supp. 150, 1997 WL 106398 (N.D. Ill. 1997); Cremin v. Merrill Lynch Pierce Fenner & Smith, Inc., 957 F. Supp. 1460, 1997 WL 88195 (N.D. Ill. 1997); Maye v. Smith Barney Inc., 897 F. Supp. 100, 109 (S.D.N.Y. 1995); Crawford v. West Jersey Health Sys., 847 F. Supp. 1232, 1242 (D.N.J. 31, 1994)(compelling arbitration of Title VII sex discrimination claim); Williams v. Katten, Muchin & Zavis, 837 F. Supp. 1430, 1443 (N.D. Ill. 1993)(compelling arbitration of claims brought pursuant to Title VII and 42 U.S.C. § 1981); Scott v. Farm Family Life Ins. Co., 827 F. Supp. 76, 77, 80 (D. Mass. 1993)(holding that alleged claims of pregnancy discrimination are arbitrable); Hull v. NCR Corp., 826 F. Supp. 303, 306 (E.D. Mo. 1993)(compelling arbitration of Title VII and state law antidiscrimination claims); DiCrisci v. Lyndon Guar. Bank, 807 F. Supp. 947, 952 (W.D.N.Y. 1992)(holding that *Gilmer* compels arbitration, and precludes direct judicial enforcement, of Title VII and state claims of sex discrimination, sexual harassment, and hostile work environment); Newton v. Southern Pac. Transp. Co., 59 Fair Empl. Prac. Cas. (BNA) 1568, 1570 (W.D. Tex. 1992)(holding that the compulsory arbitration provision of the Railway Labor Act compels arbitration and precludes direct judicial enforcement of Title

VII racial discrimination claims); Scott v. Merrill Lynch, Pierce, Fenner & Smith, Inc., No. 89 Civ. 3749, 1992 WL 245506, at *6 (S.D.N.Y. Sept. 14, 1992)(compelling arbitration of Title VII and state claims of racial discrimination); Bender v. Smith Barney, Harris Upham & Co., 789 F. Supp. 155, 160 (D.N.J. 1992)(holding that arbitration of a Title VII action is not against public policy); Roe v. Kidder Peabody & Co., 52 Fair Empl. Prac. Cas. (BNA) 1865, 1868–70 (S.D.N.Y. 1990)(holding that the *Mitsubishi* trilogy compels arbitration of Title VII racial discrimination claims).

Additionally, several courts have concluded that the FAA compels arbitration of discrimination suits brought under state laws. *See, e.g., A.G. Edwards & Sons*, 971 F.2d at 699 (upholding the district court's ruling compelling arbitration of state law claims); *Willis*, 948 F.2d at 312 (reversing the district court's denial of the defendant's motion to arbitrate state law claims); Sacks v. Richardson Greenshield Sec., Inc., 781 F. Supp. 1475, 1476, 1483 (E.D. Cal. 1991)(finding arbitration appropriate for disputes arising out of state labor code); ITT Consumer Fin. Corp. v. Wilson, 8 Individual Empl. Rights Cas. (BNA) 802, 807 (S.D.Miss.1981)(referring state invasion of privacy claims to arbitration); Spellman v. Securities, Annuities & Ins. Servs., Inc., 10 Cal. Rptr.2d 427, 433–34 (Ct.App. 1992)(holding that state law claims are subject to compulsory arbitration under the FAA); Higgins v. Superior Court, 1 Cal. Rptr.2d 57, 62 (Ct. App. 1991)(not published according to California Rules of Court)(noting that the FAA preempts conflicting state law); Cook v. Barratt Am., Inc., 268 Cal. Rptr. 629, 630, 632 (Ct. App. 1990)(not published according to California Rules of Court)(adopting federal policy to compel arbitration of a violation of the California Government Code), *cert. denied*, 500 U.S. 932 (1991); Fletcher v. Kidder, Peabody & Co., 584 N.Y.S.2d 838, 839–40 (App. Div. 1992)(compelling arbitration of state racial discrimination claim), *aff'd*, 619 N.E.2d 998 (N.Y.), *cert. denied*, 510 U.S. 993 (1993); Nelsen v. Colleary, 574 N.Y.S.2d 912, 913–14 (Sup. Ct. 1991)(directing the parties to arbitrate state discrimination claim).

19. *See* Utley v. Goldman Sachs & Co., 883 F.2d 184, 187 (1st Cir. 1989)(holding that "an employee cannot waive prospectively her right to a judicial forum at any time, regardless of the type of employment agreement which she signs"), *cert. denied*, 493 U.S. 1045 (1990); Swenson v. Management Recruiters Int'l, Inc., 858 F.2d 1304, 1309 (8th Cir. 1988)("Congress has articulated an intent through the text and legislative history of Title VII to preclude waiver of judicial remedies for violation of both federal Title VII rights and parallel state statutory rights."), *cert. denied*, 493 U.S. 848 (1989).

20. 905 F.2d 104 (5th Cir. 1990) *(Alford I), vacated and remanded*, 500 U.S. 930; *on remand*, 939 F.2d 229 (5th Cir. 1991) *(Alford II)*.

21. *See, e.g.*, Pitter v. Prudential Life Ins. Co. of Am., 906 F. Supp. 130, 139 (E.D.N.Y. 1995).

22. *Alford I*, 905 F.2d at 108.

23. *See Alford*, 500 U.S. at 930.

24. *Alford II*, 939 F.2d at 229–30.

25. Robert L. Stern et al., Supreme Court Practice, 249–50 (7th ed. 1993)(concluding that the Supreme Court does not treat a summary reconsideration order as the functional equivalent of the summary reversal order, and that a summary reconsideration order merely instructs the lower court to reconsider the case in light of intervening precedent which may or may not compel a different result); A. Hellman, *Granted, Vacated and Remanded . . .: Shedding Light on a Dark Corner of Supreme Court Practice*, 67 Judicature 389, 392–95 (1984)(concluding that while some reconsideration orders "may be tantamount to reversals, . . . it cannot be assumed that all of them are"); Board of Trustees v.

Sweeney, 439 U.S. 24. 26 (1978)(Stevens, J., dissenting)(observing that the Court issues reconsideration orders when an "intervening decision has shed new light on the law which, if [the decision] had been available at the time of the Court of Appeal's decision, might have led to a different result.").

26. Pub. L. No. 102–166, 105 Stat. 1071, 1081 (1991)(codified in scattered sections of 42 U.S.C.).

27. *Compare id. with Gilmer,* 500 U.S. at 27 (stating that the ADEA's purpose was " 'to help employers and workers find ways of meeting problems' ")(quoting 29 U.S.C. § 621(b)(1988)).

28. John A. Gray, *Have The Foxes Become the Guardians of the Chickens? The Post-Gilmer Legal Status of Predispute Mandatory Arbitration as a Condition of Employment,* 37 VILL L. REV. 113, 131 n.64 (1992); *see also* Todd H. Thomas, *Using Arbitration To Avoid Litigation,* 44 LAB. L.J. 3, 14 (1993)(arguing that the Civil Rights Act of 1991 provides "another source of authority" for compelling arbitration of statutory claims); Rebecca Hanner White, *The EEOC, the Courts, and Employment Discrimination Policy: Recognizing the Agency's Leading Role in Statutory Interpretation,* 1995 UTAH L. REV. 51, 71 (1995)("The Civil Rights Act of 1991 and the *Gilmer* decision portend the widespread future use of arbitration to resolve employment discrimination claims."); *see also* DeGaetano v. Smith Barney, Inc., 70 Fair Empl. Prac. Cas. (BNA) 401 (S.D.N.Y. 1996)(finding no evidence in Title VII's legislative history or the Civil Rights Act of 1991 that Congress intended to preclude the arbitrability of claims under Title VII).

29. 137 CONG. REC. 515, 478; *id.* at H 9548.

30. H.R. REP. No. 40, 102d Cong., 1st Sess., pt. 2, at 41 (1991).

31. H.R. REP. No. 40(I), 102d Cong., 1st Sess., pt. 1, at 97 (1991).

32. *Id.* at 104.

33. *Id.* (citations omitted).

34. *See* Amanda G. Dealy, Note, *Compulsory Arbitration in the Unionized Workplace: Reconciling* Gilmer, Gardner-Denver, *and The Americans with Disabilities Act,* 37 B.C. L. REV. 479, 502–03 (1996). *See also* Joseph R. Grodin, *Arbitration of Employment Discrimination Claims: Doctrine and Policy in the Wake of* Gilmer, 14 HOFSTRA LAB. L.J. 1, 34–35 (1996)("When the Supreme Court decided Gilmer—subsequent to the report of the Labor and Employment committee, but prior to the passage of the statute—there was no legislative reaction to that decision, presumably because by that time the deal had been struck on a compromise bill which no one was motivated to upset. Instead, legislators attempted, as usual, to make legislative history on both sides of the issue.").

35. For a discussion of post-*Gilmer* legislative attempts to restrain compulsory employment arbitration, see Bryan K. Van Engen, Note, *Post Gilmer Development in Mandatory Arbitration: The Expansion of Mandatory Arbitration for Statutory Claims and the Congressional Effort to Reverse the Trend,* 21 J. CORP. L. 391 (1996).

36. *Id.*

37. *See* Johnson v. Hubbard Broadcasting, Inc., 1996 WL 511585 (D. Minn. 1996)(rejecting attempts to use legislative history to defeat the applicability of the FAA to Title VII claims).

38. Moses H. Cone Memorial Hosp. v. Mercury Constr. Corp., 460 U.S. 1, 25 n.32 (1983).

39. 350 U.S. 198 (1956).

40. *Id.* at 205.

41. 304 U.S. 64, 79–80 (1938).

42. *Bernhardt,* 350 U.S. at 203.

43. *Erie R.R. Co.,* 304 U.S. at 77–78.

44. *Id.* at 76–77.

45. *Id.* at 78; *see also* Guaranty Trust Co. of N.Y. v. York, 326 U.S. 99, 106–07 (1945).

46. 346 U.S. 427, 435–38 (1953).

47. *Bernhardt,* 350 U.S. at 203.

48. *Id.*

49. *Id.* at 201.

50. *See supra* chapter 2.

51. 388 U.S. 395, 403–04 (1966). For a discussion of this case, see Stephen J. Ware, *Employment Arbitration and Voluntary Consent,* 25 HOFSTRA L. REV. 83, 128–38 (1996).

52. *Id.* at 399–400.

53. *Id.* at 403–04 (footnote omitted).

54. *See* Republic of the Philippines v. Westinghouse Elec. Corp., 714 F. Supp. 1362, 1367 (D.N.J. 1989)(concluding that treating an arbitration clause separable from the remainder of a contract "is not wholly logical"); Samuel Estreicher, *Arbitration of Employment Disputes without Unions,* 66 CHI.-KENT L. REV. 753, 766 (1990)(the decision in *Prima Paint* "is problematic on a number of grounds"); Ware, *supra* note 51, at 135–38 (criticizing the severability doctrine).

55. *See Prima Paint,* 388 U.S. at 405.

56. 460 U.S. 1 (1983).

57. *Id.* at 24.

58. *Id.* at 16.

59. 465 U.S. 1 (1984).

60. *Id.* at 10.

61. *Id.* at 16.

62. 115 S. Ct. 834, 835 (1995). For analysis of this case, see Lauri Washington Sawyer, Casenote, Allied-Bruce Terminix Companies v. Dobson: *The Implementation of the Purposes of the Federal Arbitration Act or an Unjustified Intrusion into State Sovereignty?,* 47 MERCER L. REV. 645 (1996).

63. *Id.* at 839–40.

64. 116 S. Ct. 1652 (1996). For discussions of this case, see Stephen J. Ware, *Arbitration and Unconscionability after* Doctor's Associates, Inc. v. Casarotto, 31 WAKE FOREST L. REV. 1001 (1996); Traci L. Jones, Note, *State Law of Contract Formation in the Shadow of the Federal Arbitration Act,* 46 DUKE L.J. 651 (1996).

65. MONT. CODE ANN. § 27-5-114 (4)(1993).

66. Casarotto v. Lombardi, 901 P.2d 596, 597–98 (Mont. 1995).

67. *Doctor's Assoc.,* 116 S. Ct. at 1656.

68. Jean R. Sternlight, *Panacea or Corporate Tool?: Debunking the Supreme Court's Preference for Binding Arbitration,* 74 WASH. U. L. Q. 637, 668 (1996).

69. *Moses H. Cone,* 460 U.S. at 24; *see Prima Paint,* 388 U.S. at 404–05.

70. *See, e.g., Willis,* 948 F.2d at 306 (allowing FAA preemption of Kentucky statute prohibiting gender discrimination); *Sacks,* 781 F. Supp. at 1483 (allowing FAA preemption of California statute prohibiting gender discrimination); *Spellman,* 10 Cal. Rptr.2d at 432–34 (allowing FAA preemption of California statute prohibiting racial discrimination); *Higgins,* 1 Cal. Rptr. 2d at 62–63 (allowing FAA preemption of California statute prohibiting gender discrimination); *Cook,* 268 Cal. Rptr. at 630–32 (allowing FAA preemption of California statute prohibiting gender discrimination); Reid v. Goldman, Sachs & Co., 590

N.Y.S.2d 497, 497–98 (App. Div. 1992)(allowing FAA preemption of New York statute prohibiting gender discrimination); *Fletcher,* 584 N.Y.S.2d at 835–41 (allowing FAA preemption of New York statute prohibiting racial discrimination); *Nelsen,* 574 N.Y.S.2d at 913–14 (allowing FAA preemption of New York statute prohibiting racial and religious discrimination).

71. *See* Perry v. Thomas, 482 U.S. 483, 492 (1987)(holding that the FAA preempted a state statute which provided that parties can maintain breach of contract claims in a judicial forum without regard to the existence of any private agreement to arbitrate).

72. *See, e.g.,* Bender v. A. G. Edwards & Sons, 971 F.2d 698, 699 (11th Cir. 1992)(compelling arbitration of common law claims of battery, intentional infliction of emotional distress, and negligent retention); Singer v. Jefferies & Co., 575 N.E.2d 98, 102–04 (N.Y. 1991)(compelling arbitration of a tort claim for damage to professional reputation); DeSapio v. Josephthal & Co., 540 N.Y.S.2d 932, 937 (Sup. Ct. 1989)(ordering arbitration of state disability law claims, breach of express contract, breach of implied contract, breach of covenant of good faith and fair dealing, wrongful discharge, and intentional infliction of emotional distress); Prudential-Bache Sec., Inc. v. Garza, 848 S.W.2d 803, 806–08 (Tex. App.—Corpus Christi 1993, no writ)(compelling arbitration of defamation and intentional infliction of emotional distress claims).

73. *See supra* notes 38–63 and accompanying text.

74. *Doctor's Assoc.,* 116 S. Ct. at 1656.

75. For a detailed discussion of this issue, see Michael R. Holden, Note, *Arbitration of State-Law Claims by Employees: An Argument for Containing Federal Arbitration Law,* 80 Cornell L. Rev. 1095, 1730–37 (1995).

76. 619 N.E.2d 998 (N.Y.), *cert. denied,* 510 U.S. 993 (1993).

77. N.Y. Exe. Law § 296 (McKinney 1993).

78. *Fletcher,* 619 N.E.2d at 1002 (footnote omitted).

79. *Id.* at 1003.

80. 825 S.W.2d 27, 29 (Mo. Ct. App. 1992); *see also* Skewes v. Shearson Lehman Bros., 829 P.2d 874, 877 (Kan. 1992).

81. No. CV92-3476 SVW(KX), 126 Lab. Cas. (CCH) ¶ 57,558, 1992 WL 464125 at *4 (C.D. Cal. Sept. 24, 1992); *see also* Huertebise v. Reliable Business Computers, Inc., 452 Mich. 405, 550 N.W.2d 243, 258 (1996)(concluding in dicta that the Michigan antidiscrimination statute evinces a legislative intent to preclude arbitration of claims brought under that statute).

82. 593 N.Y.S.2d 927, 929 (Sup. Ct. 1992).

83. *See, e.g.,* 140 Cong. Rec. 54266 (daily ed. April 14, 1994).

Chapter Five. Employment Arbitration and the National Labor Relations Act

1. 29 U.S.C. §§ 151–66.

2. *Id.* § 151.

3. *Id.* at § 157.

4. *Id.* § 153–56, 158–60.

5. NLRB Rules and Regulations and Statements of Procedure, Series 8, as last amended, Jan. 8, 1976 (1976), § 102.34.

6. *See* Universal Camera Corp. v. NLRB, 340 U.S. 474 (1951).

7. 29 U.S.C. § 150(e).

8. *Id.* § 10(e)-(f).

9. 29 U.S.C. § 157.

10. 29 U.S.C. § 158(a)(1)(emphasis added).

11. Southern S. S. Co. v. NLRB, 316 U.S. 31, 38 (1942); NLRB v. Fansteel Metallurgical Corp., 306 U.S. 240, 252 (1939).

12. Florida Steel Corp. v. NLRB, 529 F.2d 1225, 1234 (5th Cir. 1976); Corriveau & Routheir Cement Block, Inc. v. NLRB, 410 F.2d 347, 350 (1st Cir. 1969).

13. NLRB v. Electrical Workers (IBEW) Local 1229 (Jefferson Standard Broadcasting Co.), 346 U.S. 464 (1953); NLRB v. Canuth Bros., 537 F.2d 950 (7th Cir. 1976); Note, *The Boundaries of Unprotected "Disloyalty" When a Non-Striking Employee's Section 7 Concerted Activity Threatens Employee-Customer Relations,* 125 U. Pa. L. Rev. 1339 (1977); *but see* Altex Ready Mix Concrete Corp. v. NLRB, 542 F.2d 295 (5th Cir. 1976); *enforcing* 223 NLRB 696; Community Hospital of Roanoke Valley v. NLRB, 538 F.2d 607 (4th Cir. 1976), *enforcing* 220 NLRB 217 (1975).

14. Liberty Mut. Ins. Co. v. NLRB, 592 F.2d 595, 604 (1st Cir. 1979); Washington Adventist Hosp., 291 NLRB 95 (1988).

15. Patrick Hardin, The Developing Labor Law, 137–38 (3d ed. 1992).

16. 157 NLRB 1295 (1966).

17. 388 F.2d 495, 500 (2d Cir. 1967).

18. *See* Mardell Nereim, Comment, *National Labor Relations Act Section 7: Protecting Employee Activity through Implied Concert of Action,* 76 Nw. L. Rev. 813, 825 (1981); Lori A. Ciarrocca, Note, *The Struggle to Define Section 7 Concerted Activity: A Literal Definition Emerges,* 44 Wash. & Lee L. Rev. 1277, 1288 (1987).

19. 465 U.S. 882 (1984).

20. *See, e.g.,* NLRB v. Washington Aluminum Co., 370 U.S. 9 (1962)(protecting seven unorganized employees who walked off the job because the building in which they worked was cold).

21. 221 NLRB 999 (1975).

22. *Id.* at 1000.

23. *See* Ciarrocca, *supra* note 18, at 1290.

24. Self Cycle & Marine Distribution Co., Inc., 237 NLRB 75 (1978).

25. Air Surrey Corp., 229 NLRB 1064 (1977).

26. Hansen Chevrolet, 237 NLRB 584, 590 (1978).

27. Steere Dairy, Inc., 237 NLRB 1350, 1351 (1978).

28. Krispy Kream Donut Corp., 245 NLRB No. 135 (1979).

29. United Investment Corp. d/b/a/ Santa's Bakery, 249 NLRB No. 150 (1980).

30. Diagnostic Ctr. Hosp. Corp., 228 NLRB 1215 (1977).

31. Dawson Cabinet Co., 228 NLRB 290 (1977).

32. WNAC-TV Division, RKO General, Inc., 264 NLRB 216 (1982); Hotel & Restaurant Employees Local 28, 252 NLRB 1124 (1980); Flynn Paving Co., 236 NLRB 721 (1978); *see also* King Soopers, Inc., 222 NLRB 1011 (1976).

33. Country Club of Little Rock, 260 NLRB 1112 (1982).

34. Advance Carbon Products, Inc., 198 NLRB 741 (1972).

35. Apollo Tire Co., 236 NLRB 1627 (1978), *aff'd,* 604 F.2d 1180 (9th Cir. 1979).

36. B & P Motor Express, Inc., 230 NLRB 653 (1977).

37. Triangle Tool & Eng'r, Inc., 226 NLRB 1354 (1976).

38. G.V. R., Inc., 201 NLRB 147 (1973).

39. Ontario Knife Co. v. NLRB, 637 F.2d 840, 844 (2d Cir. 1980)(Section 7 requires that activity not only be for mutual aid and protection but that activity also be concerted).

40. Krispy Kream Donut Corp., NLRB 635 F.2d 304 (4th Cir. 1980)(individual em-

ployee action for benefit of fellow employees is not concerted if employee did not intend to enlist group support).

41. NLRB v. Buddie Supermarkets, 41 F.2d 714 (5th Cir. 1979).

42. A.R.O. Inc. v. NLRB, 596 F.2d 713, 1717–18 (6th Cir. 1979)(employee must actually, not impliedly, be representing views of fellow employees to be protected by Section 7 of the NLRA).

43. Pelton Casteel Inc. v. NLRB, 627 F.2d 23, 30 (7th Cir. 1980)(employees simply sharing concerns that individual employee voiced is insufficient to constitute concerted activity).

44. Dawson Cabinet Co. v. NLRB, 566 F.2d 1079 (8th Cir. 1977).

45. Becorn Beverage v. NLRB, 614 F.2d 1238 (9th Cir. 1980).

46. 268 NLRB 493 (1984), *rev'd sub nom,* Prill v. NLRB, 755 F.2d 941 (D.C. Cir.), *cert. denied,* 474 U.S. 971 (1985), *decision on remand sub nom* Meyers Indus., 281 NLRB 882 (1986), *aff'd,* 835 F.2d 1481 (D.C. Cir. 1987), *cert. denied,* 487 U.S. 1205 (1988).

47. Prill v. NLRB, 755 F.2d 941, 953 (D.C. Cir. 1985).

48. Meyers Indus., Inc., 281 NLRB 882 (1986).

49. Prill v. NLRB, 835 F.2d 1481 (D.C. Cir. 1987).

50. Hardin, *supra* note 15, at 142.

51. 271 NLRB 35 (1984).

52. 272 NLRB 931 (1984).

53. 282 NLRB No. 24 (1986).

54. 282 NLRB 413 (1986), *enforced,* 833 F.2d 1012 (6th Cir. 1987).

55. 857 F.2d 419 (7th Cir. 1988), *enforcing* 285 NLRB 550 (1987).

56. Franklin Iron & Metal Corp., 315 NLRB 819 (1994).

57. Rita Gail Smith and Richard A. Parr II, Note, *Protection of Individual Action as "Concerted Activity" under the National Labor Relations Act,* 68 CORNELL L. REV. 369, 374 (1983). *See, e.g.,* Frank Briscoe Inc. v. National Labor Relations Board, 637 F.2d 946, 950 (3d Cir. 1981).

58. 538 F.2d 1379 (9th Cir. 1976), *enforcing* 213 NLRB 752 (1975).

59. 637 F.2d at 950.

60. Smith and Parr, *supra* note 57, at 375. *See, e.g.,* NLRB v. Buddie's Supermarkets, Inc., 41 F.2d 714, 718–19 (5th Cir. 1973).

61. *See, e.g.,* NLRB v. Gibbs Corp., 284 F.2d 403, 405–06 (5th Cir. 1960)(shop steward discharged because of continued demands for special treatment).

62. *See, e.g.,* Buddie's Supermarkets, 481 F.2d at 718–19 (employee sought more favorable commission rate for himself); Inked Ribbon Corp., 241 NLRB 7 (1979)(individual employee claimed wage increase and other benefits for herself only).

63. *See, e.g.,* Pelton Casteel, Inc. v. NLRB, 627 F.2d 23, 28 (7th Cir. 1980)(employee complained about job rates and overtime).

64. Smith & Parr, *supra* note 57 at 375–76.

65. *See, e.g.,* NLRB v. Gissel Packing Co., 395 U.S. 575, 618–19 (1969).

66. *See, e.g.,* Medo Photo Supply Corp. v. NLRB, 321 U.S. 678, 686 (1944).

67. *See, e.g.,* Struksness Construction Co., 165 NLRB 1062 (1967); Blue Flash Express, 109 NLRB 591 (1954).

68. Ford Bros., 295 NLRB No. 10 (1989); Yolo Transp., 286 NLRB 1087 (1987); Lord Jim's, 259 NLRB 1162 (1982); S.M.C. Restaurant Corp. dba Poletti's Restaurant, 261 NLRB 313 (1982), *enforced mem.,* 718 F.2d 1086 (2d Cir. 1983).

69. 500 U.S.

70. *Id.*

71. Margaret A. Jacobs, *Firms with Policies Requiring Arbitration Are Facing Obstacles,* Wall St. J., Oct. 16, 1995, at B5 (quoting Rochelle Kentov, regional director of the NLRB in Tampa, Florida, as saying, "The requirement that an employee or job applicant sign a mandatory arbitration policy is an unfair labor practice, as is their discharge for not signing."); Stephen J. Ware, *Employment Arbitration and Voluntary Consent,* 25 HOFSTRA L. REV. 83, 106 n. 106 (1996); Jerry M. Hunter, *ADR, the NLRB, and Non-Union Workers,* DISP. RESOL. J., Fall 1995, at 18.

72. NLRB General Counsel Report, January to September 1995, Daily Lab. Rep. (BNA) No. 36, at E-6–7 (Feb. 23, 1996).

73. Bentley's Luggage Corp., NLRB Case No. 12-CA-16658, 1995 Daily Lab. Rep. (BNA) D-4 (Sept. 25, 1995)(issuing unfair labor practice complaint on the theory that it is an unfair labor practice for an employer to fire an employee for refusing to waive her right to bring an unfair labor practice charge to the Board); Great Western Financial Corp., NLRB Case No. 12-CA-166886, Daily Lab. Rep. (BNA) D-4 (Sept. 25, 1995)(issuing unfair labor practice complaint where employee who signed a pre-hire arbitration agreement was fired for filing an unfair labor practice charge with the Board).

74. S. 1958, 74th CONG., 1st Sess. (1935), 78 CONG. REC. 3443 (1934), *reprinted in* NLRB, LEGISLATIVE HISTORY OF THE NATIONAL LABOR RELATIONS ACT, 1935, at 15, 32–38.

75. Martin T. Moe, Note, *Participatory Work Place Decision Making in the NLRA: Section 8(A)(2), Electromation, and the Specter of the Company Union,* 68 N.Y.U. L. REV. 1127, 1136 (1993); Mark Berenberg, *The Political Economy of the Wagner Act: Power, Symbol, and Work Place Cooperation,* 106 HARV. L. REV. 1379, 1386 (1993)("the role of the company union was . . . the most important substantive issue in the political fight over the drafting and passage of the Wagner Act.").

76. In 1928, company unions represented 45 percent of organized workers; by 1935, company unions represented 60 percent of organized workers, and three-fifths of these unions had been initiated since 1933. Thomas C. Kohler, *Models of Worker Participation: The Uncertain Significance of Section 8(a)(2),* 27 B.C.L. REV. 499, 526–30 (1986); *see also* Daniel Nelson, *The Company Union Movement, 1900–1937: A Reexamination,* 56 BUSINESS HISTORY REVIEW, 335–38 (1982).

77. A. B. Cochran, III, *We Participate, They Decide: The Real Stakes in Revising Section 8(a)(2) of the National Labor Relations Act,* 16 BERKELEY J. EMP. LAW. & LAB. LAW 458, 474 (1995).

78. *Id.* at 474.

79. Richard Edwards, CONTESTED TERRAIN: THE TRANSFORMATION OF THE WORKPLACE IN THE 20TH CENTURY, 106–07 (1979).

80. Cochran, *supra* note 77, at 474.

81. Archibald D. Cox, et al., CASES AND MATERIALS ON LABOR LAW, 201 (11th ed. 1991).

82. Moe, *supra* note 15, at 1136–37; Sanford M. Jacoby, EMPLOYING BUREAUCRACY: MANAGERS, UNIONS AND THE TRANSFORMATION OF WORK IN AMERICAN INDUSTRY, 1900–1945, at 228 (1985).

83. 78 CONG. REC. 3443 (1934), *reprinted in* 1 NLRA HISTORY, *supra* note 74, at 15, 15.

84. Note, *Collective Bargaining as an Industrial System: An Argument against Judicial Revision of Section 8(a)(2) of the National Labor Relations Act,* 96 HARV. L. REV. 1662, 1678 (1983).

85. 29 U.S.C. § 158(2). This section, however, also states that "an employer shall not

be prohibited from permitting employees to confer with him during working hours without loss of time or pay." *Id.*

86. 29 U.S.C. § 152(5).

87. 29 U.S.C. § 159(a).

88. Hardin, *supra* note 15, at 291 (3d ed. 1992); Columbia Transit Corp., 237 NLRB 1196 (1978); Rakay Packaging Corp., 221 NLRB 99 (1975); Lane Aviation Corp., 211 NLRB 824 (1974); Stowe Mfg., 103 NLRB 1280 (1953), *enforced* 217 F.2d 900 (2d Cir. 1954), *cert. denied*, 348 U.S. 964 (1955).

89. *See generally* NLRB v. Yeshiva University, 444 U.S. 672 (1980).

90. General Foods Corp., 231 NLRB 1232, 1234–35 (1977); *see also* Cochran, *supra* note 77 at 478.

91. NLRB v. Streamway Div. of Scott & Fetzer Co., 691 F.2d 288, 294–95 (6th Cir. 1982); *see also* Sears, Roebuck & Co., 274 NLRB 230 (1985); Cochran, *supra* note 77 at 478; Moe, *supra* note 75, at 1175.

92. Electromation, Inc., 309 NLRB 990 (1992); Moe, *supra* 75, at 1165–66, 1174–77.

93. 117 NLRB 1633 (1957), *enforcement denied*, 256 F.2d 281 (5th Cir. 1958), *rev'd and remanded*, 360 U.S. 203 (1959).

94. 360 U.S. at 205.

95. *Id.* at 210.

96. *Id.* at 214.

97. Jerry M. Hunter, General Counsel, NLRB, Memorandum GC 93–4 (April 15, 1993), at 4 (*cited in* Cochran, *supra* note 77, at 478).

98. 442 F.2d 82, 84 (7th Cir. 1971).

99. 217 F.2d 900, 903–04 (2d Cir. 1954), *cert. denied*, 348 U.S. 964 (1955).

100. Spark's Nugget, Inc. dba John Ascuaga's Nugget, 230 NLRB 275, 276 (1977), *enforcement granted in part and denied in part, sub nom* NLRB v. Silver Spur Casino, 623 F.2d 571 (9th Cir. 1980).

101. *Id.* at 276.

102. 231 NLRB 1108 (1977).

103. *Id.* at 1120.

104. *Id.* at 1108, 1121.

105. 317 NLRB 1110 (1995).

106. *Id.* at 1114.

107. 308 U.S. 241 (1939).

108. *Id.* at 249; *see also* HARDIN, *supra* note 15, at 299.

109. Newman-Green, Inc., 161 NLRB 1062, 1065 (1966).

110. Dennison Mfg. Co., 168 NLRB 1012, 1017 (1967), *enforced* 419 F.2d 1080 (1st Cir. 1969), *cert. denied*, 397 U.S. 1023 (1970); *but see* Manuela Mfg. Co., 143 NLRB 379, 385 (1963).

111. Connor Foundry Co., 100 NLRB 146, 150 (1952); Standard Transformer Company, 97 NLRB 669, 671 (1951), *enforced*, 202 F.2d 846 (6th Cir. 1953).

112. Wheeling Steel Corp., 1 NLRB 699, 708–09 (1936)(holding that an employer's donation of 50¢ per employee per year violated Section 8(a)(2)).

113. Newtone, Inc., 112 NLRB 1153, 1170 (1955)(company permitted labor organization to use mimeograph machine); Crowley Milk Co., 88 NLRB 1049, 1061 (company permitted labor organization to use company safe), *modified*, 208 F.2d 444 (3d Cir. 1953).

114. Cochran, *supra* note 77, at 482; Ultrad Corp. v. NLRB, 454 F.2d 520, 522 (7th

Cir. 1972) citing NLRB v. Thompson Ramo Wooldridge, Inc., 305 F.2d 807, 810 (7th Cir. 1962); Coamo Knitting Mills, Inc. 150 NLRB 579, 582 (1964).

115. NLRB v. H & H Plastics Mfg. Co., 389 F.2d 678, 680 (6th Cir. 1968). The Board adopted a similar list of factors in Speigel Trucking Co., 225 NLRB 178, 179 (1976), *enforced,* 559 F.2d 188 (D.C. Circuit 1977).

116. *Keeler Brass,* 317 NLRB at 114–15.

117. 360 U.S. at 215–18.

Chapter Six. The Role of the EEOC

1. 42 U.S.C. § 2000e-2 (1994).

2. 29 U.S.C. §§ 621–34 (1994).

3. 42 U.S.C. §§ 12101–213 (1994).

4. For detailed histories of the creation of the EEOC, see Alfred W. Blumrosen, MODERN LAW: THE LAW TRANSMISSION SYSTEM AND EQUAL EMPLOYMENT OPPORTUNITY 40–92 (1993); Michael Selmi, *The Value of the EEOC: Reexamining the Agency's Role in Employment Discrimination Law,* 57 OHIO ST. L.J. 1, 5–11 (1996); Arthur Earle Bonfield, *The Origin and Development of American Fair Employment Legislation,* 52 IOWA L. REV. 1043, 1048–88 (1967); Richard K. Berg, *Equal Employment Opportunity Under the Civil Rights Act of 1964,* 31 BROOK. L. REV. 62, 62–68 (1964).

5. Pub. L. No. 88–352, § 705, 78 Stat. 241, 258 (codified as emended at 42 U.S.C. § 2000e-4 (1994)).

6. H.R. REP. NO. 7152, 88th Cong., 1st Sess. § 714(a)(1963).

7. *See* 29 U.S.C. § 156 (1994).

8. See Charles J. Morris, *The NLRB in the Doghouse—Can an Old Board Learn New Tricks?,* 24 SAN DIEGO L. REV. 9, 27–28 (1987); *but see Gould Outlines His Agenda for Change as NLRB Chairman,* Daily Lab. Rep. (BNA) 53, 53 (March 21, 1994)(promising that the NLRB will use substantive rulemaking more frequently in the future).

9. Rebecca Hanner White, *The EEOC, The Courts, and Employment Discrimination Policy: Recognizing the Agency's Leading Role in Statutory Interpretation,* 1995 UTAH L. REV. 51, 60 (1995).

10. 110 CONG. REC. 2575 (1964)(statement of Rep. Celler, who offered the amendment).

11. *Id.* (Chairman Celler, noting no objections to the amendment).

12. One Charles A. Sullivan et al., EMPLOYMENT DISCRIMINATION, § 11.2 (2d ed. 1988).

13. *See* U.S.C. § 2000e-5(b).

14. 42 U.S.C. § 2000e-5(e)(1). The 300-day requirement is applicable to employees working in states (called "deferral" states) that have established a state administrative agency parallel to the EEOC; employees working in a state that has not established such a parallel agency must file their Title VII charge within 180 days of the allegedly unlawful act. *Id.*

15. 29 C.F.R. § 1601.16(a)(1996); *see also* EEOC v. Ford Motor Credit Co., 26 F.3d 44; 47–48 (6th Cir. 1944)(permitting judicial enforcement of an EEOC administrative subpoena if the subpoena (1) seeks relevant information, (2) is not unduly burdensome, and (3) is within the statutory authority of the EEOC).

16. 29 C.F.R. § 1601.15(a); *see also* EEOC Comp. Man. (CCH) ¶ 9810, 821–32 (discussing the types and purposes of interviews during employment-related investigation).

17. Motorola, Inc. v. McLean 484 F.2d 1339, 1346 (7th Cir. 1973), *cert. denied,* 416 U.S. 936 (1974)(upholding the EEOC's right to conduct an on-site inspection); *but see*

EEOC v. Maryland Club Corp., 785 F.2d 471, 475 n.2 (4th Cir.), *cert. denied*, 479 U.S. 815 (1986)(noting that the district court refused to enforce a subpoena demand by the EEOC to tour an employer's facility).

18. *See* 42 U.S.C. § 2000e-5(b).

19. EQUAL EMPLOYMENT OPPORTUNITY COMMISSION, LEGISLATIVE HISTORY OF TITLES VII AND XI OF CIVIL RIGHTS ACT OF 1964, at 3284 (1968) [hereinafter EEOC, LEGISLATIVE HISTORY] (statement of Cong. Celler).

20. *See, e.g.*, Wheeldon v. Monon Corp., 946 F.2d 533, 535–36 (7th Cir. 1991); Marrero-Rivera v. Department of Justice, 800 F. Supp. 1024, 1028–29 (D.P.R. 1992), *aff'd*, 36 F.3d 1089 (1st Cir. 1994); Johnson-McCray v. Board of Educ., 44 Fair Empl. Prac. Cas. 1145, 1146 (S.D.N.Y. 1987); *see also* Babrocky v. Jewel Food Co., 773 F.2d 857, 863–64 (7th Cir. 1985)("allowing a complaint to encompass allegations outside the ambit of the predicate EEOC charge would circumvent the EEOC's investigatory and conciliatory role . . . as surely would an initial failure to file a timely EEOC charge"); Dickey v. Greene, 710 F.2d 1003, 1006 (4th Cir. 1983)(a plaintiff's failure specifically to list her former supervisor as a respondent in her EEOC charge was fatal to her suit against the supervisor because it did not give the EEOC an opportunity to investigate and conciliate the allegations made against the supervisor).

21. *See* Selmi, *supra* note 4, at 16, 22 (noting that each year, the EEOC files approximately 350 lawsuits, whereas private attorneys file between eight thousand and ten thousand employment discrimination cases in federal court).

22. *See* 29 C.F.R. § 1601.28(a)(1)(noting that an employment discrimination claimant can request a notice of right to sue 180 days after filing a charge of discrimination).

23. *See* 42 U.S.C. § 2000e-5(f)(1)(describing procedures for filing a court claim); McDonnell Douglas Corp. v. Green, 411 U.S. 792, 798–99 (1973)(discussing prerequisites to filing a discrimination lawsuit).

24. Francis J. Vaas, *Title VII: Legislative History*, 7 B.C. INDUS. & COM. L. REV. 431, 450–51 (1966)(referring to the "fear that the EEOC would develop into another expensive octopus like the NLRB"); *see also* EEOC v. Hearst Corp., 103 F.3d 462, 465 (5th Cir. 1997)(discussing legislative history of 1972 amendments to Title VII).

25. HOUSE COMM. ON THE JUDICIARY, ADDITIONAL VIEWS OF HON. GEORGE MEADER, H.R. REP. NO. 914, 88th Cong., 1st Sess. (1963), *reprinted in* EEOC LEGISLATIVE HISTORY, *supra* note 19, at 2043, 2057. As indicated by a member of the House Committee on the Judiciary, "a substantial number of committee members . . . preferred that the ultimate determination of discrimination rested with the Federal judiciary. Through this requirement . . . settlement of complaints w[ould] occur more rapidly and with greater frequency. In addition . . . the employer or labor union w[ould] have a fairer forum to establish innocence. . . ." HOUSE COMM. ON THE JUDICIARY, ADDITIONAL VIEWS OF HON. WILLIAM MCCULLOCH ET AL., H.R. REP. NO. 914, 88th Cong., 1st Sess., pt. 2 (1963), *reprinted in* EEOC LEGISLATIVE HISTORY, *supra* note 19, at 2122, 2150.

26. EEOC, LEGISLATIVE HISTORY, *supra* note 19, at 2029 (1968).

27. *See* STAFF OF SENATE SUBCOMM. ON LABOR OF COMM. ON LABOR AND PUBLIC WELFARE, 92d CONG., 2d SESS., LEGISLATIVE HISTORY OF THE EQUAL EMPLOYMENT OPPORTUNITY ACT OF 1972, 141–47, 251–314, 1557 (Comm. Print 1972).

28. EEOC, LEGISLATIVE HISTORY, *supra* note 19, at 10–11, 3003–04.

29. Amend. No. 656, 88th Cong., 2d Sess., 110 CONG. REC. 11,926 (1964); Amend. No. 1052, 88th Cong., 2d Sess., 110 CONG. REC. 13,310 (1964).

30. A staff member of the Senate Judiciary Committee summarized the change as

follows: "The Senate amendment struck out the power of the . . . [EEOC] to enforce this title of the bill in court suits. . . . Its function now is limited to an attempt at voluntary conciliation of alleged unlawful practices. . . . Under the Senate amendment only an aggrieved person can bring suit against an employer unless there is a pattern or practice of resistance. . . . The Commission cannot institute suit at all." 110 CONG. REC. 14,331 (1964), *quoted in* Vaas, *supra* note 24, at 452.

31. Hugh D. Graham, THE CIVIL RIGHTS ERA, 157–59, 235–36 (1990).

32. Michael I. Sovern, LEGAL RESTRAINTS ON RACIAL DISCRIMINATION IN EMPLOYMENT, 205 (1966).

33. The EEOC's reputation has not improved substantially over the years. *See, e.g.,* Selmi, *supra* note 4, at 64 (describing the EEOC as "a failure, serving in some instances as little more than an administrative obstacle to resolution of claims on the merits").

34. The purpose of the change was explained in a Senate report as follows: "The accomplishment of the stated purpose of Title VII, the elimination of employment discrimination in all areas of employment in this Nation, has not been accomplished under the present system of voluntary compliance through EEOC procedures or, in the alternative, the private law suit. Under the provisions of section 4 of the bill, the overriding public interest in equal employment opportunity would be asserted through direct Federal enforcement." 4 LARSON EMPLOYMENT DISCRIMINATION § 75.01, at 75–2 (2d ed 1995).

35. Equal Employment Opportunity Act of 1972, Pub. L. No. 92–261, §§ 1–3, 86 Stat. 103 (codified as amended in scattered sections of 5 U.S.C. and 42 U.S.C.).

36. *See* Selmi, *supra* note 4, at 16, 21 (noting that the EEOC receives approximately 90,000 charges of discrimination per year, but only files approximately 350 substantive lawsuits involving a total of approximately 450 allegations of discrimination); William M. Howard, *Arbitrating Claims of Employment Discrimination: What Really Does Happen? What Really Should Happen?,* 50 DISPUTE RESOLUTION J. 40, 45 (Oct.–Dec. 1995).

37. 500 U.S. 20 (1991)(compelling arbitration of a securities representative's suit against his employer for age discrimination).

38. *Gilmer,* 500 U.S. at 28.

39. *Id.*

40. *Id.* at 32.

41. *See* EEOC v. Tire Kingdom, Inc., 80 F.3d 449, 451–52 (11th Cir. 1996)(confirming EEOC's authority to conduct an investigation into alleged discrimination in absence of a valid charge of discrimination); EEOC v. American & Efird Mills, Inc., 904 F.2d 300 (4th Cir. 1992); *see also* R. Gaull Silberman et al., *Alternative Dispute Resolution of Employment Discrimination Claims,* 54 LA. L. REV. 1533, 1550 (1994).

42. In addition to the cases cited in the text, see also EEOC v. Cosmair, Inc., L'Oreal Hair Care Div., 821 F.2d 1085, 1090 (5th Cir. 1987)(holding that an employee's waiver of the right to file a charge with the EEOC is void as against public policy); EEOC v. McDonnell Douglas Corp., 948 F. Supp. 54, 55 (E.D. Mo. 1996)(noting that the EEOC sues not in a representative capacity, but "on its own authority to vindicate the public interest"); EEOC v. Astra U.S.A., Inc., 929 F. Supp. 512, 521 (D. Mass.)(granting EEOC's request for preliminary injunction enjoining the enforcement of provisions in settlement agreements that prohibited the employees from filing EEOC charges or assisting the EEOC in any investigation), *aff'd in part, vacated in part,* 94 F.3d 738 (1st Cir. 1996); *cf.* EEOC v. Hearst Corp., 103 F.3d 462 (5th Cir. 1997).

43. 446 U.S. 318 (1980).

44. Federal Rule of Civil Procedure 23 permits one or more members of a class to sue

or be sued as representative parties on behalf of all members of the class only if "(1) the class is so numerous that joinder of all members is impracticable, (2) there are questions of law or fact common to the class, (3) the claims or defenses of the representative parties are typical of the claims or defenses of the class, and (4) the representative parties will fairly and adequately protect the interests of the class." FED. R. CIV. P. 23(a).

45. *General Telephone,* 446 U.S. at 333–34.

46. *Id.* at 324.

47. *Id.* at 318.

48. 525 F.2d 1007 (6th Cir. 1975).

49. 29 C.F.R. § 1601.10 permits an aggrieved person to withdraw his EEOC charge only with the consent of the EEOC.

50. *McLean Trucking,* 525 F.2d at 1010 (quoting EEOC v. Kimberley-Clark Corp., 511 F.2d 1352 (6th Cir.), *cert. denied,* 423 U.S. 994 (1975))(citations omitted).

51. 813 F.2d 1539 (9th Cir. 1987).

52. *Id.* at 1544.

53. *Id.* at 1542.

54. 860 F.2d 372 (10th Cir. 1988).

55. *Id.* at 377.

56. *See, e.g.,* New Orleans S.S. Ass'n v. EEOC, 680 F.2d 23, 25 (5th Cir. 1982); *see also* Secretary of Labor v. Fitzsimmons, 805 F.2d 682, 694 (7th Cir. 1986) *(en banc)* (holding that government actions to enforce ERISA are not barred under *res judicata* principles by private ERISA litigation); Donovan v. Cunningham, 716 F.2d 1455, 1462 (5th Cir. 1983)(same), *cert. denied,* 467 U.S. 1251 (1984); United States v. Massachusetts Maritime Academy, 762 F.2d 142, 151–52 (1st Cir. 1985)(holding that the mootness of the complainant's claim in a Title IX action did not moot the Attorney General's right to continue the suit against the maritime academy for sex discrimination in student recruitment and admissions).

57. 500 U.S. 20 (1991).

58. *See also Goodyear,* 813 F.2d at 1543; *McLean,* 525 F.2d at 1011; *Astra U.S.A.,* 929 F. Supp. at 521 (stating in dicta that an employee may, in a settlement agreement, "waive the right to recover damages both in his or her own lawsuit and in a lawsuit brought by the EEOC on the employee's behalf"); *EEOC Guidance on Waivers under Civil Rights Laws,* DAILY LAB. REP. E-4 (Apr. 14, 1997)(noting that where an employee has waived or settled her claim but nonetheless files a charge with the EEOC, the employer will be "shielded against any further recovery by the charging party provided the waiver agreement or settlement is valid under applicable law. . . . However, while a private agreement can eliminate an individual's right to personal recovery, it cannot interfere with EEOC's right to enforce [the anti-discrimination laws] by seeking relief that will benefit the public and any victims of an employer's unlawful practices who have not validly waived their claims.").

59. *See* Richard C. Reuben, *Two Agencies Review Forced Arbitration—EEOC Gets Injunction against Company That Told Workers: Accept ADR or Quit,* 81 ABA J. 26, 26 (1995)(quoting EEOC Commissioner Paul Steven Miller); *see also* EQUAL EMPLOYMENT OPPORTUNITY COMMISSION, LEGAL SERVICES, OFFICE OF LEGAL COUNSEL, NOTICE NO. 915.002, at 3 (July 17, 1995)(stating that the EEOC "believes that parties must knowingly, willingly, and voluntarily enter into an ADR proceeding"); *Employers Pursue Mandatory Arbitration Despite EEOC's Opposition to Practice,* DAILY LAB. REP. D-8 (Oct. 10, 1996)(noting the EEOC's "oft-stated view that mandatory arbitration of discrimination claims conflicts with Title VII . . . and other federal laws"); *EEOC Guidance on Waivers*

under Civil Rights Laws, DAILY LAB. REP. E-4 (Apr. 14, 1997)(asserting that any agreements that would prohibit an employee from filing a charge with the EEOC or participating in an EEOC investigation violate the anti-retaliation provisions of the anti-discrimination laws, and therefore are void).

60. In addition to the *ROID* case, *see* Duffield v. Robertson Stephens & Co., No. C-95–0109-EFL (N.D. Cal.)(amicus brief filed by EEOC); Cosgrove v. Shearson Lehman Bros., No. 95–3432, 1997 WL 4783 (6th Cir. 1997)(amicus brief filed by EEOC); EEOC v. Midland Food Services, LLC, No. 1:96-MC-107 (N.D. Ohio); Johnson v. Hubbard Broadcasting, Inc., No. 4–96-cv-107 (D. Minn.)(amicus brief filed by EEOC). In the amicus brief filed in *Duffield*, the EEOC stated: "The Commission strongly favors the voluntary use of arbitration and other forms of alternative dispute resolution ('ADR') and believes that properly used it can speed and simplify the process of adjudicating discrimination claims. However, arbitration that is not knowing and voluntary deprives individuals of substantial rights provided by congress, especially where—as alleged here—the procedures are unfair and specifically designed not to safeguard statutory rights." Pierre Levy, *Gilmer Revisited: The Judicial Erosion of Employee Statutory Rights*, 26 N.M.L. REV. 455, 478 n. 193 (1996)(quoting Memorandum of Points and Authorities of the EEOC as Amicus Curiae, Duffield v. Robertson Stephens & Co., No. C-95–0109-EFL at 1 (N.D. Cal. filed Aug. 4, 1995)(EEOC Memorandum)). The amicus brief described the EEOC's objections to the procedures at issue as follows: "[Arbitration] (1) is not governed by the statutory requirements and standards of Title VII; (2) is conducted by arbitrators given no training and possessing no expertise in employment law; (3) routinely does not permit plaintiffs to receive punitive damages and attorneys' fees to which they would otherwise be entitled under the statute; and (4) forces them to pay exorbitant 'forum fees' in the tens of thousands of dollars, greatly discouraging aggrieved employees from seeking relief." *Id.* at 478 (quoting EEOC Memorandum at 3).

61. 67 Fair Empl. Prac. Cas. (BNA) 1243 (S.D. Tex. 1995). Similarly, in Johnson v. Hubbard Broadcasting, Inc., 940 F. Supp. 1447, the EEOC filed a brief as amicus curiae, arguing that the compulsory arbitration agreement at issue abrogated the plaintiff's Title VII rights. The court granted the EEOC's motion for leave to participate as amicus, but nonetheless ordered the case to arbitration.

62. *Id.*

63. *Federal Judge Issues Injunction against Employment Arbitration Policy*, 6 WORLD ARB. & MEDIATION REP. 95, 95 (1995)("Judge Norman Black found that the arbitration policy appeared to be part of an effort by the employer to penalize or dismiss workers who had filed discrimination and harassment complaints."); *Boss Can't Force Staff to Sign an ADR Clause, Court Finds, Adopting the EEOC's Argument*, 13 ALTERNATIVES TO HIGH COST LITIG. 76 (1995)(the EEOC argued that "the company imposed the policy to get even with employees who complained of sexual harassment and other discriminatory conduct").

64. *River Oaks Imaging*, 67 Fair Empl. Prac. Cas. (BNA) at 1243.

65. *Id.*

66. *See supra* note 59 and accompanying text.

67. *See* Atchison, Topeka, & Santa Fe Ry. Co. v. Pena, 44 F.3d 437, 445 (7th Cir. 1994)(Easterbrook, J., concurring); Stephen Breyer, *Judicial Review of Questions of Law and Policy*, 38 ADMIN. L. REV. 363 (1986); Colin S. Diver, *Statutory Interpretation in the Administrative State*, 133 U. PA. L. REV. 549, 565–67 (1985); Clark Byse, *Scope of Judicial Review in Informal Rulemaking*, 33 ADMIN. L. REV. 183, 191 (1981).

68. *See* Ronald M. Levin, *Judicial Review and the Uncertain Appeal of Certainty on Appeal*, 44 DUKE L.J. 1081, 1084 (1995).

69. *See, e.g.,* Regents of Univ. of Calif. v. Public Employees' Relations Bd., 485 U.S. 589, 603–04 (1988) (White, Jr., concurring); Lukhard v. Reed, 481 U.S. 368, 383 (1987) (Blackmun, Jr., concurring); Pattern Makers League v. NLRB, 473 U.S. 95, 117 (1985) (White, J., concurring).

70. 401 U.S. 424, 433–34 (1971).

71. 422 U.S. 405, 431 (1975).

72. 5 U.S.C. §§ 551–96 (1994).

73. *Albemarle,* 422 U.S. at 452 (Burger, C.J., concurring & dissenting).

74. 429 U.S. 125 (1976).

75. *Id.* at 141 and n.20.

76. *See* BLACK'S LAW DICTIONARY (6th ed. 1991); JEM Broadcasting Co., Inc. v. F.C.C., 22 F.3d 320, 326–27 (D.C. Cir. 1994); Kenneth Culp Davis and Richard J. Pierce, Jr., ADMINISTRATIVE LAW TREATISE, vol. I, § 6.4, at 248–50 (3d ed. 1994); Bernard Schwartz, ADMINISTRATIVE LAW, § 4.8, at 180–82 (3d ed. 1991).

77. 486 U.S. 107, 112, 121–22 (1988).

78. *Id.* at 112.

79. *Id.* at 115–16; *see also id.* at 125–26 (O'Connor, J., concurring).

80. 499 U.S. 244, 258 (1991).

81. *Id.*

82. *Id.* at 256–57.

83. *See, e.g.,* Garcia v. Spun Steak Co., 998 F.2d 1480, 1489 (9th Cir. 1993)(stating that courts may consider but are not bound by EEOC guidelines), *cert. denied,* 114 S. Ct. 2726 (1994); Colgan v. Fisher Scientific Co., 935 F.2d 1407, 1421 n.11 (3d Cir.)(stating that courts need not defer to the EEOC), *cert denied,* 502 U.S. 941 (1991); Rowe v. Sullivan, 967 F.2d 186, 192–94 (5th Cir. 1992)(giving deference to EEOC's opinions); Vogel v. City of Cincinnati, 959 F.2d 594, 598 (6th Cir.)(giving deference to EEOC interpretation of Civil Rights Act of 1991), *cert. denied,* 506 U.S. 827 (1992); Russell v. Microdyne Corp., 830 F. Supp. 305, 308 (E.D. Va. 1993)(giving EEOC guidelines limited deference); *rev'd on other grounds,* 65 F.3d 1229 (1995).

84. 473 U.S. 614, 628 (1985).

85. 9 U.S.C. §§ 1–16.

86. This presumption—that a statutory claim is presumed arbitrable unless the language of the statute expressly indicates otherwise—is discussed in chapter 2 parts F and G.

87. *See* Selmi, *supra* note 4, at 50 (noting the negligible value of the EEOC as a deterrent to employment discrimination).

Chapter Seven. Compulsory Employment Arbitration in the Securities Industry

1. 500 U.S. 20 (1991).

2. *Id.* at 23.

3. *Id.* at 35.

4. Lewis D. Lowenfels and Alan R. Bromberg, *Securities Industry Arbitrations: An Examination and Analysis,* 53 ALBANY L. REV. 755, 769 (1989); Deborah Masucci & Edward Morris, Jr., *Securities Arbitration at Self-Regulatory Organizations: Administration and Procedures,* in SECURITIES ARBITRATION 1988 at 309–13 (Corporate Law & Practice Course Handbook Series No. 601, 1988).

5. The American Stock Exchange (AMEX) adopted arbitration in 1964, followed by the National Association of Securities Dealers (NASD) in 1968, and the Chicago Board Options Exchange (CBOE) in 1973. Lowenfels & Bromberg, *supra* note 4, at 769; Masucci & Morris, *supra* note 4, at 309–13; NASD Manual (CCH) ¶ 3701, at 3711 (1988).

6. The move in the securities industry toward compulsory arbitration began in 1987 following the Supreme Court's decision, in Shearson/American Express, Inc. v. McMahon, 482 U.S. 220 (1987), that brokerage firms could require customers to settle their disputes through arbitration. Peter M. Mundheim, *The Desirability of Punitive Damages in Securities Arbitration: Challenges Facing the Industry Regulators in the Wake of* Mastrobuono, 144 U. PA. L. REV. 197, 200–01 (1995); George H. Friedman, *Changes in Rules on Securities Cases,* N.Y. L.J., Aug. 5, 1993, at 3, 28. In 1980, 830 securities arbitration cases were filed; that number rose to 5,300 in 1993. Mundheim, *supra,* at 201; Susan Antilla, *An Arbitration Plan Goes Begging,* N.Y. TIMES, Jan. 9, 1994, at 15.

7. HEALTH, EDUCATION AND HUMAN SERVICES DIVISION, GENERAL ACCOUNTING OFFICE, EMPLOYMENT DISCRIMINATION: HOW REGISTERED REPRESENTATIVES FARE IN DISCRIMINATION DISPUTES (1994) [hereinafter 1994 GAO REPORT].

8. *See* Mundheim, *supra* note 6, at 201 n.23.

9. *Id.*

10. *Id.* at 1.

11. *Id.* at 1 (noting that registered representatives constitute approximately thirty-two percent of securities industry employees in the largest fifty securities firms in the United States).

12. *Id.* at 4; *see* Securities Exchange Act of 1934, 15 U.S.C. § 78(f) (1994)(providing that no registration of a national securities exchange shall be granted or remain in force unless its rules provide for the expulsion, suspension, or discipline of a member for conduct inconsistent with just and equitable principles of trade).

13. 15 U.S.C. § 78s (b) (providing that SROs must file proposed rule changes with the SEC). The SEC has the power to "abrogate, add to, and delete from" SRO rules. William A. Gregory and William J. Schneider, *Securities Arbitration: A Need for Continued Reform,* 17 NOVA L. REV. 1223, 1247 (1993)(quoting 15 U.S.C. § 78s(c)). The SEC must first notify the SRO, publish notice of the proposed amendment in the Federal Register, and hold a public hearing for comment. 15 U.S.C. § 78s(c)(1).

14. *See id.* (the SEC can amend any rule it deems "necessary . . . to insure the fair administration" of the SROs).

15. *See* Masucci and Morris, *supra* note 4, at 309, 313; *Securities Arbitration at Self-Regulatory Organizations: Administration and Procedures,* in SECURITIES ARBITRATION 1988 at 309.

16. Constantine N. Katsoris, *The Arbitration of a Public Securities Dispute,* 53 FORD-HAM L. REV. 279, 283 (1984).

17. *See* Securities Exchange Act Release No. 12, 528, 9 SEC DOCKET 833, 834 (June 9, 1976); Exchange Act Release No. 34–26805, 54 Fed. Reg. 21144, 21145 (1989); Constantine N. Katsoris, *The Arbitration of a Public Securities Dispute,* 53 FORDHAM L. REV. 279, 283–84 (1984).

18. Exchange Act Release No. 34–12974, [1976–1977 Transfer Binder] Fed. Sec. L. Rep. (CCH) ¶ 80807 (Nov. 15, 1976); David A. Lipton, *The Standard on Which Arbitrators Base Their Decisions: The SROs Must Decide,* 16 SEC. REG. L. J. 3, 5 (1988).

19. Securities Exchange Act Release No. 12, 974, 10 SEC DOCKET 955–56 (Nov. 15, 1976).

20. FIFTH REPORT OF THE SECURITIES INDUSTRY CONFERENCE ON ARBITRATION, 2 (Apr. 1986) [hereinafter SICA REPORT NO. 5].

21. *Id.* at 2–3.

22. GENERAL GOVERNMENT DIVISION, GENERAL ACCOUNTING OFFICE, SECURITIES ARBITRATION: HOW INVESTORS FARE, 15 n.2 (1992) [hereinafter 1992 GAO REPORT].

23. PROPOSALS TO ESTABLISH A UNIFORM SYSTEM FOR THE RESOLUTION OF CUSTOMER DISPUTES INVOLVING SMALL CLAIMS, Exhibit D (Nov. 15, 1977); Constantine N. Katsoris, *SICA: The First Twenty Years,* 23 FORDHAM URBAN L. J. 483, 489 (1996).

24. Katsoris, *supra* note 16, at 283–84.

25. UNIFORM CODE OF ARBITRATION, § 13 [hereinafter UCA], *reprinted in* SECURITIES INDUS. CONFERENCE ON ARBITRATION REPORT NO. 6, at 5–12 (1989).

26. SICA REPORT NO. 5, *supra* note 20, at 4; SECURITIES INDUSTRY CONFERENCE ON ARBITRATION, EIGHTH REPORT, 1 (April 1986) [hereinafter SICA REPORT NO. 8].

27. 482 U.S. 220 (1987). This case is discussed in greater detail in chapter 2.

28. Lowenfels and Bromberg, *supra* note 4, at 772; N.Y. TIMES, May 11, 1989, at D2, Col. 5; N.Y. TIMES, Nov. 15, 1988, at D1, Col. 6; N.Y. TIMES, Sept. 22, 1988, at D7, Col. 5; N.Y. TIMES, July 13, 1988, at D15, Col. 1; *see also NASAA Proposes Ban on Mandatory Predispute Arbitration Agreements,* 20 Sec. Reg. & L. Rep. (BNA) No. 22, at 850 (June 3, 1988).

29. *See SEC Tables Proposal to Bar Brokers from Mandating Predispute Agreements,* 20 Sec. Reg. & L. Rep. (BNA) No. 22, at 832 (June 3, 1988) (discussing initial proposal to ban compulsory arbitration agreements); *Boucher Introduces Bill Barring Mandatory Arbitration Clauses,* 20 Sec. Reg. & L. Rep. (BNA) No. 27, at 1053 (July 8, 1988).

30. *See* 134 CONG. REC. E2233 (Daily ed. June 30, 1988) (statement of Rep. Boucher setting forth analysis of bill).

31. *SIA Says There's No Data to Support Bar on Predispute Arbitration Clauses,* 20 Sec. Reg. & L. Rep. (BNA) No. 26, at 1025 (July 1, 1988); *Boucher Introduces Bill, supra* note 29, at 1053 (noting the unanimous disapproval of the bill by the SEC).

32. Lowenfels and Bromberg, *supra* note 4, at 773; *Self-Regulatory Organizations; Order Approving Proposed Rule Changes by the New York Stock Exchange, Inc., National Association of Securities Dealers, Inc., and the American Stock Exchange, Inc., Relating to the Arbitration Process and the Use of Predispute Arbitration Clauses,* Exchange Act Release No. 26, 805 [1989 Transfer Binder] Fed. Sec. L. Rep. (CCH) ¶ 84,414, at 80,100 (May 10, 1989) [hereinafter SEC Release No. 26]; Securities Industry Ass'n v. Connolly, 703 F. Supp. 146, 148 n.3 (D. Mass. 1988), *aff'd,* 883 F.2d 1114 (1st Cir.), *cert. denied,* 495 U.S. 956 (1990).

33. SEC Release No. 26, *supra* note 32, at 80, 100, 80, 111–13 n.51.

34. *Id.* at 80, 114.

35. Megan L. Dunphy, Comment, *Mandatory Arbitration: Stripping Securities Industry Employees of Their Civil Rights,* 44 CATH. U. L. REV. 1169, 1172 (1995).

36. Mark D. Fitterman and Robert Asher Love, The Regulatory Framework of Securities Arbitration, in SECURITIES ARBITRATION: PRACTICE AND FORMS, §1.01, at 1–1, 1–4 (Anthony Djinis and Joseph A. Post eds., 1994); NATIONAL ASSOCIATION OF SECURITIES DEALERS: CODE OF ARBITRATION PROCEDURE, 4; § 1 (Dec. 1993) [hereinafter NASD CAP]; NEW YORK STOCK EXCHANGE, INC., CONSTITUTION AND RULES (CCH) ¶ 2347 rule 347 (Nov. 1, 1993) [hereinafter NYSE RULES.]

37. Kuehner v. Dickinson & Co., 84 F.3d 316, 318 (9th Cir. 1996) (quoting NASD CAP, pt. I, § 1 & pt. II, § 8).

38. *See NASD Announces SEC Approval of Rules Making Employment Disputes Arbitrable*, 25 Sec. Reg. & L. Rep. (BNA) 1250, 1252 (Sept. 17, 1993) [hereinafter *SEC Approval*].

39. 1992 GAO REPORT, *supra* note 7, at 3, 5, 13, 25.

40. *See* Securities Exchange Act of 1934, 15 U.S.C. § 78b.

41. Letter from Robert L. D. Colby, Deputy Director, Securities & Exchange Commission, to Linda G. Morra, Director, Education and Employment Issues, GAO 5 (Dec. 30, 1993), *reprinted* in 1994 GAO REPORT, *supra* note 7, app. at 25.

42. 1994 GAO REPORT, *supra* note 7, at 13–16.

43. *See, e.g.,* Dunphy, *supra* note 35, at 1173 and sources cited at 1173 n.17. For example, Marc Steinberg states: "[M]ounting evidence shows that many investors emerge victorious from arbitration, even recovering punitive damages in appropriate cases. The lack of intensive pre-trial discovery (at least as compared to the court setting) and the more expeditious time frame in which arbitration proceeds may favor the public investor who cannot match the brokerage firms litigation resources. Moreover, the inapplicability of strict pleading rules, along with the informality of arbitration, may result in the arbitrators seeking to be 'fair' whereas such claims may have been dismissed by a court." Marc I. Steinberg, *Securities Arbitration: Better for Investor Than the Courts?*, 62 BROOKLYN L. REV. 1505–6 (1996)(citations omitted). Steinberg thus concludes that "investors today likely fare better in arbitration than they would in federal court." *Id.* at 1531.

44. *See* Mundheim, *supra* note 6, at 203.

45. *See* C. Edward Fletcher, ARBITRATING SECURITIES DISPUTES, 106–07 (Leary D. Soderquist, ed., 1990); 15A David A. Lipton, BROKER-DEALER REGULATION, §4.02, at 4–20 (1995); Mundheim, *supra* note 6, at 203.

46. *See generally* Robert R. Gregory, *Arbitration: It's Mandatory But It Ain't Fair*, 19 SEC. REG. L. J. 181 (1991); Jacobs and Siconolfi, *Investors Fare Poorly Fighting Wall Street —And May Do Worse*, WALL ST. J. (Feb. 8, 1995), at A1; *see* Steinberg, *supra* note 43, at 1506; Report of the Arbitration Policy Task Force to the Board of Governors, National Association of Securities Dealers, Inc. [1995–96 Transfer Binder], Fed. Sec. L. Rep. (CCH) ¶ 85,735, at 87,475 (1996); *but see* Norman J. Poser, *When ADR Eclipses Litigation: The Brave New World of Securities Arbitration*, 59 BROOKLYN L. REV. 1095, 1111 (1993)(stating that "it would not be fair to describe [arbitration] as a deck stacked in favor of the brokerage firms").

47. Dunphy, *supra* note 35, at 1193–94; Richard A. Bales & Reagan Burch, *The Future of Employment Arbitration in the Non-Union Sector*, 45 LAB. L. J. 627, 631 (1994).

48. *See, e.g.,* Dunphy, *supra* note 35, at 1194–1200.

49. David E. Robbins, SECURITIES ARBITRATION PROCEDURE MANUAL § 10.04 at 10–9 (2d ed. 1995); Masucci, *supra* note 4, at 321.

50. *See* Marilyn Blumberg Cane and Patricia A. Shub, SECURITIES ARBITRATION: LAW AND PROCEDURE, 369 (1991) ("word of mouth and current panelists' recommendations of new arbitrators generally is [sic] used" in the recruitment process).

51. *See* Bowsher v. Synar, 478 U.S. 714 (1986).

52. 1994 GAO REPORT, *supra* note 7, at 8.

53. *See, e.g.,* William M. Howard, *Arbitrating Employment Discrimination Claims: Do You Really Have To? Do You Really Want To?*, 43 DRAKE L. REV. 255, 276–77 (1994); *see also* Olson v. American Arb. Ass'n, 876 F. Supp. 850, 852 (N.D. Tex. 1995) (rejecting

plaintiff's claims under the Texas Deceptive Trade Practices Act that AAA's arbitrators were biased), *aff'd*, 71 F.3d 877 (1995).

54. Federal Arbitration Act, 9 U.S.C. § 10 (1994).

55. As of mid-1993, 90.6 percent of federal circuit court judges, and 90.1 percent of federal district court judges, were men. *See Report of the Special Committee on Gender to the Gender, Race, and Ethnic Bias Task Force Project in the D.C. Circuit*, 84 GEO. L. J. 1657, 1678 (1996) (citing Alliance for Justice, *AFJ Mid-Year 1994 Report*, July 1, 1994, at table 3). Similarly, as of mid-1994, 90 percent of federal circuit court judges, and approximately 85 percent of federal district court judges, were white. *Report of the Special Committee on Race and Ethnicity to the D.C. Circuit Task Force on Gender, Race, and Ethnic Bias*, 64 GEO. WASH. L. REV. 189, 202 (1996) (citing *Report on the Federal Judiciary of the Alliance for Justice*).

56. *See* Judith P. Vladeck and Theodore O. Rogers, *Employment Discrimination*, 63 FORDHAM L. REV. 1613, 1626–27, 1628 (1995).

57. UCA, *supra* note 25, § 8(a)(2).

58. *Id.* § 8(a)(3); *see also Guidelines for Classification of Arbitrators*, DEPARTMENT OF ARBITRATION, NEW YORK STOCK EXCHANGE, INC., ARBITRATION RULES: GUIDELINES FOR CLASSIFICATION OF ARBITRATORS No. 5 (May 10, 1989) [hereinafter NYSE GUIDELINES].

59. Fletcher, *supra* note 45, at 109–10.

60. By "panel," I mean the arbitrators who have been selected to decide a given dispute. In labor arbitration, the word "panel" refers to the list of potential arbitrators that the parties receive.

61. NASD CAP, *supra* note 36, §§ 4, 9.

62. Cane and Shub, *supra* note 50, at 13.

63. NASD CAP, *supra* note 36, § 9(b)(ii).

64. *Id.* § 19(b).

65. Dunphy, *supra* note 35, at 1196; *SEC Approval, supra* note 38, at 1252.

66. UCA, *supra* note 25, § 13.

67. *Id.* § 13(c).

68. *Id.* § 9; *see also* Mundheim, *supra* note 6, at 230.

69. Dunphy, *supra* note 35, at 1199 n.170.

70. NASD CAP, *supra* note 36, § 23(a).

71. UCA, *supra* note 25, §§ 9, 11(d).

72. UCA, *supra* note 25, § 10.

73. *See* Mundheim, *supra* note 6, at 226 (discussing bias in the context of investor suits against brokerage firms, and stating that "[f]orcing investors to bring their complaints to forums [sic] that are in the 'brokerage firm's proverbial backyard' invites skepticism about the opportunity for customers to receive unbiased treatment" (quoting Brief Amicus Curiae in Support of Petitioners by the Public Investors Arbitration Bar Association at 25–26, Mastrobuono v. Shearson Lehman Hutton Inc., 115 S. Ct. 1212 (1995) (No. 94–18)). In this context, however, the General Accounting Office has found no evidence that any such bias has affected case outcomes. The GAO compared arbitration results in arbitrations conducted by SROs with the results in arbitrations conducted by the independent American Arbitration Association and concluded that "the forum in which a case [is] arbitrated [is] not a factor that affect[s] whether investors receive [ ] an award or the proportion of any award the investor receive[s]." 1992 GAO Report, *supra* note 7, at 35.

74. See Frank Elkouri and Edna Asper Elkouri, HOW ARBITRATION WORKS, 135–37 (4th ed. 1989).

75. G. Richard Shell, *ERISA and Other Federal Employment Statutes: When is Commercial Arbitration an "Adequate Substitute" for the Courts?*, 68 TEX. L. REV. 509, 569 (1990). In an interview with BNA, SEC Commissioner Isaac Hunt criticized employment arbitration in the securities industry and noted that "If you look at the makeup of the industry, you're not going to have the most diverse group of employees and employers in the world." *Arbitration: SEC Commissioner Says Industry Panels Not Qualified to Handle Job Bias Claims*, 59 DAILY LAB. REP. A-5 (March 27, 1997) [hereinafter SEC Commissioner].

76. *See* 1994 GAO REPORT, *supra* note 7, at 3 (stating that neither the NASD nor NYSE "systematically assigns arbitrators to panels on the basis of subject matter expertise"); SEC Commissioner, *supra* note 75 (asserting that "securities industry-dominated panels are . . . uniquely unqualified to arbitrate employment discrimination claims" because securities arbitrators have "very little experience" with employment law). The SROs require arbitrators initiated into the arbitrator pool to take an initial mandatory training program to ensure that they have been trained adequately in the arbitration process. NASD, INTRODUCTORY TRAINING FOR ARBITRATORS, 2 (1994). However, there is no requirement that arbitrators receive similar training in specific areas of the law. *Id.* (stating that while training is an ongoing process and an introductory session is required, second level training, which is "a more in-depth study of selected topics," such as employment law, is encouraged but currently not required). The SROs presently are attempting to provide arbitrators with current literature, case law developments, and periodic *voluntary* training opportunities in specific areas of the law. SECURITIES ARBITRATION, *supra* note 4, §1.06[1], at 1–37; 1994 GAO REPORT, *supra* note 7, app. II at 28 (noting that the NASD has begun training its arbitrators on employment law issues); *but see* Vladeck, *supra* note 56, at 1628–30 (noting the difficulty of creating qualified employment arbitrators in a two-hour training session).

77. 1992 GAO REPORT, *supra* note 7, at 6.

78. *Id.* at 8.

79. *See* 1994 GAO REPORT, *supra* note 7.

80. *Levitt's Views Sought Regarding Changes to Industry Arbitration Process*, 26 SEC. REG. & L. REP. (BNA) 876 (1994) (quoting Letter from Rep. Edward Markey (D-Mass.), Rep. Marjorie Margoelis-Mezvinsky (D-Pa.), and Lynn Schenk (D-Calif.) to Arthur Levitt, Chair, Securities & Exchange Commission (June 9, 1994)).

81. 1994 GAO REPORT, *supra* note 7, at 12.

82. *Id.*

83. FED. R. CIV. P. 30.

84. FED. R. CIV. P. 31.

85. FED. R. CIV. P. 33.

86. FED. R. CIV. P. 34.

87. Cane and Shub, *supra* note 50, at 10 (noting that discovery "is generally limited to the exchange of documents and the identification of witnesses"); 2 N.Y.S.E. Guide (CCH) ¶ 2636, at 4328 (Rule 636 (a)(6)(1995) ("Pre-Arbitration discovery is generally more limited and different from court proceedings")).

88. UCA, *supra* note 25, § 20; *see also* Cane and Shub, *supra* note 50, at 35–36.

89. Cane and Shub, *supra* note 50, at 10; Reginald Alleyne, *Statutory Discrimination Claims: Rights "Waived" and Lost in the Arbitration Form*, 13 HOFSTRA LAB. L.J. 381, 411 (1996).

90. The rules of the exchanges do not specifically provide for depositions, but they do empower arbitrators to issue any order that "is necessary to permit any party to fully develop its case." American Stock Exchange, Inc., Arbitration Rules, Rule 607(e), 2 Am. Stock Ex.

Guide (CCH) ¶ 9545A (July 31, 1989) [hereinafter AMEX Arbitration Rules]; New York Stock Exchange, Inc., Arbitration Rules, Rule 619(e), 2 N.Y.S.E. Guide (CCH) ¶ 2619 (Nov. 30, 1989) [hereinafter NYSE Arbitration Rules]. The SEC approved this language "based on our clear understanding that depositions will now be available as a matter of routine to parties in appropriate cases." Exchange Act Release No. 34–26805, 54 Fed. Reg. 21144, 21150 (1989). The NASD has similarly represented to the SEC that depositions are permitted under its arbitration rules. *Id.*

91. Cane and Shub, *supra* note 50, at 10.

92. UCA, *supra* note 25, § 20(d).

93. UCA, *supra* note 25, § 20(e).

94. *Gilmer,* 500 U.S. at 31 (quoting Mitsubishi Motors Corp. v. Soler Chrysler-Plymouth, Inc., 473 U.S. 614, 628 (1985)).

95. *See, e.g.,* Jennifer A. Marler, Note, *Arbitrating Employment Discrimination Claims: The Lower Courts Extend Gilmer v. Interstate/Johnson Lane Corp. to Include Individual Employment Contracts,* 74 Wash. U. L. Q. 443, 471, 473 n. 238 (1996); *see also* Robbins, *supra* note 49, § 9.01 at 9–2 (stating that the "[e]xtensive pretrial discovery permitted in the courts is not available in securities arbitration proceedings . . . [b]ecause it could be expensive and burdensome, a stalling tactic, a nuisance, an effort to wear down one's opponent, and, in short, contrary to the objective of arbitration as an expeditious, cost-effective alternative to the courts").

96. *See, e.g.,* Dunphy, *supra* note 35, at 1203; 140 Cong. Rec. E1753–54 (daily ed. Aug. 17, 1994) (statement of Rep. Markey).

97. *See, e.g.,* Texas Dep't of Community Affairs v. Burdine, 450 U.S. 248, 253–54 (1981)(stating that plaintiff has the burden of establishing a prima facie case of disparate treatment); McDonnell Douglas Corp. v. Green, 411 U.S. 792, 802–03 (1973) (holding that plaintiff established a prima facie showing that the employer refused to hire him because of his race).

98. Christine G. Cooper, *Where Are We Going with Gilmer?—Some Ruminations on the Arbitration of Discrimination Claims,* 11 St. Louis U. Pub. L. Rev. 203, 218 (1992).

99. *See, e.g.,* Griggs v. Duke Power Co., 401 U.S. 424, 431 (1971) (holding that an employment practice excluding Negroes is prohibited if it cannot be shown to be related to job performance).

100. Cooper, *supra* note 98, at 218.

101. Securities Industry Conference on Arbitration, The Arbitrators' Manual, 26 (1992).

102. *Id.* The "manifest disregard" standard applies when a party seeks to overturn an arbitral award on the basis of the arbitrator's failure to apply the law correctly. The FAA also permits arbitration awards to be overturned on other grounds, such as where the award was procured by corruption or fraud, where the arbitrator refused to let a party present his case, or where the arbitrator exceeded his authority. 9 U.S.C. § 10.

103. *See, e.g.,* Siegel v. Titan Indus. Corp., 779 F.2d 891, 892–93 (2d Cir. 1986).

104. *Mitsubishi,* 473 U.S. 614, 628 (1985), quoted in *Gilmer,* 500 U.S. at 26.

105. Howard, *supra* note 53, at 275.

106. Because the FAA does not require arbitrators to issue written opinions, there is no meaningful appellate process in other types of FAA arbitration as well. This issue is discussed further in chapter 9.

107. *See* Cane and Shub, *supra* note 50, at 116 (noting that "[t]here is a significant problem in defining the proper role of judicial review in an arbitral system that does not require the arbitrators to explain the basis upon which their decisions rest.").

108. UCA, *supra* note 25, § 28(d).

109. *Id.* at § 28(e).

110. *See, e.g.,* 21 Sec. Reg. L. Rep. (BNA) at 1252 (1989).

111. *See* Exchange Act Release No. 34–26805, 54 Fed. Reg. 21154, 21151 (1989); Fahnestock & Co., Inc. v. Waltman, 935 F.2d 512, 516 (2d Cir. 1991), *cert. denied,* 502 U.S. 942 (1991) and 503 U.S. 1120 (1992); Alleyne, *supra* note 89, at 412–14.

An exception exists for "large and complex" arbitration cases. In June 1990, the SROs adopted new procedures that permit either party in such a case to request written findings of fact and conclusions of law. *Rules Changed to Make Written Findings Easier to Obtain in Larger Arbitrations,* 22 Sec. Reg. L. Rep. (BNA) 816 (June 1, 1990). The request does not require the consent of any other party, and an arbitrator who refuses the request may be replaced. *Id.* The findings of fact and conclusions of law are made public along with the award statement.

These changes do not affect routine, non-complex arbitration proceedings. *Id.* Although a party to such a case may request written findings of fact and conclusions of law, the other parties and the arbitrator must agree to the request. Even if all parties agree on the need for a written opinion, the arbitrator cannot be compelled to provide one. *Id.; see also* Cane and Shub, *supra* note 50, at 117.

Cases that qualify for "large and complex" status are determined on a case-by-case basis. Such cases may include "class actions, cases involving multiple parties, cases dealing with a novel legal theory, and disputes involving potentially large sums of money." Comment, *Should Mandatory Written Opinions Be Required in All Securities Arbitrations?: The Practical and Legal Implications to the Securities Industry,* 45 AM. U. L. REV. 151, 167 (1995), *relying on Rudder Urges Rules to Allow Arbitrators to Refer Complex Cases to Court System,* 20 Sec. Reg. L. Rep. (BNA) 1087 (1988).

112. Merrill Lynch, Pierce Fenner & Smith Inc. v. Bobker, 808 F.2d 930, 933 (2d Cir. 1986 (citing Bell Aerospace Col. Div. of Textron v. Local 516, 356 F. Supp. 354, 356 (W.D.N.Y. 1973), *rev'd on other grounds,* 500 F.2d 921 (2d Cir. 1974)).

113. *See* Wall Street Assoc., L.P. v. Becker Paribus, Inc., 818 F. Supp. 679, 685 (S.D.N.Y. 1993), *aff'd,* 27 F.3d 845 (2d Cir. 1994).

114. *See* Margaret A. Jacobs, *Men's Club—Riding Crop and Slurs: How Wall Street Dealt with a Sex-Bias Case,* WALL ST. J., June 9, 1994, at A-1.

115. Harris v. Forklift Sys. Inc., 510 U.S. 17, 21 (1993); *see* Meritor Sav. Bank v. Vinson, 477 U.S. 57, 66, 73 (1986).

116. Jacobs, *supra* note 114, at A-1.

117. *Gilmer,* 500 U.S. at 33.

Chapter Eight. Compulsory Arbitration as Part of a Broader Employment Dispute Resolution Process: The Brown & Root Example

1. The number of employees varies due to the project-based nature of the company's work. Approximately 20,000 of the company's employees are "core" personnel. The remaining 5,000 to 10,000 employees work for Brown & Root on a project-to-project basis. The turnover rate for these project-based employees is extremely high.

2. William L. Bedman, *From Litigation to ADR: Brown & Root's Experience,* 50 DISPUTE RESOLUTION J. 8, 8 (Oct.–Dec. 1995).

3. *Id.*

4. *Id.*

5. *Id.*

6. *Id.* at 8–9. AAA later became the private supplier of Brown & Root's external

mediators and arbitrators, while Sheppards Associates assisted in announcing Brown & Root's dispute resolution program and then educating the company's supervisors about it.

7. *See* Bedman, *supra* note 2, at 9.

8. I have relied on two documents, both published by Brown & Root, for my discussion of the substance of the Program (1) Brown & Root, *Dispute Resolution Plan and Rules* (Sept. 1994); and (2) Brown & Root, *Resolution: Brown & Root Dispute Resolution Program* (undated). The first is the formal set of rules governing the Program; the second is the less formal booklet that Brown & Root uses to explain the Program to employees. I also have relied on several informal discussions with William Bedman, Brown & Root's associate general counsel in charge of employment matters.

9. Letter from T. E. Knight to All Brown & Root Employees (May 1, 1993) (on file with author).

10. *Id.*

11. Some commentators have argued that an employer, by amending the at-will employment relationship in any way, risks converting the relationship to a just-cause relationship. *See* Stephen L. Hayford and Michael J. Evers, *The Interaction between the Employment-At-Will Doctrine and Employer-Employee Agreements to Arbitrate Statutory Fair Employment Practices Claims: Difficult Choices for At-Will Employers,* 73 N.C.L. REV. 443 (1995). This issue is discussed in chapter 9.

12. *See* Stewart J. Schwab, *Wrongful Discharge Law and the Search for Third-Party Effects,* 74 TEX. L. REV. 1943, 1966–72 (1996) (discussing the reluctance of courts to recognize causes of action protecting internal whistleblowers, and why it is in the best economic interest of employers to encourage internal whistleblowing by protecting the whistleblowers). Retaliation for opposing unlawful employment practices and participating in any proceeding to enforce the employee's statutory rights is proscribed by Title VII and other such employment statutes. *See, e.g.,* 42 U.S.C. § 2000e-3(a)(Title VII); 29 U.S.C. § 1140 (ERISA); 29 U.S.C. § 215(a)(3) (FLSA); 29 U.S.C. § 660(c)(1)(OSHA); *see generally* R. Bales, *A New Standard for Title VII Opposition Cases: Fitting the Personnel Manager Double Standard into a Cognizable Framework,* 35 S. TEX. L. REV. 95, 98–117 (1994)(discussing the elements of a retaliation cause of action under Title VII). Courts have not yet been confronted with the issue of whether participation in arbitration or arbitration-related processes pursuant to a compulsory arbitration agreement constitutes protected activity under these statutes. In any case, the Brown & Root antiretaliation guarantee extends further than these statutory provisions, because the Brown & Root guarantee proscribes retaliation for *all* uses of the company's dispute resolution program, regardless of whether a statutory right is at issue.

13. John W. Zinsser, *Employment Dispute Resolution Systems: Experience Grows But Some Questions Persist,* 12 NEGOTIATION J. 151, 155 (1996).

14. For a discussion of the role of ombudspersons, see E. Patrick McDermott, *Survey of 92 Key Companies: Using ADR to Settle Employment Disputes,* 50 DISPUTE RESOL. J. 8, 9–10 (Jan. 1995); Mary P. Rowe, *The Ombudsman's Role in a Dispute Resolution System,* 7 NEGOTIATION J. 353–60 (1991).

15. Zinsser, *supra* note 13, at 156.

16. Brown & Root's program for reimbursing employees for attorneys' fees is described in Brown & Root, *Employment Legal Consultation Plan* (1994). It is a qualified plan under the Employment Retirement Income Security Act of 1974 ("ERISA"), 29 U.S.C. §§ 1001–1461 (1994).

17. This practice is discussed further in chapter 9.

18. Brown & Root, *Dispute Resolution Plan and Rules* § 8(c), at 10 (Sept. 1994).

19. *See, e.g.,* Meat Cutters & Butcher Workmen of N. Am., Dist. Local No. 540 v. Neuhoff Bros. Packers, Inc., 481 F.2d 817, 820 (5th Cir. 1973) (noting the "great flexibility" afforded to labor arbitrators on issues of the admissibility of evidence); *see generally* Frank Elkouri and Edna Asper Elkouri, HOW ARBITRATION WORKS, 296–98, 319–23 (4th ed. 1985).

20. Brown & Root, *Dispute Resolution Plan and Rules* § 19(A) at 13 (Sept. 1994).

21. *Id.* at § 19(C).

22. Zinsser, *supra* note 13, at 161.

Chapter Nine. Creating a Fair (and Enforceable) Arbitration Agreement

1. 500 U.S. at 33. See subsection G in chapter 2 for a detailed discussion of *Gilmer.*

2. 67 Fair Empl. Prac. (BNA) 189, 190–91 (N.D. Tex. 1994).

3. 835 F. Supp. 1104, 1106 (D. Minn. 1993).

4. 711 S.W.2d 227 (Tex. 1986).

5. *Id.* at 229. *See also* Jennings v. Minco Technology Labs., Inc., 765 S.W.2d 497, 592 (Tex. App.—Austin 1989, writ denied) (enforcing employer's unilateral implementation of drug testing policy).

6. 9 U.S.C. §§ 1–16 (1994).

7. *Id.* § 3 (emphasis added).

8. 25 F.3d 1437, 1439–40 (9th Cir.), *cert. denied,* 115 S. Ct. 638 (1994).

9. *Id.* at 1439 (quoting Genesco, Inc. v. T. Kakiuchi & Co., 815 F.2d 840, 846 (2d Cir. 1987)); Durkin v. Signa Property & Casualty Corp., 942 F. Supp. 481 (D. Kan. 1996).

10. *Id.*

11. *See also* Brown v. KFC National Management Co., 921 P.2d 146, 159 (Hawaii 1996)(enforcing a written arbitration agreement where the underlying employment relationship was at-will); White-Weld & Co. v. Mosser, 587 SW.2d 485, 486–87 (Tex. Civ. App. 1979, writ ref'd n.r.e.) (enforcing written arbitration agreement where the underlying employment agreement was oral), *cert. denied,* 446 U.S. 966 (1980).

12. 942 F. Supp. 481 (D. Kan. 1996).

13. *Id.* at 483–84.

14. *Id.* at 487–88.

15. *See, e.g.,* Johnson v. Hubbard Broadcasting. Inc., 940 F. Supp. 1447, 1454 (D. Minn. 1996) ("By signing her name [to an employment agreement containing an arbitration clause, plaintiff] unequivocally and positively expressed an intent to enter into a binding employment agreement. While [plaintiff] represents that she neither read nor understood [the arbitration clause], her affirmations cannot insulate her from the contractual obligations which she has incurred as a result of signing the Agreement.").

16. *See* Volt Info. Sciences, Inc. v. Board of Trustees of Leland Stanford Junior Univ., 489 U.S. 468, 479 (1989) ("Arbitration under the [Federal Arbitration] Act is a matter of consent, not coercion, and parties are generally free to structure their arbitration agreements as they see fit. Just as they may limit by contract the issues which they will arbitrate, so too may they specify by contract the rules under which that arbitration will be conducted.") (citation omitted).

17. Sheller v. Frank's Nursery & Crafts, Inc., 957 F. Supp. 150, 1997 WL 106398 (N.D. Ill. 1997) (compelling arbitration pursuant to arbitration clause in plaintiff's employment application; "By accepting employment . . ., Plaintiffs assented to be bound by their

prior agreement that, if employed, they would submit all calims to arbitration."); *Brown,* 921 P.2d 146, 159, 163–64 (compelling arbitration of plaintiff's discriminatory discharge claim based on arbitration provision contained in plaintiff's employment application); *White-Weld,* 587 S.W.2d at 486–87 (compelling arbitration of plaintiff's breach of employment contract claim where arbitration provision was contained in his employment application).

18. *See, e.g.,* Michele M. Buse, Comment, *Contracting Employment Disputes Out of the Jury System: An Analysis of the Implementation of Binding Arbitration in the Non-Union Workplace and Proposals to Reduce the Harsh Effects of a Non-Appealable Award,* 22 PEPPER-DINE L. REV. 1485, 1526–27 (1995) ("Employers may opt to make individual contracts with their employees, asking them to acknowledge the new arbitration policy and agree to be bound by its terms. This, however, must be supported by independent consideration to make the contract valid.").

19. *See e.g.,* Hellenic Lines, Ltd. v. Louis Dreyfus Corp., 372 F.2d 753, 758 (2d Cir. 1967) ("Hellenic's promise to arbitrate was sufficient consideration to support Dreyfus's promise to arbitrate."); *Durkin* (holding that plaintiff's continued employment provided sufficient consideration to support her arbitration agreement); Golenia v. Bob Baker Toyota, 915 F. Supp. 201, 204 (S.D. Cal. 1996) (upholding arbitration agreement in a claim alleging violations of the Americans with Disabilities Act); Lacheney v. ProfitKey Int'l, 818 F. Supp. 922, 925 (E.D. Va. 1993) ("The agreement of one party to a contract to arbitrate disputes is sufficient consideration to support the other party's agreement to do the same."); *cf.* Stirlen v. Supercuts, Inc., 60 Cal.Rptr.2d 138, 51 Cal.App.4th 1519 (Cal. App. 1 Dist. 1997) (voiding agreement by which the employee, but not the employer, agreed to arbitrate all future claims).

20. *Durkin,* 942 F. Supp. at 487–88 (mutuality of contract present where both parties were bound to arbitration provision); Albert v. National Cash Register Co., 874 F. Supp. 1324, 1326 (S.D. Fla. 1994)(same); *cf.* Hull v. Norcom, Inc., 750 F.2d 1547, 1549 (11th Cir. 1985)(arbitration agreement void because not mutually binding).

21. *See, e.g.,* Woolley v. Hoffmann-La Roche, Inc., 491 A.2d 1257, 1264 (N.J.) (enforcing termination clauses, including the procedure required before termination occurs, within the company's policy manual), *modified,* 499 A.2d 515 (N.J. 1985); Weiner v. McGraw-Hill, Inc., 443 N.E.2d 441, 446–47 (N.Y. 1982) (holding that plaintiff had a breach of contract claim where he was discharged without the "just and sufficient cause" or the rehabilitative efforts specified in personnel handbook); Toussaint v. Blue Cross & Blue Shield of Mich., 292 N.W.2d 880, 885 (Mich. 1980) (enforcing provision of employment contract providing that employee shall not be discharged except for cause).

22. *See, e.g.,* Owens v. Brookwood Med. Ctr. of Tampa, Inc., 11 I.E.R. Cas. 1310, 1996 WL 376772 (M.D. Fla. 1996) (holding that the arbitration agreement in the employee handbook was not binding, but ordering the case to arbitration because the employee had signed an acknowledgment form containing an arbitration agreement); Federal Express Corp. v. Dutschmann, 846 S.W.2d 282, 284 (Tex. 1993) (holding that the employee manual did not create an enforceable contract).

23. 452 Mich. 405, 550 N.W.2d 243 (1996).

24. *Id.* at 247.

25. *See, e.g., Owens* 11 I.E.R. Cas. 1310, 1996 WL 376772; Reese v. Commercial Credit Corp., 955 F. Supp. 567, 1997 WL 85786 (D.S.C. 1997) (enforcing arbitration clause which was both contained in handbook and mailed separately to employee).

26. 942 F. Supp. 762 (D. Conn. 1996).

27. *Id.* at 765.

28. Margaret A. Jacobs, *Executives Are Often Successful in Wrongful-Termination Suits*, WALL ST. J., April 15, 1996, at B5.

29. Buse, *supra* note 18, at 1516.

30. *Id.; see also Gilmer*, 500 U.S. at 33.

31. *See* Gateson v. ASLK-Bank, N.V./(GER-Banque S.A.), No. 94 Civ. 5849, 1995 WL 387720 (S.D.N.Y. June 29, 1995) (compelling arbitration pursuant to an agreement to arbitrate controversies, "arising out of or related to" the employment agreement).

32. 70 Fair Emp. Prac. Cas. (BNA) 401 (S.D.N.Y. 1996).

33. *Id.* at 407 (alteration in original).

34. *Id.*

35. *See* Maye v. Smith Barney Inc., 897 F. Supp. 100, 103 (S.D.N.Y. 1995); *see also* Jennifer A. Marler, Note, *Arbitrating Employment Discrimination Claims: The Lower Courts Extend Gilmer v. Interstate/Johnson Lane Corp. to Include Individual Employment Contracts*, 74 WASH. U.L.Q. 443, 472 (1996); Note, *Agreements to Arbitrate Claims under the Age Discrimination in Employment Act*, 104 HARV. L. REV. 568, 586 (1990).

36. 993 F.2d 1253, 1254–55 (7th Cir. 1993); *cf.* Kidd v. Equitable Life Assurance Soc'y of Am., 32 F.3d 516, 519 (11th Cir. 1994); Rudolph v. Alamo Rent A Car, Inc., 952 F. Supp. 311 (E.D. Va. 1997) (refusing to compel arbitration of statutory dispute where employment contract provided only for arbitration of contractual disputes); Bright v. Norshipco & Norfolk Shipbuilding & Drydock Corp., 951 F. Supp. 95 n.1 (E.D. Va. 1997) (discussing same).

37. 42 F.3d 1299, 1305 (9th Cir. 1994). For a discussion of this case, see Catherine Chatman, Note, *Mandatory Arbitration of Title VII Claims: A New Approach*, 1996 J. DISP. RESOL. 255.

38. *See* Hoffman v. Aaron Kamhi, Inc., 927 F. Supp. 640, 645 (S.D.N.Y. 1996).

39. For examples of 'adhesive' arbitration agreements that have been held to be unenforceable adhesion contracts, see *Broemmer v. Abortion Servs. of Phoenix, Ltd.*, 840 P.2d 1013, 1015–17 (Ariz. 1992) (en banc) (arbitration agreement between physician and patient) and *Patterson v. ITT Consumer Fin. Corp.*, 18 Cal. Rptr. 2d 563, 565–67 (Ct. App. 1993), *cert. denied*, 510 U.S. 1176 (1994).

40. *See, e.g.*, William M. Howard, *Arbitrating Employment Discrimination Claims: Do You Really Have To? Do You Really Want To?*, 43 DRAKE L. REV. 255, 266–69 (1994); Katherine Van Wezel Stone, *Mandatory Arbitration of Individual Employment Rights: The Yellow Dog Contract of the 1990s*, 73 DENVER L. REV. 1017, 1036 (1996) ("Many pre-hire arbitral agreements are blatant contracts of adhesion."); Robert J. Lewton, Comment, *Are Mandatory, Binding Arbitration Requirements a Viable Solution for Employers Seeking to Avoid Litigating Statutory Employment Discrimination Claims?*, 59 ALB. L. REV. 991, 1019–21 (1996).

41. Neal v. State Farm Ins. Co., 10 Cal. Rptr. 781, 784 (Dist. Ct. App. 1961); *see also* RESTATEMENT (SECOND) OF CONTRACTS § 211 (1979)(defining standardized agreements); Todd D. Rakoff, *Contracts of Adhesion: An Essay in Reconstruction*, 96 HARV. L. REV. 1173, 1173 (1983) (contracts of adhesion are "standard form contracts presented on a take-it-or-leave-it basis").

42. *See* Graham v. Scissor-Tail, Inc., 623 P.2d 165, 172 (Cal. 1981).

43. *See id.* at 172–73; *see also* Williams v. Walker-Thomas Furniture Co., 350 F.2d 445, 449–50 (D.C. Cir. 1965) (holding that contract is unenforceable where unconscionability is present at time contract is made); Stirlen v. Supercuts, Inc., 60 Cal.Rptr.2d 138, 51 Cal.App.4th 1519 (Cal. App. 1 Dist. 1997)(discussing meaning of unconscionability); RE-

STATEMENT (SECOND) OF CONTRACTS § 211(3) ("[w]here the other party has reason to believe that the party manifesting such assent would not do so if he knew that the writing contained a particular term, the term is not part of the agreement"). *Cf. Brown*, 921 P.2d 146, 167 (noting that a contract of adhesion is unenforceable only if it is both the result of coercive bargaining between parties of unequal bargaining strength and it unfairly advantages the stronger party); Buraczynski v. Eyring, 919 S.W.2d 314, 318–21 (Tenn. 1996) (same).

44. *See* Mago v. Shearson Lehman Hutton, Inc., 956 F.2d 932, 934 (9th Cir. 1991); Cohen v. Wedbush, Noble, Cooke, Inc., 841 F.2d 282, 286 (9th Cir. 1988).

45. *Gilmer*, 500 U.S. at 32–33; *see also* Webb v. R. Rowland & Co., 800 F.2d 803, 807 (8th Cir. 1986) ("The use of a standard form [arbitration] contract between two parties of admittedly unequal bargaining power does not invalidate an otherwise valid contractual provision."); Hoffman v. Aaron Kamhi, Inc., 927 F. Supp. 640, 643–44 (S.D.N.Y. 1996) (holding that an arbitration clause is not unconscionable simply because it is drafted by an employer); Katz v. Shearson Hayden Stone, Inc., 438 F. Supp. 637, 641 (S.D.N.Y. 1977); Rust v. Drexel Firestone, Inc., 352 F. Supp. 715, 718 (S.D.N.Y. 1972).

46. *Gilmer*, 500 U.S. at 33, (citing Mitsubishi Motors Corp. v. Soler Chrysler-Plymouth, Inc., 473 U.S. 614, 627 (1985)).

47. Prima Paint Corp. v. Flood & Conklin Energy Mfg. Co., 388 U.S. 395, 400 (1967).

48. *Id.* at 399–400; *see also* Hampton v. ITT Corp., 829 F. Supp. 202, 204 (S.D. Tex. 1993)(finding that plaintiffs were not unfairly induced to sign the arbitration clauses separately from the employment agreements).

49. *See* Samuel Estreicher, *Arbitration of Employment Disputes Without Unions*, 66 CHI. KENT L. REV. 753, 766 (1990).

50. *Gilmer*, 500 U.S. at 32–33.

51. 897 F. Supp. 100 (S.D.N.Y. 1995).

52. *Id.* at 106.

53. *Id.* at 107.

54. *Id.* at 108 (quoting Metzger v. Edna Ins. Co., 227 N.Y. 411, 125 N.E. 14, 816 (1920)); *see also* Johnson v. Hubbard Broadcasting, Inc., 940 F. Supp. 1447, 1444–45 (D. Minn. 1996).

55. 942 F. Supp. 963.

56. *Id.*

57. 915 F. Supp. 201, 204 (S.D. Cal. 1996).

58. *Id.*

59. *Id.; see also Brown*, 921 P.2d at 167 (noting that the terms of an arbitration agreement could not be unfair if they applied equally to both parties); Leong v. Kaiser Found. Hosp. 71 Haw. 240, 788 P.2d 164, 169 (1990)(same).

60. 921 S.W.2d 817, 819 (Tex. App.—San Antonio 1996, n.w.h.).

61. *See, e.g.*, Saint Mary's Honor Ctr. v. Hicks, 113 S. Ct. 2742, 2749 (1993).

62. Frank Elkouri and Edna Asper Elkouri, HOW ARBITRATION WORKS, 661–63 (4th ed. 1985).

63. Stephen L. Hayford and Michael J. Evers, *The Interaction between the Employment-At-Will Doctrine and Employer-Employee Agreements to Arbitrate Statutory Fair Employment Practices Claims: Difficult Choices for At-Will Employers*, 73 N.C. L. REV. 443 (1995).

64. Elkouri and Elkouri, *supra* note 62, at 652 (quoting Atwater Mfg. Co., 13 LA 747, 749 (Donnelly, 1949)).

65. Aristotle, for example, wrote: "[e]quity is justice in that it goes beyond the written law. And it is equitable to prefer arbitration to the law court, for the arbitrator keeps equity in view, whereas the judge looks only to the law, and the reason why arbitrators were appointed was that equity might prevail." THE ARBITRATOR'S MANUAL i (1989).

66. *See, e.g.*, Perling v. Citizens and Southern Nat'l Bank, 300 S.E.2d 649, 652 (Ga. 1983).

67. 2 Mark A. Rothstein et al., EMPLOYMENT LAW, § 9.6 (1994) (noting that only about one-fifth of the states have recognized the doctrine).

68. Hayford and Evers, *supra* note 63, at 483.

69. *Id.* at 486–87; *see also* cases cited therein at 487 n.191.

70. *See* Swanson v. Liquid Air Corp., 826 P.2d 664, 668 (Wash. 1992).

71. *See, e.g.*, McDonald v. Santa Fe Trail Transp. Co., 427 U.S. 273 (1976).

72. *Hicks*, 113 S. Ct. at 2749.

73. *See, e.g.*, Hayford and Evers, *supra* note 63, at 506.

74. These problems are discussed in chapter 8.

75. Hayford and Evers, *supra* note 63, at 500. Hayford and Evers take this argument even further, arguing that the resulting pattern of frequent arbitrations "will create in the minds of protected-group members the same type of reasonable expectation of fair treatment in discharge matters that is generally deemed to constitute an enforceable implied-in-fact term of employment," and that, moreover, arbitrators will be compelled by nondiscrimination principles to extend this protection to persons who are outside of protected groups. *Id.* at 506, 520.

76. *See* Alexander v. Gardner-Denver Co., 415 U.S. 36, 47 n.6 (1974).

77. *Gilmer*, 500 U.S. at 30 (quoting *Mitsubishi*, 473 U.S. at 634).

78. *Id.* at 30–31.

79. *Id.* at 30 (alteration in original) (quoting 9 U.S.C. § 10(b)).

80. 968 F.2d 877, 882 (9th Cir.), *cert. denied*, 506 U.S. 986 (1992).

81. *Id.* at 882 (quoting *Gilmer*, 500 U.S. at 34 n.5).

82. *Gilmer*, 500 U.S. at 33.

83. Reginald Alleyne, *Statutory Discrimination Claims: Rights "Waived" and Lost in the Arbitration Forum*, 13 HOFSTRA LAB. L.J. 381, 426 (1996); Sarah Rudolph Cole, *Incentives and Arbitration: The Case against Enforcement of Executory Arbitration Agreements between Employers and Employees*, 64 UMKC L. REV. 449, 476–79 (1996); Joseph R. Grodin, *Arbitration of Employment Discrimination Claims: Doctrine and Policy in the Wake of* Gilmer, 14 HOFSTRA LAB. L.J. 1, 43–44 (1996); Dennis O. Lynch, *Conceptualizing Forum Selection as a "Public Good": A Response to Professor Stone*, 73 DENVER L. REV. 1071, 1073 (1996). On the importance of bilateral repeat player status in the context of labor arbitration, see Bernard D. Meltzer, *Ruminations about Ideology, Law, and Labor Arbitration*, PROC. OF THE 20TH ANNUAL MEETING OF THE NAT'L ACAD. OF ARB. 1, 3–4 (1967); Julius G. Getman, *Labor Arbitration and Dispute Resolution*, 88 YALE L.J. 916, 929–30 (1979).

84. Martin H. Malin, *Arbitrating Statutory Employment Claims in the Aftermath of Gilmer*, 40 ST. LOUIS U. L.J. 77, 97–98 (1996); Estreicher, *supra* note 49, at 765; Grodin, *supra* note 83, at 44; Lynch, *supra* note 83, at 1073.

85. 876 F. Supp. 850 (N.D. Tex.), *aff'd*, 71 F.3d 877 (5th Cir. 1995).

86. *Id.* at 852.

87. *Id.*

88. *See* Elkouri and Elkouri, *supra* note 62, at 135.

89. 837 F. Supp. 1430, 1433 (N.D. Ill. 1993); *see also Pony Express*, 921 S.W.2d 1433, 821–22 (holding that an arbitration clause allowing AAA to select the arbitrator was not unconscionable because it favored neither party).

90. *Williams*, 837 F. Supp. at 1443. The compulsory arbitration clause at issue in *Williams* specified that an arbitrator was to be chosen according to the AAA Labor Arbitration Rules. *Id.* at 1439. Rule 17 of the AAA Labor Arbitration Rules, as amended January 1, 1992, provides: "No person shall serve as a neutral arbitrator in any arbitration under these rules in which that person has any financial or personal interest in the result of the arbitration. Any prospective or neutral arbitrator shall immediately disclose any circumstance likely to affect impartiality, including any bias or financial or personal interest in the result of arbitration. Upon receipt of this information from the arbitrator or any other source, the AAA shall communicate the information to the parties and . . . [u]pon objection of a party to the continued service of a neutral arbitrator, the AAA, after consultation with the parties and the arbitrator, shall determine whether the arbitrator should be disqualified and shall inform the parties of its decision, which shall be conclusive." *Id.* at 1439–40 n.13. AAA's Labor Arbitration Rules were designed for use in the collective bargaining context. The AAA has designed a separate but similar set of rules for use in the noncollective bargaining agreement employment context. AMERICAN ARBITRATION ASSOCIATION, NATIONAL RULES FOR THE RESOLUTION OF EMPLOYMENT DISPUTES 15–16 (1996) (hereinafter AAA NATIONAL RULES). Rule 11(c) of the AAA National Rules, which covers the selection of arbitrators, is similar to the Labor Arbitration rule at issue in *Williams*.

91. Brown & Root's arbitration agreement, discussed in chapter 8, contains such a provision.

92. Orley Ashenfelter and David Bloom, Lawyers as Agent of the Devil in a Prisoner's Dilemma Game, 11–19 (National Bureau of Economic Research Working Paper No. 4447 (Sept. 1993); Richard N. Block and Jack Stieber, *The Impact of Attorneys and Arbitrators on Arbitration Awards*, 40 INDUS. & LAB. REL. REV. 543 (1987).

93. *See* Ronald J. Gilson and Robert H. Mnookin, 94 COLUM. L. REV. 509, 566 n.42 (1994).

94. Ashenfelter and Bloom, *supra* note 92, at 21.

95. Christine G. Cooper, *Where Are We Going with* Gilmer?—*Some Ruminations on the Arbitration of Discrimination Claims*, 11 ST. LOUIS U. PUB. L. REV. 203, 218 (1992). *See* McDonnell Douglas Corp. v. Green, 411 U.S. 792, 802 (1973) (specifying the elements the plaintiff must prove to establish *prima facie* case of racial discrimination); *see also* St. Mary's Honor Ctr. v. Hicks, 509 U.S. 502, 506 (1993) (discussing plaintiff's burden of proof).

96. Cooper, *supra* note 95, at 218.

97. *See, e.g.*, Griggs v. Duke Power Co., 401 U.S. 424, 436 (1971) (holding that employers are prohibited from requiring a high school education or passing a standardized general intelligence test as a condition of employment).

98. Cooper, *supra* note 95, at 218.

99. *See* Wards Cove Packing Co. v. Atonio, 490 U.S. 642, 650–51 (1989) (it is a comparison "between the racial composition of the qualified persons in the labor market and the persons holding at-issue jobs" that generally "forms the proper basis for the initial inquiring in a disparate-impact case").

100. *Gilmer*, 500 U.S. at 31.

101. *Id.* (quoting *Mitsubishi*, 473 U.S. at 628); *see also Pony Express*, 921 S.W.2d at 822 (holding that an arbitration clause prohibiting discovery was not unconscionable on its

face, but remanding for a factual determination of whether the arbitration agreement as a whole was unconscionable).

102. The arbitration agreement in *Williams* incorporated the AAA rules for labor arbitration. *See* Williams, 837 F. Supp. at 1439. The AAA rules for employment dispute resolution similarly do not contain any provision specifically permitting or denying discovery. They, like the labor arbitration rules, do permit an arbitrator to subpoena witnesses and documents either independently or upon request of a party. AMERICAN ARBITRATION ASSO-CIATION, EMPLOYMENT DISPUTE RESOLUTION RULES § 19, at 18 (January 1, 1993).

103. AAA's employment arbitration Rule 7 provides: "The arbitrator shall have the authority to order such discovery, by way of deposition, interrogatory, document produc-tion, or otherwise, as the arbitrator considers necessary to a full and fair exploration of the issues in dispute." AAA NATIONAL RULES, *supra* note 90, at 12–13.

104. *Williams,* 837 F. Supp. At 1439.

105. Marler, *supra* note 35, at 471, 473 n.238; Thomas H. Stewart, *Arbitrating Claims Under the Age Discrimination in Employment Act of 1967,* 59 CINN. L. REV. 1415, 1436–37 (1991).

106. *See* Ronald Turner, *Compulsory Arbitration of Employment Discrimination Claims with Special Reference to the Three A's—Access, Adjudication, and Acceptability,* 31 WAKE FOREST L. REV. 231, 289 (1996); Cynthia L. Estlund, *Wrongful Discharge Protections in an At-Will World,* 74 TEX. L. REV. 1655, 2670 (1996); Robert A. Gorman, *The Gilmer Decision and the Private Arbitration of Public-Law Disputes,* 4 U. ILL. L. REV. 635, 661–62 (1995); *see also* Jean R. Sternlight, *Panacea or Corporate Tool?: Debunking the Supreme Court's Preference for Binding Arbitration,* 74 WASH. U. L. Q. 637, 683–84 (emphasizing impor-tance of discovery to consumers when they are arbitrating claims against a company); Mark E. Bunditz, *Arbitration of Disputes between Consumers and Financial Institutions: A Serious Threat to Consumer Protection,* 10 OHIO ST. J. OF DISP. RESOL. 267, 283–84 (1995)(same).

107. *Gilmer,* 500 U.S. at 31; *see also* United Steelworkers of Am. v. Enterprise Wheel & Car Corp., 363 U.S. 593, 597 (1960) (noting that arbitrators "have no obligation to the court to give their reasons for an award"); George Goldberg, A LAWYER'S GUIDE TO COMMERCIAL ARBITRATION 62 (1977); *but see* David E. Feller, *Arbitration and the Exter-nal Law Revisited,* 37 ST. LOUIS U.L.J. 973, 981 (1993) (stating that, the law notwithstand-ing, "any labor arbitrator who hears a grievance and then just comes out with an award saying 'grievance denied,' or 'grievance granted' will never be hired by any employer or union again").

108. *Gilmer,* 500 U.S. at 31. Agreeing with Gilmer's argument, one commentator explained: "Imagine a sexual harassment case in private arbitration. If the arbitrator ruled that the employer did not perform an adequate investigation of the sexual harassment complaint, who will learn what kind of investigation should have been performed? Indeed, in the typical commercial arbitration, where arbitrators are discouraged from writing opinions containing findings of fact and conclusions of law, not even the immediate parties would know that the wrong committed was an inadequate investigation: they would know only that the employer lost the sexual harassment case." Cooper, *supra* note 95, at 215 (footnotes omitted).

109. *Gilmer,* 500 U.S. at 31; *see also* Cooper, *supra* note 95, at 215–18 (explaining why effective appellate review is hampered).

110. *Gilmer,* 500 U.S. at 31; *see also* Cooper, *supra* note 95, at 218 (Arbitrators "are completely inadequate to develop the law. Could an arbitrator have come up with the

disparate impact theory of discrimination? With an understanding that environmental sexual harassment is sex discrimination?") (footnotes omitted).

111. *Gilmer,* 500 U.S. at 31–32.

112. *See* Uniform Code of Arbitration, *reprinted in* SECURITIES INDUS. CONFERENCE ON ARBITRATION REPORT. NO. 6, at § 28(e); *see also* George Goldberg, A LAWYER'S GUIDE TO COMMERCIAL ARBITRATION, 57–60 (2d ed.) (describing the procedures and content of an arbitration award).

113. *See* Peter M. Mundheim, Comment, *The Desirability of Punitive Damages in Securities Arbitration: Challenges Facing the Industry Regulators in the Wake of Mastrobuono,* 144 U. PA. L. REV. 197, 202 (1995); Alleyne, *supra* note 83, at 413. AAA requires that its arbitrators issue "written reasons for the award unless the parties agree otherwise." AAA NATIONAL RULES, *supra* note 90, at 25–26 (Rule 32).

114. *Gilmer,* 500 U.S. at 32.

115. *Id. But see* Cooper, *supra* note 95, at 222 ("settlement is based on a prediction of the outcome of litigation; arbitration [when it is the product of the employer's coercion and the employer's expectation that she will more likely win in arbitration than litigation] is based on an avoidance of the outcome of litigation.").

116. *See* Alexander v. Gardner-Denver Co., 415 U.S. 36, 51 n.13 & 55 (1974) (noting the "therapeutic value" of arbitration); United Steelworkers v. American Mfg. Co., 363 U.S. 564, 568 (1960) (same); Elkouri and Elkouri, *supra* note 62, at 280–82; Roger I. Abrams, et al., *Arbitral Therapy,* 46 RUTGERS L. REV. 1751, 1756–95 (discussing the value of the therapeutic value arbitration has) (1994); Susan A. Fitzgibbon, *The Judicial Itch,* 34 ST. LOUIS U. L.J. 485, 506 (1990) (a written "arbitral opinion contributes to the therapeutic effect on the process and the continuing relationship of the parties by explaining the reasoning behind the award, demonstrating that the arbitrator heard and considered the arguments of each side").

117. Richard E. Speidel, *Arbitration of Statutory Rights under the Federal Arbitration Act: The Case for Reform,* 4 OHIO ST. J. ON DISP. RESOL. 157, 198 (1989).

118. Judith P. Vladeck and Theodore O. Rogers, *Employment Discrimination,* 63 FORDHAM L. REV. 1501, 1638 (1995) [hereinafter "Symposium"].

119. *Gilmer,* 500 U.S. at 32 n.4; *see also* Cooper, *supra* note 95, at 216–17.

120. 9 U.S.C. § 10 (1994). For a comprehensive discussion of the standards governing judicial review of arbitral awards, see Stephen L. Hayford, *Law in Disarray: Judicial Standards for Vacator of Commercial Arbitration Awards,* 30 GEO. L. REV. 731 (1996).

121. *See* Bowles Fin. Group, Inc. v. Stifel, Nicolaus & Co., 22 F.3d 1010, 1012 (10th Cir. 1994) (noting that these FAA provisions are not interpreted literally); Jenkins v. Prudential-Bache Secs., Inc., 847 F.2d 631, 634 (10th Cir. 1988) (same).

122. *See, e.g., Burchell v. Marsh,* 58 U.S. 344, 349 (1854) ("[i]f an award is within the submission, and contains the honest decision of the arbitrators, after a full and fair hearing of the parties, a court of equity will not set it aside for error, either in law or fact"); *Forsythe Int'l, S.A. v. Gibbs Oil Co.,* 915 F.2d 1017, 1020 (5th Cir. 1990) ("In reviewing the district court's vacatur, we posit the . . . question . . . [of] whether the arbitration proceedings were fundamentally unfair."); *Hoteles Condado Beach v. Union de Tronquistas Local 901,* 763 F.2d 34, 40 (1st Cir. 1985)("Vacatur is appropriate only when the exclusion of relevant evidence 'so affects the rights of a party that it may be said that he was deprived of a fair hearing' ") (citation omitted); *National Post Office Mailhandlers v. United States Postal Serv.,* 751 F.2d 834, 841 (6th Cir. 1985) ("[T]he standard for judicial review of arbitration procedures is merely whether a party to arbitration has been denied a fundamentally fair hearing."); *Hall*

v. Eastern Air Lines, Inc., 511 F.2d 663, 663–64 (5th Cir. 1975) ("review is not absolutely foreclosed where petitioner alleges a denial of fundamental due process"); *Bell Aerospace Co. Div. of Textron v. Local 516, Int'l Union*, 500 F.2d 921, 923 (2d Cir. 1974)("an arbitrator need not [observe] all the niceties [of] . . . federal courts. . . . he need only grant the parties hearing").

123. *Bowles*, 22 F.3d at 1013; *see* Robbins v. Day, 954 F.2d 679, 685 (11th Cir.) ("the Federal Arbitration Act allows arbitration to proceed with only a summary hearing and with restricted inquiry into factual issues"), *cert. denied*, 506 U.S. 870 (1992); Employers Ins. of Wausau v. National Union Fire Ins. Co., 933 F.2d 1481, 1491 (9th Cir. 1991) (fair hearing is based on notice, opportunity to be heard and to present evidence, and lack of biased decision making); Sunshine Mining Co. v. United Steelworkers of Am., 823 F.2d 1289, 1295 (9th Cir. 1987) ("a hearing is fundamentally fair if it meets the 'minimal requirements of fairness'—adequate notice, a hearing on the evidence, and an impartial decision") (quoting Ficek v. Southern Pacific Co., 338 F.2d 655, 657 (9th Cir. 1964), *cert. denied*, 380 U.S. 988, (1965)); Hoteles Condado Beach, 763 F.2d at 38–39 (arbitrator must give each party an adequate opportunity to present evidence and arguments).

124. Estreicher, *supra* note 49 at 777–78; Cynthia L. Estlund, *Wrongful Discharge Protections in an At-Will World*, 74 Tex. L. Rev. 1655, 1655 (1996) (discussing the public interest underlying employment laws designed to ensure racial and sexual equality); Feller, *supra* note 107, at 983; *see also* Cole v. Burns Int'l Security Services, 105 F.3d 1465, 1476 (D.C. Cir. 197) ("The fundamental distinction between contractual rights, which are created, defined, and subject to modification by the same private parties participating in arbitration, and statutory rights, which are created, defined, and subject to modification only by Congress and the courts, suggests the need for a public, rather than private, mechanism of enforcement for statutory rights.").

125. General Telephone Co. v. EEOC, 446 U.S. 318, 326 (1990).

126. Estreicher, *supra* note 49, at 777. David Feller asks: what happens if the parties have stipulated that the arbitration decision shall be final and binding, but the decision is wrong on the legal merits? He concludes that courts are likely to review arbitral decisions concerning statutory clams more closely than courts currently review labor arbitration decision, because of the "much larger social policies involved." Feller, *supra* note 107, at 982–83.

The D.C. Circuit reached the same conclusion in *Cole*, 105 F.3d at 1487. After noting the pronouncements in *Gilmer* that "by agreeing to arbitrate a statutory claim, a party does not forgo the substantive rights afforded by the statute; it only submits to their resolution in an arbitral, rather than a judicial, forum," and that "although judicial scrutiny of arbitration awards necessarily is limited, such review is sufficient to ensure that arbitrators comply with the requirements of the statute," the circuit court concluded that "[t]hese twin assumptions regarding the arbitration of statutory claims are valid only if judicial review under the 'manifest disregard of the law' standard is sufficiently rigorous to ensure that arbitrators have properly interpreted and applied statutory law." Additionally, the court stated that a higher standard of review would not significantly undermine the finality of arbitration because most employment discrimination claims center on factual, rather than legal, disputes. *Id.* For further discussion of this point, see Martin H. Malin, *Arbitrating Statutory Claims in the Aftermath of Gilmer*, 40 St. Louis U. L.J. 77, 104 (1996); Michele Hoyman and Lamont E. Stallworth, *The Arbitration of Discrimination Grievances in the Aftermath of Gardner-Denver*, 39 Arb. J. 49, 53 (Sept. 1984).

127. 473 U.S. 614 (1985).

128. *Id.* at 636–37.

129. *See id.* at 637.

130. *Id.* at 638.

131. *Id.*

132. *See, e.g.,* Gingiss Int'l, Inc. v. Bormet, 58 F.3d 328, 333 (7th Cir. 1995); Ainsworth v. Skurnick, 960 F.2d 939, 940 (11th Cir. 1992), *cert. denied,* 507 U.S. 915 (1993); Robbins v. Day, 954 F.2d 679, 683 (11th Cir. 1992), *cert. denied,* 506 U.S. 870 (1992); National R.R. Passenger Corp. v. Chesapeake & Ohio Ry. Co., 551 F.2d 136, 143 (7th Cir. 1977); Republic of Korea v. New York Navigation Co., Inc., 302, 469 F.2d 377 (2d Cir. 1972); Regina M. Lyons, Testamentary Trust Inc. v. Shearson Lehman Hutton, Inc., 809 F. Supp. 302 (S.D.N.Y.1993).

133. The manifest disregard of the law standard was first mentioned in dictum by the Supreme Court in Wilko v. Swan, 346 U.S. 427, 436–37 (1953). The Court in *Wilko* recognized that courts have limited power to vacate arbitration awards, but stated that "[w]hile it may be true . . . that a failure of the arbitrators to decide in accordance with [applicable law] would 'constitute grounds for vacating the award pursuant to Section 10 of the Federal Arbitration Act,' that failure would need to be made clearly to appear. . . . [T]he interpretations of the law by the arbitrators in contrast to manifest disregard are not subject, in the federal courts, to judicial review for error in interpretation." *Id.* (footnotes omitted).

134. Merrill Lynch, Pierce, Fenner & Smith, Inc. v. Jarros, 70 F.3d 418, 421 (6th Cir. 1995); Folkways Music Publishers, Inc. v. Weiss, 989 F.2d 108, 111 (2d Cir. 1993); Carte Blanche (Singapore) PTE., Ltd. v. Carte Blanche Int'l, Ltd., 888 F.2d 260, 265 (2d Cir. 1989); O.R. Securities, Inc. v. Professional Planning Associates, Inc., 857 F.2d 742, 746 (11th Cir. 1988); First Interregional Equity Corp. v. Haughton, 842 F. Supp. 105, 108 (S.D.N.Y. 1994); Pompano-Windy City Partners Ltd. v. Bear Stearns & Co., Inc., 794 F. Supp. 1265, 1272 (S.D.N.Y. 1992).

135. Siegel v. Titan Indus. Corp., 779 F.2d 891, 892–93 (2d Cir. 1985) (citations omitted); *see also* Prudential Bache Sec., Inc. v. Tanner, 72 F.3d 234, 239 (1st Cir. 1995); Health Servs. Management Corp. v. Hughes, 975 F.2d 1253, 1267 (7th Cir. 1992)(to vacate an arbitration award for manifest disregard of the law, "it must be demonstrated that the majority of arbitrators deliberately disregarded what they knew to be the law in order to reach the result they did."); Marshall v. Green Giant Co., 942 F.2d 539, 550 (8th Cir. 1991); Advest Inc. v. McCarthy, 914 F.2d 6, 9 (1st Cir. 1990) (finding that a brokerage house failed to show that arbitrators manifestly disregarded the law when they ordered restoration as part of the remedy for wrongful liquidation of an investor's holdings); Merrill Lynch, Pierce, Fenner & Smith, Inc. v. Bobker, 808 F.2d 930, 933 (2d Cir. 1986); San Martine Compania de Navegacion v. Saguenay Terminals, Ltd., 293 F.2d 796, 801 (9th Cir. 1961).

136. Hayford, *supra* note 63, at 776; Brad A. Galbraith, Note, *Vacator of Commercial Arbitration Awards in Federal Court: Contemplating the Use and Utility of the "Manifest Disregard of the Law" Standard,* 27 IND. L. REV. 241, 252 (1993).

137. META §§ 1(4), 3(a)(1991).

138. *Id.* § 7(b).

139. *Id.* § 6.

140. *Id.* § 8(c).

141. Theodore J. St. Antoine, *The Making of the Model Employment Termination Act,* 69 WASH. L. REV. 361, 378 (1994); Theodore J. St. Antoine, *Employment-At-Will—is the Model Act the Answer?,* 23 STETSON L. REV. 179, 194 (1993).

142. Estreicher, *supra* note 49, at 778 n.74.

143. *Cf.* Malin, *supra* note 84, at 99–105 (arguing that courts should review arbitral interpretations of law on a *de novo* basis).

144. G. Richard Shell, *ERISA and Other Federal Employment Statutes: When Is Commercial Arbitration an "Adequate Substitute" for the Courts?*, 68 Tex. L. Rev. 509, 568 (1990).

145. *Id.*

146. *Gilmer,* 500 U.S. at 32.

147. *Id.* ("[E]ven if the arbitration could not go forward as a class action or class relief could not be granted by the arbitrator, the fact that the [ADEA] provides for the possibility of bringing a collective action does not mean that individual attempts at conciliation were intended to be barred.") (quoting Nicholson v. CDC Int'l Inc., 877 F.2d 221, 241 (3d Cir. 1989)). The Court also noted that arbitration agreements would not preclude the EEOC from bringing actions seeking class-wide and equitable relief. *Id.* However, as discussed in chapter 6, the EEOC threat is not particularly potent because the agency files suit in so few of the complaints it receives.

148. Richard A. Bales and Reagan Burch, *The Future of Employment Arbitration in the Nonunion Sector,* 45 Lab. L. J. 627, 633 (1994); Jacobs, *supra* note 28, at B-5; *see also* Jill Hodges, *EEOC Argues against Hubbard Policy; Race Discrimination Suit Questions KSTP-TV's Employment Agreement,* Star Tribune, May 18, 1996 at 1D (noting that a television station had requested employees to sign an agreement limiting recovery to "out of pocket damages").

149. Baravati v. Josephthal, Lyon & Ross, Inc., 28 F.3d 704, 709 (7th Cir. 1994)(citations omitted).

150. Heather J. Haase, Note, *In Defense of Parties' Rights to Limit Arbitral Awards under the Federal Arbitration Act:* Mastrobuono v. Shearson Lehman Hutton, Inc., 31 Wake Forest L. Rev. 309, 331 (1996); *see also* Volt Info. Sciences, Inc. v. Board of Trustees, 489 U.S. 468, 479 (1989) (by permitting courts to " 'rigorously enforce' such agreements according to their terms . . . we give effect to the contractual rights and expectations of the parties without doing violence to the policies behind the FAA").

151. *See* Alexander v. Gardner-Denver Co., 415 U.S. 36, 52 n.15 (1974).

152. *See, e.g.,* Schwartz v. Florida Bd. of Regents, 807 F.2d 901, 906 (11th Cir. 1987) (sex discrimination claim); Rogers v. General Elec. Co., 781 F.2d 452, 454 (5th Cir. 1986) (sex discrimination claim); Williams v. Vukovich, 720 F.2d 909, 926 (6th Cir. 1983) (racial discrimination claim). *See also* United States v. Allegheny-Ludlum Indus., Inc. 517 F.2d 826, 853 (5th Cir. 1975), *cert. denied,* 425 U.S. 944 (1976); Watkins v. Scott Paper Co., 530 F.2d 1159, 1172 (5th Cir.), *cert. denied,* 429 U.S. 861 (1976); Cox v. Allied Chem. Corp., 538 F.2d 1094, 1098 (5th Cir. 1976), *cert. denied sub nom.* Allied Chem. Corp. v. White, 434 U.S. 1051 (1978); Baker v. Chicago Fire & Burglary Detection, Inc., 489 F.2d 953, 955–56 (7th Cir. 1973).

153. *Gilmer,* 500 U.S. at 26 (alteration in original) (quoting *Mitsubishi,* 473 U.S. at 628).

154. 115 S. Ct. 1212 (1995). For a discussion of this case, see G. Richard Shell, *Federal versus State Law in the Interpretation of Contracts Containing Arbitration Clauses: Reflections on* Mastrobuono, 65 U. Cin. L. Rev. 43 (1996).

155. *Id.* at 1219.

156. *Id.* at 1218–19.

157. *Id.* at 1219.

158. *Id.* at 1223 (Thomas, J., dissenting).

159. *Id.* at 1219.

160. *See* Garrity v. Lyle Stuart, Inc., 353 N.E.2d 793, 794 (N.Y. 1976); *but see* Singer v. Salomon Bros. Inc., 593 N.Y.S.2d 927, 930 (N.Y. Sup. Ct. 1992) (permitting arbitrator to award punitive damages in a disability discrimination claim).

161. *See, e.g.,* DiCrisci v. Lyndon Guar. Bank of N.Y., 807 F. Supp. 947, 953–54 (W.D.N.Y. 1992); Chisolm v. Kidder, Peabody Asset Management, Inc., 810 F. Supp. 479, 485 (S.D. N.Y. 1992); Mulder v. Donaldson, Lufkin & Jenrette, 611 N.Y.S.2d 1019, 1021–22 (N.Y. Sup. Ct. 1994); *see also* Marler, *supra* note 35, at 478 (arguing that arbitrators in this situation should resolve all liability issues, then send the case to a judicial forum for resolution of all damages issues).

162. 67 Fair Empl. Prac. Cas. (BNA) 189 (N.D. Tex. 1994).

163. 29 U.S.C. § 206(d) (1994).

164. Tex. Lab. Code Ann. §§ 21.001–.306 (Vernon 1996).

165. *Kinnebrew,* 67 Fair Empl. Prac. Cas. at 190.

166. *Id.*

167. *Id.* at 191.

168. 43 F.3d 1244, 1246 (9th Cir. 1994); *see also* Stirlen v. Supercuts, Inc., 60 Cal.Rptr.2d 138, 51 Cal.App.4th 1519 (Cal. App. 1 Dist. 1997) (striking as unconscionable an arbitration agreement which withdrew from employees the right to recover punitive damages); *but see* Great Western Mortgage Corp. v. Peacock, 110 F.3d 122, 1997 WL 153012 (3d Cir. 1997) (the waiver in an arbitration agreement of the right to recover punitive damages "is separate and apart from the issue of whether an employee has agreed to an arbitral forum, and hence, is for the arbitrator to decide").

169. 15 U.S.C. §§ 2801–2806 (1994).

170. *Graham Oil,* 43 F.3d at 1247.

171. *Id.* at 1247–48.

172. *Id.* at 1247.

173. *Id.* at 1249.

174. 940 F. Supp. 1447 (D. Minn. 1996).

175. The employee also challenged the agreement for imposing a 180-day statute of limitations on the filing of an EEOC charge. The normal statute of limitations is 300 days.

176. *Johnson,* 940 F. Supp. 1447, 1462.

177. *See* Shearson Lehman Hutton, Inc. v. McKay, 763 S.W.2d 934, 939 (Tex. App.— San Antonio 1989, no writ) ("Once forced to trial, the benefits of arbitration are forever lost: the speed and economy of first going to arbitration are defeated.").

178. Michele L. Giovagnoli, *To Be or Not to Be?: Recent Resistance to Mandatory Arbitration Agreements in the Employment Arena,* 64 UMKC L. Rev. 547, 573 (1996).

Chapter Ten. The Policy Implications of Compulsory Employment Arbitration

1. William M. Howard, *Arbitrating Employment Discrimination Claims: Do You Really Have To? Do You Really Want To?,* 43 Drake L. Rev. 255, 269–79 (1994).

2. Richard Delgado et al., *Fairness and Formality: Minimizing the Risk of Prejudice in Alternative Dispute Resolution,* 1985 Wis. L. Rev. 1359, 1387–89.

3. Issue one may be decided by the judge only if no rational jury could disagree as to the fact at issue; if rational disagreement is possible, the issue must be decided by the jury. Similarly, issue three (damages) is initially decided by the jury, but the damage award may be modified by the judge if, again, no rational jury could have rendered the original award. In most tort cases, the legal standard is that of a reasonable person. This means that, in addition

to deciding what the defendant did (issue one), the jury also must decide what a reasonable person in defendant's position would have done, and whether the defendant's conduct departed from that standard.

4. *See* 42 U.S.C. § 1981a(c)(1994).

5. Richard A. Bales and Reagan Burch, *The Future of Employment Arbitration in the Nonunion Sector,* 45 LAB. L.J. 627, 633 (1994).

6. *See* Oliver Wendell Holmes, THE COMMON LAW, 124 (1946) ("A judge who has long sat as *nisi prius* ought gradually to acquire a fund of experience which enables him to represent the common sense of the community in ordinary instances better than an ordinary jury.").

7. PRICE WATERHOUSE LAW FIRM & LAW DEPARTMENT SERVICES GROUP, 1993 LAW DEPARTMENT SPENDING SURVEY OF 201 MAJOR COMPANIES, *cited in* William M. Howard, *Arbitrating Claims of Employment Discrimination: What Really Does Happen? What Really Should Happen?,* 50 DISP. RES. J. 40, 42 (Oct.-Dec.1995) [hereinafter *Arbitrating Claims*]; *see also* George Rutherglen, *From Race to Age: The Expanding Scope of Employment Discrimination Law,* 24 J. LEG. STUD. 491, 503 (1995) (noting that juries are no more favorable to plaintiffs than judges on the issue of liability, although they might make larger damage awards once they find liability); Harry Kalven, Jr., *The Dignity of the Civil Jury,* 50 VA. L. REV. 1055, 1065–67 (1964) (same); *see also* Kevin M. Clermont and Theodore Eisenberg, *Trial by Jury or Judge: Transcending Empiricism,* 77 CORNELL L. REV. 1124, 1137–38, 1140–41, 1175 (1992).

8. Brown & Root's experience with the arbitration of employment claims indicates that employees are more likely to prevail on the issue of liability in arbitration than they are in litigation, but that damage awards are smaller in arbitration.

9. Frank Elkouri and Edna Asper Elkouri, HOW ARBITRATION WORKS, 285–90, 688–91 (4th ed. 1995).

10. *See* Charles Alan Wright, Arthur Miller, and Richard L. Marcus, FEDERAL PRACTICE & PROCEDURE, § 2001, at 41 (1994) (hereinafter, FEDERAL PRACTICE & PROCEDURE)("The basic philosophy underlying [the discovery rules adopted in 1938] was that prior to trial, every party to a civil action is entitled to the disclosure of all relevant information in the possession of any person, unless the information is privileged").

11. Burns v. Thiokol Chem. Corp., 483 F.2d 300, 304 (5th Cir. 1973).

12. Morrison Export Co. v. Goldstone, 12 F.R.D. 258, 259 (S.D.N.Y. 1952).

13. Nutt v. Black Hills Stage Lines, Inc., 452 F.2d 480, 482 (8th Cir. 1971).

14. Hickman v. Taylor, 329 U.S. 495, 500 (1947); *Nutt,* 452 F.2d at 483; Gary Plastic Packaging Corp. v. Merrill Lynch, Pierce, Fenner & Smith, Inc. 756 F.2d 230, 236 (2d Cir. 1985).

15. FEDERAL PRACTICE & PROCEDURE, *supra* note 10, § 2001, at 40.

16. *Id.* at 46; In re Halkin, 598 F.2d 176, 192 (D.C. Cir. 1979); Mid-West Paper Prods. Co. v. Continental Group, Inc., 596 F.2d 573, 579 (3d Cir. 1979); Martin v. Reynolds Metals Corp., 297 F.2d 49, 56 (9th Cir. 1961).

17. FEDERAL PRACTICE & PROCEDURE, *supra* note 10, at § 2001, at 41; *see also* FED. R. CIV. P. 26(b)(1); United States v. Proctor & Gamble Co., 356 U.S. 677, 682–83 (1958); *Hickman,* 329 U.S. at 500.

18. *See* FED. R. CIV. P. 26–37.

19. *See* FED. R. CIV. P. 26(a)(1).

20. *See* Ronald Turner, *Compulsory Arbitration of Employment Discrimination Claims with Special Reference to the Three A's—Access, Adjudication, and Acceptability,* 31 WAKE

FOREST L. REV. 231, 289 (1996); Cynthia L. Estlund, *Wrongful Discharge Protections in an At-Will World*, 74 TEX. L. REV. 1655, 2670 (1996); Robert A. Gorman, *The Gilmer Decision and the Private Arbitration of Public-Law Disputes*, 4 U. ILL. L. REV. 635, 661–62 (1995); *see also* Jean R. Sternlight, *Panacea or Corporate Tool?: Debunking the Supreme Court's Preference for Binding Arbitration*, 74 WASH. U. L. Q. 637, 683–84 (emphasizing importance of discovery to consumers when they are arbitrating claims against a company); Mark E. Bunditz, *Arbitration of Disputes between Consumers and Financial Institutions: A Serious Threat to Consumer Protection*, 10 OHIO ST. J. OF DISP. RESOL. 267, 283–84 (1995)(same).

21. *See Gilmer v. Interstate/Johnson Lane Corp.*, 500 U.S. at 31–32.

22. AMERICAN ARBITRATION ASSOCIATION, NATIONAL RULES FOR THE RESOLUTION OF EMPLOYMENT DISPUTES: ARBITRATION AND MEDIATION RULES Rule 7, at 12–13 (1996).

23. *See* Drinane v. State Farm Mut. Auto. Ins. Co., 606 N.E.2d 1181, 1183 (Ill. 1992).

24. *See, e.g.*, Wetzel v. Liberty Mutual Ins. Co., 511 F.2d 199, 202–03 (3d Cir. 1975), *vacated on other grounds*, 424 U.S. 737 (1976) (stating that lay persons should not be denied access to the federal courts because of a technical error); Ang v. Proctor & Gamble Co., 932 F.2d 570 (6th Cir. 1991)(noting that courts often interpret the law liberally to protect claimants who are "unschooled in the technicalities of the law and [who] proceed without counsel"); *but see* Baldwin County Welcome Ctr. v. Brown, 466 U.S. 147 (1984) (dismissing, on procedural grounds, an employment discrimination case filed by a *pro se* plaintiff).

25. *See Arbitrating Claims, supra* note 7, at 42.

26. Turner, *supra* note 20, at 289.

27. Richard A. Posner, THE FEDERAL COURTS: CRISIS AND REFORM, 59 (1985).

28. Irving R. Kaufman, *Reform for a System in Crisis: Alternative Dispute Resolution in the Federal Courts*, 59 FORDHAM L. REV. 1, 4–6 (1990).

29. ADMIN. OFFICE OF THE U.S. COURTS, FEDERAL JUDICIAL WORKLOAD STATISTICS, 2–3 (1993); John J. Donohue and Peter Siegelman, *The Changing Nature of Employment Discrimination*, 43 STAN. L. REV. 983, 983–84 (1991); *see also* Stanley Sporkin, *Reforming the Federal Judiciary*, 46 SMU L. REV. 751, 757 (1992) (discussing the overload of employment discrimination suits).

30. Turner, *supra* note 20, at 284. As of 1989, the median time between the filing of a lawsuit and trial (not including appeals) was fourteen months; ten percent of cases lasted more than three years. For cases concluded before trial (for example, by settlement or summary disposition), the median time between filing and disposition by the trial court was eight months; ten percent of cases lasted more than twenty-eight months. 1989 DIRECTOR ADMIN. OFFICE. U.S. COURTS ANN. REP., app. I, at 10, 212, 233.

31. Clyde Summers, *Effective Remedies for Employment Rights: Preliminary Guidelines and Proposals*, 141 U. PA. L. REV. 457, 480 (1992).

32. Turner, *supra* note 20, at 284.

33. Summers, *supra* note 31, at 488.

34. *See, e.g.*, Elkouri and Elkouri, *supra* note 9, at 9 & n.36.

35. See discussion in Chapter 6.

36. Summers, *supra* note 31, at 461.

37. David E. Robbins, SECURITIES ARBITRATION PROCEDURE MANUAL, § 9.01 at 9–2 (2d ed. 1995).

38. *See* Turner, *supra* note 20, at 286.

39. *See id.* at 468–69.

40. *Id.* at 467.

41. James N. Dertzouzos et al., THE LEGAL AND ECONOMIC CONSEQUENCES OF WRONGFUL TERMINATION, 37–48 (1988) (hereinafter THE RAND STUDY).

42. *See, e.g.,* Theodore J. St. Antoine, *Arbitration Back to the Future,* 39 U. MICH. L. QUAD. NOTES 62, 67 (1996) (stating that the successful defense of a jury case may cost $100,000 to $200,000).

43. Summers, *supra* note 31, at 468. Like settlement, an employer's *loss* of an employment case may similarly encourage other employees to challenge the employer's personnel decisions. George Rutherglen, *From Race to Age: The Expanding Scope of Employment Discrimination Law,* 24 J. LEG. STUD. 491, 514 (1995) [hereinafter *From Race to Age*]. This significantly raises the stakes for an employer in any given employment dispute, and probably contributes to the high cost of employment litigation.

44. *See id.* at 468–69.

45. *See, e.g.,* William L. Bedman, *From Litigation to ADR: Brown & Root's Experience,* 1995 DISP. RES. J. 8, 8 (Oct.-Dec. 1995) (noting that the high cost of litigating a particular case was one factor inducing Brown & Root to implement a dispute resolution program that included compulsory arbitration).

46. Estlund, *supra* note 20, at 1673. Approximately 60 percent of employment discrimination claims are brought by recently discharged employees. Donohue & Siegelman, *supra* note 29, at 1015–17 (1991); *From Race to Age, supra* note 43, at 494, Table 2 (noting that discharge is involved in an even larger percentage of age discrimination cases). This is probably because incumbent employees have more to lose and better access to evidence, and therefore more reason to sue, than applicants for employment. George Rutherglen, *Discrimination and Its Discontents,* 81 VA. L. REV. 117, 135 (1995). Moreover, incumbent employees are more likely to hold high-paying jobs that will support a large damage award than are employment applicants who, by definition, are looking for work and may find searching for another job more attractive than pursuing litigation. *Id.*

47. Summers, *supra* note 31, at 467. One survey of plaintiff's attorneys indicated that the average requirements for accepting an employment discrimination case included minimum provable damages of $60,000–65,000, a required retainer of $3000–3600, and a 35 percent contingency fee. *Arbitrating Claims, supra* note 7, at 44.

48. *See, e.g.,* MODEL RULES OF PROFESSIONAL CONDUCT, Rule 4.2 Cmt. 2 (1983) (prohibiting communication with persons having a managerial responsibility on behalf of the organization, or with any other person whose act or omission in connection with the matter about which information is being sought may be imputed to the organization for purposes of civil or criminal liability); Texas State Bar Ass'n, Op. 342 (1968), *reprinted in* O. Maru, 1970 SUPPLEMENT TO THE DIGEST OF BAR ASSOCIATION ETHICS OPINIONS, 297 (hereinafter 1970 DIGEST) (forbidding ex parte interviews if employee is person whose acts or omissions led to the lawsuit); New York City (County) Year Book, Op. 528 (1965), *reprinted in* 1970 DIGEST, at 241–42 (proscribing ex parte interviews with a corporate party's employees).

49. *See, e.g.,* Wilson v. Monarch Paper Co., 939 F.2d 1138, 1143 (5th Cir. 1991) (distinguishing the employment setting from other settings and indicating that a higher standard of liability will be imposed in the employment setting); *see also* Keeton et al., PROSSER & KEETON ON TORTS (5th ed. 1984 & 1988 Supp.) (stating that "the work culture in some situations may contemplate a degree of teasing and taunting that in other circumstances might be considered cruel and outrageous."); J. Wilson Parker, *At-Will Employment and the Common Law: A Modest Proposal to De-Marginalize Employment Law,* 81

IOWA L. REV. 347, 352)(1995)(noting that lawyers and courts often distinguish employment law from ordinary tort and contract law).

50. 42 U.S.C. § 1981a(b).

51. 42 U.S.C. § 2000e-5(k) (1994).

52. *See, e.g.,* Branch-Hines v. Hebert, 939 F.2d 1311, 1322–23 (5th Cir. 1991)(remanding for modification of the judgment to reflect special damages of $7000 while affirming an award of $10,098 for attorneys' fees).

53. *See generally* Summers, *supra* note 31, at 485–89.

54. *See* City of Burlington v. Dague, 505 U.S. 557, 561–62 (1992).

55. *See, e.g.,* Hensley v. Eckerhart, 461 U.S. 424, 440 (1983); Catlett v. Missouri Highway & Transp. Comm'n, 828 F.2d 1260, 1270 (8th Cir. 1987), *cert. denied,* 485 U.S. 1021 (1988); Uviedo v. Steves Sash & Door Co., 753 F.2d 369, 370 (5th Cir. 1985) *cert. denied,* 474 U.S. 1054 (1986); Walje v. City of Winchester, 773 F.2d 729, 732 (6th Cir. 1985); King v. McCord, 707 F.2d 466, 467 (11th Cir. 1983).

56. MODEL CODE OF PROFESSIONAL CONDUCT, Rules 1.2(a) & 1.4 cmt. (1995).

57. Evans v. Jeff D., 475 U.S. 717, 755–56 (1986) (Brennan, J., dissenting)("allowing defendants in civil rights cases to condition settlement of the merits on a waiver of statutory attorney's fees will diminish lawyer's expectations of receiving less. . . . Even the [majority] acknowledges [this].").

58. *See* Theodore Eisenberg, *Litigation Models and Trial Outcomes in Civil Rights and Prisoner Cases,* 77 GEO. L.J. 1567, 1578–84 (1989); Estlund, *supra* note 20, at 1673; *see also* Great Western Mortgage Corp. v. Peacock, 110 F.3d 222, 1997 WL 153012 (3d Cir. 1997)(noting that the employee "agreed to arbitration not because of coercion on the part of [the employer], but because of the fees that she would have been charged had she resorted to other legal proceedings"). In Bright v. Norshipco & Norfolk Shipbuilding & Drydock Corp., 951 F. Supp. 95, 1997 WL 35519 (E.D. Va. 1997), the court stated: "[A]ccess to the courts now is neither affordable nor expeditious. In many federal district and state courts, years pass before an aggrieved party can even have the proverbial day in court. In the meantime, the process grinds along, inflicting staggering legal expenses on the parties. Except for the very rich (and very poor, in some circumstances), we have simply priced the court system beyond the reach of most citizens, because the cost of litigation far exceeds the value of the decision itself. Indeed, even the most resourceful parties often decline to pursue legal rights. . . . In short, our current legal system for resolving disputes is losing the respect of the public and is rapidly approaching failure."

59. THE RAND STUDY, *supra* note 41, at 20–21.

60. *See* Summers, *supra* note 31, at 468; *see also* Roberto L. Corrada, *Claiming Private Law for the Left: Exploring* Gilmer's *Impact and Legacy,* 73 DENVER L. REV. 1051, 1052–53 (1996) (describing the difficulties that employees face in obtaining legal representation, and concluding that employees may be better off arbitrating their claims rather than litigating them); Joseph R. Grodin, *Arbitration of Employment Discrimination Claims: Doctrine and Policy in the Wake of* Gilmer, 14 HOFSTRA LAB. L.J. 1, 43–44 (1996) ("The number of employees with viable statutory claims who are able to retain competent lawyers to represent them in litigation, is undoubtedly small compared with the total number of such employees, many of whom would be well advised to forego litigation in favor of a fairly constructed arbitration."). James W. Meeker and John Dombrink, *Access to the Civil Courts for Those of Low and Moderate Means,* 66 S. CAL. L. REV. 2217, 2218 (1993) (discussing how access to the legal system is limited to those who can afford to pay the high cost of litigation); Michael Yelnosky, *Filling an Enforcement Void: Using Testers to Uncover and Remedy Discrimination*

in Hiring for Lower-Skilled, Entry-Level Jobs, 26 U. MICH. J.L. REF. 403, 412 (1993) (because lower-skilled entry-level "jobs typically pay lower wages, the plaintiff may have difficulty paying a lawyer.").

61. *Arbitrating Claims, supra* note 7, at 42.

62. Elkouri and Elkouri, *supra* note 9, at 19.

63. *ADR Techniques Gaining Favor in Non-Traditional Settings,* DAILY LAB. REP. (BNA), March 15, 1993, at 2.

64. *See* Turner, *supra* note 20, at 283–84.

65. See Michael Selmi, *The Value of the EEOC: Reexamining the Agency's Role in Employment Discrimination Law,* 57 OHIO ST. L.J. 1, 10–11, 25 (1996).

66. Employers tempted to draft arbitration agreements requiring employees to commence arbitration proceedings within a specified time frame should review *EEOC v. River Oaks Imaging and Diagnostic,* Civ. A. No. H-95-755, 1995 WL 264003 at *1 (S.D. Tex. Apr. 19, 1995), in which the court invalidated an arbitration agreement requiring employees to initiate arbitration within one year of the complained-of incident. This case is discussed in chapter 6.

67. FEDERAL PRACTICE & PROCEDURE, *supra* note 10.

68. The Brown & Root Dispute Resolution Program, discussed in chapter 8, contains such an agreement.

69. *See* Turner, *supra* note 20, at 284.

70. Bedman, *supra* note 45, at 11.

71. *Id.*

72. *Id.*

73. *See id.*

74. Bales and Burch, *supra* note 5, at 633.

75. *See* REPORT AND U.C. RECOMMENDATIONS OF THE COMMISSION ON THE FUTURE OF WORKER-MANAGEMENT RELATIONS, *reprinted in* Special Supplement to DLR No. 6, Jan. 10, 1995, at 30 (noting that "[private arbitration] may . . . allow even the most contentious disputes to be resolved in a manner which permits the complaining employee to raise the dispute without permanently fracturing the employee's working relationship with the employer.").

76. Adverse selection problems probably will cause the employer's risk of exposure to lag significantly behind the rate of employee participation in the program, because litigation-prone employees may be less likely to participate.

77. *See, e.g.,* Maye v. Smith Barney, Inc., 897 F. Supp. 100 (S.D.N.Y. 1995).

78. Jean R. Sternlight, *Panacea or Corporate Tool? Debunking the Supreme Court's Preference for Binding Arbitration,* 74 WASH. U.L.Q. 637, 676 (1996); Melvin A. Eisenberg, *The Limits of Cognition and the Limits of Contract,* 47 STAN. L. REV. 211, 241–43 (1995) (arguing that a rational receiver of a standard form contract will choose to remain ignorant of its terms because of the relatively high costs of ascertaining the terms' meaning and the low probabilities of the terms becoming relevant or of negotiating a revision); Stephen J. Ware, *Employment Arbitration and Voluntary Consent,* 25 HOFSTRA L. REV. 83, 119–20 (1996); RESTATEMENT (SECOND) OF CONTRACTS § 211 cmt. b (1970) ("A party who makes regular use of a standardized form of agreement does not ordinarily expect his customers to understand or even to read the standard terms."); *but see* EZ Pawn Corp. v. Mancias, 934 S.W.2d87, 90 (Tex. 1996) ("[Plaintiff's] failure to read the agreement does not excuse him from arbitration. We presume a party, like [Plaintiff], who has the opportunity to read an arbitration agreement and signs it, knows its contents."); Ware, *supra,* at

119–20 ("If . . . the duty to arbitrate is prominantly displayed near the signature line of the standardized agreement, the employee probably consents to arbitrate. If . . . the duty to arbitrate is buried among many pages of fine print, then the employee probably does not consent to arbitrate.").

79. Matthew W. Finkin, *Commentary on "Arbitration of Employment Disputes Without Unions,"* 66 CHI.-KENT L. REV. 799, 809 (1990).

80. Kenneth G. Dau-Schmidt, *Employment Security: A Comparative Institutional Debate,* 74 TEX. L. REV. 1645, 1649 (1996); *see also* J. Hoult Verkerke, *An Empirical Perspective on Indefinite Term Employment Contracts: Resolving the Just Cause Debate,* 1995 WIS. L. REV. 837, 898 (noting that, under established theories on the resolution of cognitive dissonance, "people prefer not to think about unpleasant possibilities").

81. *See* Sarah Rudolph Cole, *Incentives and Arbitration: The Case against Enforcement of Executory Arbitration Agreements between Employers and Employees,* 64 UMKC L. REV. 449, 479–82 (1996).

82. Joseph E. Herman, *Arbitrate, Don't Litigate, at Work,* N.Y. TIMES, Apr. 14, 1991, at F11.

83. *Id.*

84. *See, e.g.,* Peter M. Mundheim, Comment, *The Desirability of Punitive Damages in Securities Arbitration: Challenges Facing the Industry Regulators in the Wake of* Mastrobuono, 144 U. PA. L. REV., 197, 203 (1995) (discussing arbitration in the securities industry).

85. Some of the suggestions made in chapter 9 include putting the agreement in writing and making certain that it is clearly drafted, permitting ample discovery, requiring the arbitration to issue a written opinion, and not restricting the arbitrator's ability to award relief.

Index

231